The Myth Makers

Myth Makers
A Greek Tale
Copyright © 2023 by Charles Peter Zaloumis

All rights reserved. No part of this book may be reproduced or transmitted in any form or by any means without written permission from the publisher and author.

Additional copies may be ordered from the publisher for educational, business, promotional or premium use.
For information, contact ALIVE Book Publishing at:
alivebookpublishing.com

Book and cover design by Alex P. Johnson

ISBN 13
978-1-63132-219-8

Library of Congress Control Number: 2023920087

Library of Congress Cataloging-in-Publication Data
is available upon request.

First Edition

Published in the United States of America by ALIVE Book Publishing
an imprint of Advanced Publishing LLC
3200 A Danville Blvd., Suite 204, Alamo, California 94507
alivebookpublishing.com

PRINTED IN THE UNITED STATES OF AMERICA

10 9 8 7 6 5 4 3 2 1

The Myth Makers

A GREEK TALE
—
PETER'S ODYSSEY

Charles Peter Zaloumis

Alive Book Publishing

Contributions By
Elayne Becker
Nicole S. Jones (Zaloumis)
Anthony P. Zaloumis

CONTENTS

Dedications   11
Choral Foreword: The Music Makers
Prologue: Theme, Structure, Encoded Wisdoms:

PASSAGE I – THE INNOCENCE OF BECOMING   19
Choral Foreword: The Homeland
Foreword: Greece's Missing Men
Nights Awake, Nights Alone
Lesbos - Still Shrouded in Mystery
Homer's Classic Tale – The Odyssey
The Kafenio – Introductions
The Secluded Virgins

PASSAGE II – SOULFUL AGONIES   65
Choral Foreword: Whispers From Beyond
Introductory Poem: Chant – Socrates
The Choking Shreds of Tradition
Shadow Whispers
Kyrie Eleison – Have Mercy
The Twin Lies
His Perfect Will

PASSAGE III – LOVE CHANGES EVERYTHING   101
Choral Foreword: The Madness of Love
Introductory Poem: Greek Proverb
Epic Helplessness
Innocence of Young Love
To Life, To Love

Hail O'Liberty
The Spiritual Cards

PASSAGE IV – THE ODYSSEY BEGINS   139
Choral Foreword: The Journey
Poem: "Rehearsing for Death"
Even Heroes Cry
When Destiny Calls
The Trickers
The Faint of Heart
Expectations
The Launch

PASSAGE V – DESTINY'S LIFEPLAN UNFOLDS 165
Choral Foreword Poem: "Who I Am"
Goodbye Greece, Hello World
The Crossroads
The Spiritual Calling
Knowing You, Knowing Us
"ODD"
Antigone - The Vision
Living the Dream

PASSAGE VI – INTERLUDES: EARLY MORNING MOMENTS   189
Choral Foreword Poem: Rehearsing for Death
The Hetaerae
Golden Arrows
Love's Enchanted Key
Divine Pleasures
A Fragile World

PASSAGE VII – THE SPECTOR OF DEATH   221
Choral Forward: Poem: Tortured Souls
Night of the Long Knives
Was it All a Dream
For Freedom
Eyes Empty of Light
The Guiding Hand of Fate

PASSAGE VIII – ELEFTHERIA I THANATOS – FREEDOM OR DEATH   249
Choral Foreword: Poem: "The War Hymn"
For Freedom, Sons of Greece
Sir, Yes Sir
The Heart of a Warrior
The Smell of Death
The Burials
The Intelligence Report

PASSAGE IX – WHY GOD, WHY ALL THE MADNESS?   293
Introductory Poem: "The End of the Journey"
The Intelligence Report II- Psychological Warfare
The Historic Record
The Dark Passions of Fear
The Wailing Wall
The Point of No Return
A Spiritual Reveal
The Eternity of the Moment

PASSAGE X – DISTANT SHORES   331
Choral Foreword: Introduction: Life is a Moment
A Sermon on a Hillside
Forestalling Death Homer's Essence

Trickster and the Little Birds of Fate
Let's Celebrate, Let's Dance

PASSAGE XI – RIDING THE WAVES 353
Choral Foreword: Nothing Changes
Back in the Kafeno
The Magic of Boldness
Realities Illusions

PASSAGE XII – THE INSANITY OF LOVE 373
Choral Foreword: The Needlepoint in Life
Introductory Poem: "The Muses"
Nothing to Lose
Reaching for a Dream

PASSAGE XIII – FINDING A LIFE STAR 389
Choral Forward: Taking Control of Destiny
A Nee Dream Begins
Longs for Yourself
The Trickster
Play of the Game
Traveling the Crossroads
A Man Possessed by his Spirit
Hubris was a Trap

PASSAGE XIV – THE SWEETNESS OF LOVE AND IT"S MADNESS 425
The Trickster's Trap
The Sweetness of Love
Peter's Calypso Fantasy
As in a Dream
Epilogue: Celebrating the Odyssey
Epilogue: The Poetry of Peter's Tale

Ode: (The Music Makers)

We are the music-makers, and we are the dreamers of dreams,
Wandering by lone sea breakers, and sitting by desolate streams;
World-losers and world forsakes, on whom the pale moon gleams,
Yet we are the movers and the shakers of the world forever, it seems."
To the old of the new world's worth; for each age is a dream that is dying, Or one that is coming to birth.

~Arthur O'Shaughnessy

DEDICATIONS

This book is dedicated to my father Peter Charles Zaloumis and my mother Viola Bessie Zaloumis who were the loving music-makers of our family. Some spiritualist and man regression hypnotist say we got to choose the family we will be born into as children. If that be true, then my brothers and sister chose wisely. They were great parents and gave us a wonderful childhood.

They were the loving muses who taught us to be dreamers of dreams and to be the music-makers of our lives. It is our expression of love and thanks for a fabulous childhood that they created and maintained for us. We hold dear to ourselves our "heart-felt" memories of them.

This book is about my father's journey. He knew at an early age that he would have to leave Greece. At a young age, he was forced to take a spirit journey; something Greeks call an Odyssey. He experienced many adventures on his journey and many hardships. He came to know what immigrants must endure on their way to somewhere, anywhere.

This book is also dedicated to the brave immigrants of the world who risk their lives to find a safe and sustainable place in the world for themselves and their families. We salute their courage in braving the dangers that they had to face, endure, and overcome. We recognize and honor their historic contributions for the betterment of the world. To all those brave souls who tried and didn't make it, we honor your spirit and wish you "God Speed."

THE LIFE AND JOURNEY
OF PETER CHARLES ZALOUMIS

(1897 – 1973)

This book is a celebration of the life and journey of Peter Charles Zaloumis, who by example, taught us that life is a journey and an adventure to be lived to its fullest.

We start Peter's story with a Tagore's epigraph: My heart has spread its sails to the idle winds for the shadowy island of anywhere.

PROLOGUE

THEME, STRUCTURE, ENCODED WISDOMS

This book is a Greek tale that was inspired by the 'true life' story of my father Peter Charles Zaloumis. The theme of the book is based on the ancient Greek belief that everything in the universe is spiritually connected.

The terms 'tale' and 'Odyssey' take on new meanings in this book. A tale is defined as a story based on reality, which eventually becomes crowned with grandeur by real experiences and on mythological interpretations of these experiences. Peter's Odyssey is a biography. His Odyssey is a long and dangerous journey with many stops and adventures in mythical settings.

Poetry is a mirror of life and it has been used throughout the book to reflect and illuminate the meaning of Peter's mystical encounters and adventures. His life and personality are true to life, but some of the people he met on his journey and the conversations with them should be viewed as mythology.

The historic background of Peter's story is- the Ottoman occupation of Greece – and it is told in order to understand the setting in which my father and my mother Vera (Viola Photinellis} were born and raised. It is about the hardships caused by the occupation of Greece by the Ottoman Empire. His story is about his fight for freedom and independence. It is against this backdrop of the Turkish occupation of

Greece that this biography begins.

Most young Greek boys knew that they had to leave Greece and find a better place to live (characterized as Greece's 'Missing Men'). Peter also became aware at an early age that he too was meant to escape 'Ottoman-occupied' Greece and that he would have to take great risks and face many dangers. His dangerous journey tracked the story of the mythical Greek literary hero Odysseus and like Odysseus he survive many dangers, pitfalls and life-threatening' situations following his dreams. He started his personal journey as a young immigrant boy seeking his Ithaca - his rightful place in the world.

Structure of the Book

I used Greek mythology to interpret the events in Peter's journey. The book starts with Nietzsche's description of the "innocence of becoming" and proceeds with the trials and tribulations of his personal Odyssey. He learned how to embrace the events – good or bad- that he determined was his destiny, which in essence meant accepting and living fully in the present moment without fear of the future or remorse about the past. His realization and acceptance of his mortality marked his personality and was his truth, which is considered by the Greeks to be the highest form of wisdom that mankind can attain.

Interpreting the meaning of the events in Peter's biography, I looked to the wisdom encoded in the ancient Greek myths and found that these myths provided clarity and revealed that there are universal truths that govern everyone's life. These mythical art forms remind us of these truths and why they are still relevant in everyone's life.

The ancient Greek hymns, myths and poetry contain many encoded wisdoms which illuminate the meaning and purpose of life and they are an artful way of conveying and interpreting the events in Peter's life, his journey and the unfolding of his destiny. They are used and studied in epistemology (the theory of knowledge) and it is this basis that the references from the ancient Greek myths and poetry are being used as connections, comparisons and current touchstones of knowledge and the meaning of life.

This approach drew me into the massive vault of the ancient Greek myths and poetry, which comes to us as a legacy of encoded wisdoms from the past. In this majestic library of exciting tales, they imbedded encoded wisdoms which have been passed down from generation to generation and have become a code of life for the Greek people and the Western European countries. To this day and, perhaps for all time, these encoded wisdoms will continue to have relevance and will light the way for humanity.

Another ancient literary technique was used to provide clarity and to make the point that Peter's life was like the journey all immigrants must take. In fact, the journey we call life is an odyssey we all take. From the early Greek stage plays, I took and used the technique of a choral foreword to provide state the meaning of a particular phase in Peter's journey and life and alludes to the meaning of the events to come. The role of the chorus foreword is continued throughout the story by means of epigraphs at the top of the first page of each chapter.

The use of a 'choral inspired' foreword was first used in the middle of the 6th century BC. The poet - Thespis - reputedly became the first true actor when he engaged in dialogue with the chorus leader. Choral performances continued to dominate the early plays until the time of Aeschylus (5th century B.C.), who added a second actor and reduced the chorus from 50 to 12 performers.

Sophocles, who added a third actor, increased the chorus to 15 but reduced it to a mainly commentarial role in most of his plays (for an example of the distinction between the passivity of the chorus and the activity of the actors is central to the artistry of the Greek tragedies. While the tragic protagonists act out their defiance of the limits subscribed by the gods for man, the chorus expresses the fears, hopes, and judgment of the polity, the average citizens.

The Encoded Wisdoms

The meaning of life was discussed in the book. We looked to the thoughts and work of ancient Greek literatures for revelation and confirmation of the purpose of life. Many of the themes deal with the pain and suffering in life. The ancient myth makers believed that the gods knew that mankind needed 'hard lessons' to evolve and that purpose of life was about loving one another and preparing for the next reincarnation on earth.

Aeschylus, one of the great Greek writer and philosopher, profound thoughts about wisdom from pain and suffering still rings true:

"Even in our sleep, pain which cannot forget falls drop by drop upon the heart, until in our own despair, against our will, comes wisdom through the awful grace of God."

The ancient wisdoms found in Greek mythology and poetry have experienced a resurgence in the theories and language of the emerging trends in today's scientific theories about the creation of the universe and the realities of life.

Prologue

This book delves into how spirituality is replacing Darwin's materialistic theory of creation and survival of the fittest as the engine of evolution.

The themes of a spiritual and energetic universe are a constant refrain found in Greek mythology and poetry and upon close examination are similar to the concepts now being espoused in Quantum Mechanics. Bathed in love is the connectivity of all things in the universe and beyond.

The concept of the Divine spark of creation and the illusionary nature of everything are mythological themes known to the ancients, which now appears in modern scientific theories and language. These subjects give a modern touch to Peter's tale and his Odyssey.

PASSAGE I

THE INNOCENCE OF BECOMING

Choral Forward: The Homeland

Lesbos was the cradle of many tribes. The Pelasgians were considered pre-Greek. The Indo-European invaders came. These tribes were the Dorians, Aeolians, Ionians and other related peoples who savagely destroyed and replaced the Stone Age indigenous people of Greece. A number of different prehistoric peoples who inhabited Greece during the Neolithic period such as:

The Island of Lesbos has been described as a spiritual island. It is a myth, a poetic truth and a paradise of serenity and a harmony of beauty and dreams.

The poets called it the "flower of an eternal spring set on the blue waters of the Aegean"

It is a vision that opens wide its modest beauty to the horizon" offering an invitation to love and promise. Some have even gone so far as to call it an ethereal substance made from the very breath of God. The poets claim has the power to shape the lives of its inhabitants and influence their destinies.

The poets compose songs about the island that was molded from light. They say that the island is made of soft tones and sweet shadowing which emerged from the embrace of the sea.

The island achieves its spiritual quality in a melding of

myth and truth, contemplation and dreams, imagination and reality. Even Nature and its seasons need to pause in the face of such beauty; where the gods of joy and sun were worshipped, and Sapphic grief was heard in the incomparable 'Aeolian' melodies.

Peter was born in the port City of Plomari, Lesbos on September, 1897, which at the time was occupied by forces of the Ottoman Empire. Plomari is located at the southernmost tip of Lesbos. It is a lovely water front community that serves as the face of a large mountainous and wooded island of phenomenal wonderment.

Plomari was originally named 'Potamos' (which means river).It was built in the middle of the 19th century when some of the inhabitants decided to leave the island village of Megalochori (which is still sometimes referred to as the old Plomari) and go down to what was then known as the 'wet valley'. Plomari is the second largest town on the island, the first being the capital Mytilene. It is built right on the edge of the Aegean Sea and was and is an important port and a vibrant commercial and industrial town.

The chapters that comprise this Passage in Peter's life tells of the influences that helped shape Peter's early years.

Lesbos – the land of poets, lovers, dreams and yearnings

GREECE'S MISSING MEN

"The saddest of all our island's tears are the ones that come from the souls of our enslaved people."

Life in Greece was about deprivation and sacrifice. Greece was poor and lack the natural resources to build a viable economic base. Consequently, many men had to leave Greece and work in other countries to support their families.

There were many stories about Greece's missing men. Their absence was a tragedy and it adversely impacted the Greek people throughout the ages. In ancient times, the Greek men fought off invaders. They left Greece for long periods of time and were the invaders. They traded goods. At times, they attacked and took the resources of other peoples and tribes living around the Mediterranean Sea. The costs were high; many never returned.

Ancient words echoed through Greece and the world. The ancient Greek poets of tragedy wrote about the suffering of the wives of the missing Greek men – those who went to war.

Sophocles wrote these timeless words:

"I nurse fear after fear, always worrying over him. I have a constant relay of troubles: some each night dispels – each night brings others on. We have children now, when he sees at times, like a farmer working on an outlying field, who only sees it when he sows and reaps. This has been his life that only brings him home to send him out again, to serve some man or other."

The poets of the time tried to justify the pain and losses with beautiful words and concepts. But the stark reality of what was happening was: 'only tragedy after tragedy.'

Being subservient to the Ottoman Empire was too heavy a 'cross' for the Greek people to carry. Under the rule of the Ottoman Empire the country of Greece was slowly dying. Something had to be done to save the Greek nation and culture.

The cause and voice for Greek independence ended up being a high point for the Romantic Movement at an international level. World-wide enthusiasm and hope for Greece was inspired by the romantic poets of the time; but Lord Byron was the only one who had the courage to join the Greek resistance. He fought and died for Greece. His poetry was stirring:

Tis something in the dearth of fame,
Though link'd among a fetter race,
To feel at least the patriot's shame,
Even as I sing, suffuse my face;
For what is left the poet here?
For Greeks a blush—for Greece a tear.

Shelly wrote that "we are all Greeks" meaning that the world had an obligation to the Greeks for all that it did for Western Europe and the world. Keats wrote in a Vision "I think that if I could be given a month in Antiquity and leave to spend where I chose, I would spend it in Byzantium a little before Justinian opened St Sophia and closed the Academy of Plato. They did not make the sacrifice that Lord Byron made, and participate in the great adventure; but together the poets helped to galvanize world opinion to the cause of Greek independence.

Lesbos: Time to Say Goodbye

Peter's father - Charles (George) Zaloumis – had to leave and become one of these missing men. He went to the United States, which was building its industrial and transportation base and was in dire need of workers and laborers. He quickly found employment in this expanding and fast-paced nation. He worked various jobs including that of a laborer on the railroads and was one of those hard-working men who helped build America.

He had to go. It was a matter of economic survival. Like many immigrants, he had to face the dangers of the journey to a foreign land and the pain of loneliness. All the sons of the missing men grew up knowing that they too would have to leave their homes in Greece. It was a childhood fear that influenced many of their decisions and their 'life-altering' actions.

Peter's mother was a Gaia woman. These brave women were named after the Spiritual Goddess of the Earth. The vision of Gaia in Greek mythology is of a goddess who personifies nature and imbues spirit into the world of things. These thoughts and the beliefs and perceptions underlying these thoughts eventually found expression in the prayers of Greek religion which viewed Gaia as one of the Greek primordial deities and the great mother of earth.

The Gaia women were strong- both mentally and physically. They worked relentlessly, raised their families and kept the economy of Greece vibrant. The Gaia women saved the Greek nation and its culture and preserved its unique historical legacy. Even in the unknowing abyss of absence without communication, there was a strong bond between these Gaia women and their husbands. The family units remained intact waiting for the return and the reunions with the fathers.

Peter and his brother George knew that their father had no choice but to leave. It was a matter of economic survival. They believed that their mother and father were victims of Fate. Their father had to leave alone and go to a strange new world. Their mother was left to raise the family and managing their olive groves and business. Every night, she worried. Would she ever see him again?

NIGHTS AWAKE, NIGHTS ALONE

"The tigers come to us at night and rip our hearts apart. At night, we nurse fear after fear."

Peter's father wanted a family 'get togetherness session' on his last day in Greece. He wanted to connect with his family and, particularly, with his sons before he left for the United States.

The family met in the small yard behind their home. At the request of Charles, Deme served her husband and her two boys. Their father was making a point. They were now the men of the family. Peter managed to drink his cup of coffee and George spit it out. Charles thought that it was symbolic, George wasn't ready, but Peter was.

Charles told his sons that he wanted to prepare them for life by teaching them three things that would be helpful in different situations: how to sing the Greek National Anthem, how to learn how to swear and, most important, how to tell a woman he loves her.

Deme and Yaya join in with them and they sang the Greek National Anthem a couple of times. Charles taught the boys some swear words while Deme and Yaya made breakfast. The ladies return for the crucial moment; how to tell a woman they love her. Deme said, "Tell her: 'My little bird, I love you very much." Lessons over, they ate breakfast.

The boys started to cry knowing that their father was leaving them, perhaps for good. He tried to comfort them by tell them; "We will always be connected and nothing will ever change that. You are my sons. You will always be in my thoughts, heart and prayers."

Deme felt her sons' pain. She told them that they were bonded together as a family and would always be connected at a soul level. She said; "The three of you are "old souls born again". Your personalities are the same and none of you are burdened with an overly serious nature. I see the three of you revel in the joys of each day. Your 'lighthearted' natures and even your spiritual wisdom are woven into the fabric of your destinies. The three of you are as one."

She stopped for a moment to collect her final thoughts and then said; "Charles, my dear, I've always loved who you are as a person. You will always be a romantic in your heart. You let your dreams inspire you, guide you and motivate you into taking bold steps. May your journey and your sacrifices be successful and may you be able to return to us soon. "

Charles was deeply touched by Deme's words. He told her that he loved her and always would. He told the boys; "I have to finish making arrangements for my trip. I may not be able to get back before you go to sleep, but I will try. If I don't I will send you a letter from the United States telling you I made it there successfully."

Peter walked with him to the door and told his Dad; "I will follow you to the United States someday. His Dad said; "We will see each other here or over there." Then he hugged his son and left.

He walked back to the garden to finish breakfast. He looked at his mother and hs Yaya in a different way. He thought that his mother and Yaya were attractive women with fine, sharp features and deep dark eyes and chiseled faces and features. His mother's face was framed by her long, straight black hair, which gave her a look of great strength and will power; all of which she had.

Like many other Greek women, Peter's mother bore her pain bravely. She remained stoic to the end of her days and did what she needed to do to save her family. Peter believed that his mother had an angel's spirit in her. Her smile was captivating. Peter could look into his mother's deep, brown eyes and see a loving soul.

Yaya, his grandmother, still dressed in tribal clothing- a long colorful robe accented by a head band. She was an old crone, wise with a cynical perception of life. She had survived the hardships of being a widow in occupied Greece. Her wisdom came from years of pain and suffering. She was not an added burden for Deme. She helped her when she could and she was important to the family dynamic.

Peter thought of her as a loving soul who had acquired practical common sense the hard way; albeit, she delivered her wisdom and guidance within the veneer of sarcasm and at times ridicule. Her different interpretations, her sarcasm timed perfectly and delivered in a loving way. She entertained Peter with her humor mingled with her wisdom. He knew her to be a tribal woman and a character. Dressed in long, colorful robes with a matching head bands, she was a sight to behold.

He loved her "biting" comments and humorous observations. Yaya was always a source of earthly wisdom, always accessible and a necessary 'counterbalance' to his mother's more disciplined approach to life. She believed that life was an illusion and that everything was make-believe and insanely funny; but she was still acutely aware that life has its sharp edges of cruelty.

As Peter grew older, he quickly came to understand the plight of Greek women. They suffered loneliness, hard work and deprivation. During their days, they tilled the orchards and fields and maintain the country's economy, while their husbands and sons left for foreign lands. It was their sacrifices for the well-being of their family. Their sacrifices instilled in him a profound respect for women; although he would occasionally joke about how crazy they all were.

One morning, Peter had breakfast with his Yaya and he told her that he heard his mother crying softly in her bedroom. He asked his Yaya: "Why did she cry and why only at night?"

Yaya told him that she cried at night so that she could appear strong in the daytime. She went on and said; "She doesn't want you to know fear at your young age. Greek men should be brought up to be strong and not fearful and too careful. They need a little craziness to be free.

Your mother and I know that when you are young you think that the world is safe and that God is loving and forgiving. When you are young you think that he will hold you in his arms and protect you from harm. But you should know that the world doesn't work that way. He allows suffering and pain to exist. Being Greek, we think that the suffering is good. It makes us wise. Always remember Peter that your fears are tigers and they come out at night and rip your heart apart. Your mother is trying to tame her tigers."

She went on and said, "She misses your dad. There are Greek songs that cry about our plight. The music is sad. There is one song that sings of the pain that Greek women feel about their 'missing' men. In a Yianni Papaionou song, the chorus sings:

"Nights I stay awake without hope. Lonely I walk the streets. In front of the bars of your window, I spend sad hours. How I long to meet you again, to find your joy once more, to give you my kisses again, so my black sadness will leave me. But there where you in a strange place, who knows where you wander now? I wonder if you still think of me.

….. Or suffer for someone else."

The words of this song are — 'oh so Greek'. They capture the feelings of Greek women whose husbands had to leave Greece to find work in foreign lands. Their great fear was: "Would their husbands find other women; would they desert them?"

Peter couldn't know that their fears are the "tigers" that haunt Greek women and almost destroyed the Greek culture as the men left to foreign lands – some to return, others to bring their families over and still others to disappear forever. Many of these fears were born in the fatigue of sleepless nights and the intense longing to hold their husbands again, even for one short moment.

As they grew older, Peter and his younger brother George became more aware of the pain and loneliness of his mother and the tragedy of their father's separation. One night during supper George asked his mother and grandmother a curious question: "Why do you cry when you hear Greek music.

Deme tried to answer, "Sometimes George … music makes us happy and peaceful, but then sad songs sometimes make the 'hurt' much worse. Greek music brings whatever is inside us out and when we feel our joy we appear happy, but when we need to feel our pain music makes us weep."

Yaya added, "We laugh to hide our pain and weep whenever we can. We cry because love is hopeless and, yet, the dream of love is so very beautiful." Deme smiled and said, "Love was put on earth to keep us together and make life bearable. True love quiets our soul. It dominates our dreams, lodges in the heart and embraces and enhances life." It adds poetry to life and is the background music of everyday life. It is something 'preciouses between people."

There were many nights when Peter could hear his mother crying softly in her room. She never shared her feelings with Peter and George and always tried to wear the 'mask' with the brave face. Nights were her time and with bitter tears she 'cradled' her love for her husband. She released her anxieties in the sanctity of her bedroom. Peter didn't have the kind of relationship that allowed him to go into her bedroom and comfort her. He felt that she would be upset if he knew she was in pain with tears.

Peter came to know that his mother and many Greek women were the 'rock' and 'touch stone' of the family. This view was supported by what he saw as a child and that was the cultivation of soil was and still is in many parts of the world primarily in the hands of women. For centuries, the women of Greece held the country together and raised their families with their blood, sweat and tears. Surely, they rang a bell and surely all the bells ring for these brave women who sacrificed themselves to raise their children and save the family and the culture of Greece.

He realized that Greek women were very brave. They had their fears; but they learned to muster the will and the courage to proceed in life without imposing their grief on anyone else. Peter realized that his mother was courageous and loving in her efforts to protect him from her fears.

His feelings for his mother were deep. He knew her virtues. She was a woman who bore her burdens, responsibilities and sadness quietly with dignity and grace. He realized that she had to be stoic and strong to keep the family together, safe, and, above all, she needed to maintain their livelihood – the protection of their orchards and the management of their olive oil business.

LESBOS - STILL SHROUDED IN MYSTERY

"There is a sweet innocence to 'young life' and a tolerance of their 'young thoughts and actions' in their struggle to become."

Peter started the day at school and was interested in what Sophia's lecture was about. She was giving a lecture about the early settlers of Greece. Not so much about the primitive people who inhabited the land; but more about the tribes who came south from Indo-Europe through the Balkans into Greece.

He was intrigued about Greece's early history and the savage horsemen who invaded Greece. Sophia described them as savage horsemen who held a beast, an angel and a madman in them. Her main point was that beauty tamed them. When they saw the haunting beauty of Greece, a rich and mystical land, with miles of coast, its rocky cliffs and its many islands, the angels came out and took possession of them.

Sophia paused to collect her thoughts. She went on; "They called Greece *"pontos"* which means passage or road. *Pontos* gave them access to the Aegean Sea. These tribes became lovers of Greece's beauty and were tamed by its essence. Eventually, they became historic Greece, which all the world came to admire, adopt and celebrate all its intellectual accomplishments.

Peter got lost in his own thoughts. He imagined himself to be strong and capable as these savage horsemen; but quickly became aware of 'life's hard realities. He enjoyed his youthful fantasies, wishful yearnings for greatness and wealth and other unreachable life longings. As a teenager he had his dreams, but was slowly becoming a realist who did not let his wishes and illusions govern his actions.

Sophia interrupted his day dreams. It was his name day; a time for celebration. The year was 1908 and it was more significant than birthdays (date of birth). Name days are celebrated on the coinciding saint's day with gifts, sweets and parties and it is customary to wish a person on his name day Hronia Polla (meaning 'enjoy many happy years').

She let him leave class early to celebrate his name day. Leaving school early added an intense sense of excitement about the day. He had some time to do anything he wanted, but there was one thing that always captured his imagination and motivated him. Right after he was released from school, he went straight to the Plomari port site near the rocks which danced with the crashing waves.

He stayed as close to the water as he could without falling into it. There he would sit quietly for hours on a rock jetty letting his thoughts and imagination run wild. It was his way of finding a peaceful world within which he could contemplate his problems and find a release for his thoughts and his swirling emotions.

His mother had prepared a lunch for him as she knew by experience that his name day would be a long day outing for him. She knew that Sophia would release him early from school and she knew that he would go to the Port. She asked him before he went to school; "What is it about the Port that attracts you? What do you feel there?" Peter answered, "I feel free. I'm in another world. There is nothing to fear. I have no cares. It is hard to describe, but I sink into the dark and quiet of the sea and I journey to a hidden reality."

Deme kissed him goodbye and told him to be very careful.

After he left, his Yaya chimed in with the observation that, "He is experiencing the solitude of a 'small death'. There is a liberating feeling when you can let go of everything. Life and death are always is a struggle to be free." Deme cautioned her. "Don't talk like that to him. It will scare him. He's still young."

Yaya had a different view of where he was at his age; "He is still young and unafraid. He doesn't know that life is a struggle and that in the struggle we find our essence." Deme couldn't disagree. She said; "If he lives his life to its fullest; he'll have no regrets when it's over." Yaya shook her head 'yes'.

Sometimes, Deme didn't understand her mother. "Mom, sometimes you are a romantic and other times you are a sceptic. Yaya responded; "There is no difference between a sceptic and a romantic; except that a sceptic is a romantic; who is disappointed with the way things are." Deme commented with the observation; "Okay Mom. If you say so."

Peter was on his way to the port. It was about clearing his mind and aligning his thoughts. His focus was on the joy of his new discoveries about life and on his teacher's last lesson, which was the wonderful story and journey of Odysseus. There were also some statements that his mother made earlier in the week about the mystical nature of Lesbos. Peter was at an age where he was trying to learn who he was, what the world was all about and where he was going. He was trying to imagine his way forward in this great, short and scary adventure called life.

When he arrived at the Port area, he found a location on a rock jetty stretching into the bay. He was staring at the boats coming into and out of the port harbor and fell under the spell of his daydreams. He focused on the people who were on the boats and it occurred to him that maybe the story of the Odyssey was a key to the riddle of life. His thought was, "We are all on an Odyssey and every journey will be filled with adventures, challenges and moments of glory.

There will be moments of tragedy and sadness. There will be relief from our inner worries and preoccupation with our own 'stuff'. Periods of time when we have intense romance and captivating love. When all is said and sadly when the journey is over and done we then are forced to lie down and move into the great, last dark adventure called death."

This was a transformative day for him. When he was on a rock jetty and could feel the mist of the crashing waves, he could escape from time. The past, present and future became one and time disappeared. He found his peace from the cares of the world in this spiritual place of contemplation.

He sat alone on a rock jetty and listened to the birds singing as a full chorus in the background. He looked back at the land behind him to listen to their songs and it occurred to him that he had never listened to the birds sing before and he wondered why. He listened to the birds chirped and sing their songs.

He looked over the calm deep blue waters of the port and surprisingly experienced a wave of awareness overcome him. He could swear that he heard a choir of angels singing and then a feeling of awe came over him. He asked himself; "Could he look up at the sky and would he see the face of God?" He was suddenly enveloped by and aware of the other world of spiritual beauty and mystery. He never knew that it existed.

At that moment, Peter felt a great love for Lesbos. He remembered the stories he was told about Lesbos. The island was sometime called 'Emerald Green' and it was one of those magical places in the world where people live close to the land and in the cradle of the earth. He was aware of the fact that Greece was poor in resources. That the fields and the land were poor and few; yet there were many monuments, olive trees and vineyards that filled the landscape.

His mother and Yaya, his grandmother, told him, "Lesbos is an enchanting island where many of the myths of Greece found inspiration and were born through hope, fears and tears. We live on a beautiful island in the Aegean Sea where the poets say the mountains, springs and flowered dwells are haunted by hidden fairy forms."

As he stared at the water, suddenly he heard a loud shriek of a seagull and he snapped out of his reverie. He looked up to see a large sea gull dive head long into the water and grab a small fish and then watched this large sea bird fly straight up and out of sight. He wondered, "What kind of world do we live in? We must eat each other to survive." Then he looked across the water and saw some small fish jumping out of the water and said to himself, "Don't show off. Something will get you if you do."

It was getting late and the sun was setting over the calm 'wine-dark' water. An unseen bird sang for a moment and then everything was still. As the sunset faded, a dark mist was forming and began to cover the landscape. The darkness revealed another world that had the majesty and freshness of a surreal dream. All Peter's senses were awakened as he made his way home. He found a world within a world; one of peace and quiet near the port waters and away from the turmoil of life. Finding a quiet place near the water would be his sanctuary in life when he needed to quiet his mind and restore his inner being.

Peter discovered a way to access an alternative reality where he could still his mind, restore his sense of balance, go inside and know his truth as to where he was, where he wanted to go and then reenter his conscious reality. It was now time to go home.

He believed that he lived in an earthly paradise under the loving guidance of his mother; but he knew that all paradises have a black core of darkness. His early years were times of crises. He lived under the long shadow of the oppressive Ottoman regime. During his youth the Greek underground and their overseas sponsors were laying the foundations for a war against the Ottoman Empire and everything was tense. The Balkan Wars of 1912 and 1913 and the fight for independence were about to start and these wars would impact and change Peter's life as he engaged in and witnessed the horrors and losses of men and treasure in the great wars for independence.

The major influence in his life was his mother whose name was Demeter or Deme for short, after the goddess of the harvest who presided over the grains and the fertility of the earth. She had jet black hair which she combed straight back. Her dark piercing black eyes, sharp features and a 'no nonsense' countenance and demeanor evoke comparisons to the early Greek warriors who had the determination to conquer the known world under Alexander the Great.

Deme was a remarkable woman who was empowered by a powerful internal will that came from heartaches, suffering, toil and the crushing and intense need to care for her family. Her husband went to the United States to work as a laborer leaving her with the responsibility for managing the olive groves and business and raising their two young sons, Peter and his brother George. She was more than equal to the task and executed her responsibilities in a highly disciplined and efficient manner. But under that rigid persona was a big heart that Peter and George could access when they needed emotional love and support.

Because Lesbos was still under the control of the Ottoman Turks, Peter's mother was always careful. She was keenly aware of what was happening in Plomari and she did her best to protect him and his brother George from danger. She tried to keep them away from the men at the kafenio because of what she perceived was their bad influences and devious motives. They were promoting the war for independence and all young Greek men and boys were being recruited for the armed conflict that was brewing. Her boys were too young for a call to battle and possible death in the killing fields and trenches of the upcoming war.

Peter's first awareness of the fragile nature of life came when his mother told him how the Ottoman Empire conquered Greece and how life became very precarious for the Greek people. There was always a tragic overhang of sadness in Greece because of the Turkish practice of bondage known as "Devşirme" which was a system of slavery (literally meaning collecting in Turkish) also known as the "blood tax or tribute in blood" which was the annual practice of abducting boys and girls of their Christian subjects and raising them as Muslin slaves and subjects.

Deme and all the Greek people were aware of the Ottoman Turks horrendous practices as an occupying force. She always worried when Peter or George came home late in the day or evening. They knew that when they were late for any reason, she would be waiting at the door for them.

It was a policy of necessity that she translated into 'tough-love' discipline.

It was her belief that they needed to keep their heads down and out of view. Anonymity was important to their security and she was determined to live life as an ordinary family to the extent possible away from the evil eyes of the Ottoman Turks who could cause great harm to her and her children. The constant dangers and restraints of a life under occupation turned Peter and his younger brother George into rebels and questioners of authority who hated oppression in all its many forms.

HOMER'S CLASSIC TALE – THE ODYSSEY

"The poetry of the earth is never dead" …. Keats.

Peter thought that his teacher Sophia was beautiful in a subtle way. Her long wavy brown hair comb back *away* from her pretty face fascinated him. When people talked about her, they said she was special, a talented didaskalos (which means to instruct) and that she had the spiritual gift of teaching and the unique ability to clearly instruct and communicate knowledge and meaning to the inquiring minds of her young students.

Sophia's lecture that day was about the Greek myth of Odysseus whose name means "man of pain." The tale tells of his adventures and the terrifying obstacles he had to overcome to get to through many dangerous escapes and return to his home in Ithaca. Home meant to him reuniting with his beloved wife and son.

She started her lecture with the statement that Odysseus

was a war hero at the battle of Troy. The gods conspired against him during the conflict, but like many brave souls he bravely endured the pains inflicted by the god Poseidon and with one clever trick after another he managed to escape the traps set by Poseidon. She made the point that the "Odysseus' tale" is a mythical quest by a Greek warrior Odysseus who faced and survived many dangerous tests sent his way be angry Greek gods.

She described the many dangers he faced. She emphasized his torment from a range of conflicting emotions dealing with the issues of survival, love and death, heaven and hell. His struggle to survive was told as a spiritual quest. It is the head and heart of the story first told by the blind poet Homer."

There was a short pause to collect her thoughts. She continued, "All journeys have crossroads that lead the traveler to different destinations. Odysseus how to choose a path and avoid the many pitfalls, traps and dangerous byways that he encountered along the way.

"All of you will have an Odyssey and spiritual journey through life and will face many hardships. There are important warnings and lessons conveyed by the myth. Homer is making a point about the horrors of war and how one can never preserve one's sanity after experiencing and witnessing the horrors and brutalities of war and death. He describes how the combatants are hacked to pieces; how their bones cracked, their eye sockets pierced by spears and how the victors 'gloats' over the felled bodies of the enemy.

Sophia made the point that even after countless wars generations of men still lust for war. This passion for war and the resulting destruction has continued through the ages. Homer is telling a story about the individual warrior.

Once the 'chest beating' is over and the horrors of war have taken their toll, the struggle to survive becomes a warrior's ultimate battle. The need to get home is a way to recover his sanity and live a peaceful, loving life again.

She discussed the crossroads of life. Homer's tale is also a clever warning about temptations. Many times they throws the traveler off his rightful life path. Odysseus was wise enough to overcome temptation of the opportunity for youthful immortality with the beautiful goddess named Calypso and her willing maidens. He found the will to escape and continue his quest to get home to his love, his faithful wife Penelope, and where he was meant to be.

The lecture was over. Sophia open the discussion to questions. A pretty girl in the back of the class stood and asked, "Why did Homer add this instance to his poem? It's about love."

Sofia smiled, gathered her thoughts and answered, "Perhaps he was making the point that love is the strongest force in the world; even more powerful than immortal life or eventual death." That seemed to satisfy her, and she sat down with a look of satisfaction.

She added an observation that, "We are all born as seekers, travelers, mariners and adventurers on the great journey of life and, yet, we are creatures that always look homeward and yearn to be with our family, hearth and the good life. However, we must all leave home and take the journey to become who we are meant to be. Life is a spiritual journey to discover self"

After Sophia finished her teaching rendition of the Odysseus myth, the class discussion turned to Homer. Peter was intrigued by her statement that much of his trip, as Homer told it, could be traced back to actual events and places in Greece and not some mythical land that did not exist. That added a degree of truth to the story of Odysseus.

His brilliance at the battlefields of Troy and his idea of the wooden horse that turned the tide of the war, the perils of his journey back to Ithaca and everything that happened in between was inspirational and it would eventually form the basis of Peter's perception of life, his personality, his dreams, his struggles for survival and a mariner's journey that became part of his life story.

Sophia had a personal thought to share with the class. She went on to say; "The world, the planets, the stars, the earth and actually everything is interconnected in a single consciousness. That's what I believe. Everything is connected at a spiritual level. We all have experienced an opening that must have brought you a sense of wonder and a growing revelation of a far larger and more marvelous world and, perhaps, even a sense of your spiritual identity. When we access this mystic opening and allow ourselves to enter it without any fear, we see that we are all part of something bigger than ourselves. We are all playing a part in the grand story of the universe and we are all unique and essential to its divine music. We are bound together acting out a grand and profound adventure story."

"Let me end this lecture with one more thing; "He was both a myth and there is evidence he was a real person. The ancient Greeks tell us that the hero of Homer's epic poem was anchored in truth. His home was on the Island of Ithaca in the Ionian Sea off the northwest coast of Greece. The remains of his palace with steps carved out of rock have been found which date back to the 8th century BC roughly the period in which Odysseus is believed to have been king of Ithaca." Sophia continued, "Many Greek myths *are* about a glorious quest and the struggle to survive.

As it relates to all of you, the message of Homer's great poem is that we are all on a spiritual journey and that there will be pain, heartache and adventures in our journey. The theme of his great classical story is that we must all be brave and cunning like Odysseus to survive this long, wonderful, exciting journey called life. Like all Greek heroes, we must accept the challengers of life, be aware that we have a life plan, a destiny and know that there is salvation in life that comes with death."

Sophia's lecture on Odyssey had an impact on Peter; particularly when she made the point that the story is based upon real events and ancient places. Like all young teenagers his age, Peter thought that the world revolved around him; but there came a time when he became aware of the spiritual commanding forces of life and he realized that he was a part of something bigger, something confusing and something very mysterious.

Her lecture brought awareness. Life suddenly became a little scarier when he realized that his existence and his destiny were no longer under his complete control. There were greater powers and many conflicting forces that were influencing and governing his life. But he was determined to be brave, face life' challenges and not be restrained by an overly cautious approach to life. He knew there was still a small child's enjoyment of life in him and he reveled in the joy of each day's new challenges and discoveries.

He had an adventures calling, a romantic by nature, he let his dreams inspire him, guide and motivate him into taking bold steps and actions in his journey to become free from Ottoman rule, live out his destiny and find his purpose and place in life.

THE KAFENIO – INRRODUCTIONS

"The ways of a man we all can tell. Your hearts in your stomach, every one, and you'll do any one if you're not first done. We know what the jokes are you love to make, and how you each fancy yourself a rake." Aristophanes: Chorus of Thesmophoriazusae

Peter was anxious to get on with his soulful journey. Somewhere deep inside he felt like his story was going to be adventurous like the mythical hero Odyssey. He was over being a kid hanging on to his mother's apron strings It was time to find a job and help his mother with all the family expenses..

He decided to tell his mother and his Yaya at breakfast and not diner. Nighttime was 'crying time' around the house and he didn't want to get caught up in tears. They would know that it would be a matter of time before he had to leave and become one of Greece's 'missing men'.

At breakfast, he started with a usual light touch. Most times, when he enjoyed a lecture, Peter would tell his mother and his Yaya about it. They had fun discussing the topic and the meaning of it. He enjoyed their usual 'unusual takes' on his lessons.

Peter told them his version of the Odyssey and asked them what they made of it. His Yaya was first to answer; "The Greek myths are 'heaven sent' and like everything that is "heaven sent" the adventures come with a price: danger, pain and madness."

Deme added a bit of folk wisdom; "We cannot know what it means to be sane until we know what madness is.

We find out quickly what Greek madness is." She paused for a moment and added; "One thing about us Greeks is that we all think we are warriors, poets and philosophers. We are full of ourselves and it quickly gets us in trouble."

In her usual sarcastic way, Yaya said. "Yes, but Greeks, particularly Greek men, think they are too great to get in trouble. They think that they know everything. They are really only a bunch of 'know-it-alls'."

She went on to say; "The men at the kafenio are the same. I grew up with them. They were 'mungas'; 'wharf rats' chasing girls and raising hell all the time." Deme interrupted her; "Peter, the men at the kafenio are sweet men. They changed over the years they have become kind and loving – especially to young kids."

Yaya told Peter; "If you are serious, go see Alex for job at the kafenio. He knew your father and will probably hire you. It will be a good education. Peter was pleased with the suggestion. He was serious and he was at an age where he wanted a part-job. It would make him feel important and. at some level, he may have wanted to be around these old men to hear their fanciful stories intermingled with some helpful advice and guidance.

The kafenio in Plomari was a typical café that was a social and meeting place. By tradition, it only catered to men. Its menu consisted of different types of Greek coffee, including frappe, as well as beer, the awful-tasting retsina, and ouzo. It sometimes provided meze or free snacks but rarely served full meals.

The kafenio was a family-run business and it was housed in premises that were furnished quite simply. The walls were whitewashed, and the tables and chairs were battered by time and wear. As simple as the premises were, they were always clean from the kitchen and the bar to the outer patio.

Most kafenio reflect the personality of their owners. The Plomari kafenio was owned by a fine man named Alex, which was short for Alexander. He left the teaching profession to own and operate the kafenio.

Alex was always smiling and enjoyed operating the kafenio. He was a big man with a huge personality. He always said that he was born to be a proprietor of a kafenio. Peter came by the kafenio so many times and knew that it would be a good place tp work.

When he arrived at the kafenio, Alex, the proprietor, greeted him with a big smile. He knew right away that he was the son of his good friend, Peter's Dad. After a very short conversation, Alex offered him a 'part time' job waiting and cleaning the tables that were on the eating areas of the kafenio; but still part of the kafenio. Peter was excited by the offer. It would be his first job and he immediately said, "Yes."

Alex had a big smile and gave Peter a huge handshake. It was time for introductions. He escorted Peter through the noisy patio's eating area to a small messy area at the back of the kafenio for a somewhat formal greetings and a job orientation session. After the formalities were done, Alex said; "Peter you seemed a little confused by the shouting taking place between the men." Peter nodded yes he was.

Alex smiled and said, "Let me reassure you it is all good. The shouting and arguments is an old ritual. The men play cards and other games and they all know that:

"The art of the game is to cheat at cards, the joy of the game is to shout and accuse each other of cheating. At the end of the game, they forgive each other and emerge as comrades. Come their passage, a spiritual bond of love and understanding has been created between these men."

Alex, a former teacher, loved the ancient Greek myths and poetry. At the outset of Peter's interview he quoted Hesiod in his 'Works and Days' as a description of the type of men who frequented the kafenio. The poem addressed what happens to these men after their death. They became as pure spirits:

"But after earth had covered this generation — they are called pure spirits dwelling on the earth, and are kindly, delivering from harm, and guardians of mortal men; for they roam everywhere over the earth, clothed in mist and keep watch on judgments and cruel deeds…."

Peter nodded his head in agreement with Hesiod's poem even though he didn't believe that the disheveled old men at the kafenio became 'holy ghosts' who roamed the land doing good deeds. He told Alex; "My mother use to say that these men had over their lifetimes faced many hardships and dangers. As they approached death, they had become kind and loving spirits." Alex was pleased with Peter's response. They were off to a good start.

He asked Peter if he had any questions. Peter said; "No, not really. Alex smiled and said; "Welcome Peter. Let's make our time together happy and productive. It's time for introductions. Let's go."

As they walked, Peter noticed that Alex was holding back his tears. He later found out that Alex's son left Greece and went to Australia to start a new life. His son was among Greece's missing men. He found out that Alex filled the hole in his heart by employing, training and helping young men.

Alex led Peter to his workplace, the kitchen. Peter would start his business career and journey as a dishwasher. He introduced Peter to Christos, another young teen who worked at the kafenio. In no time at all, they became 'fast friends'. Christos was maybe two or three years older than Peter, but that age difference didn't hamper a close, almost immediate bonding between them. Peter's inner voice was telling him that Christos was a kindred soul and that he would play an important role in his life.

After the introduction was done, Alex led Peter to the patio eating area. He told Peter that the old men of the kafenio came from all walks of life; but they had one thing in common. They always stood ready to help fellow Greeks in need. Alex said; "There is something about these men that evokes the image of the 'loving father'. They have worked hard and suffered through their pains, bore their sorrows bravely and in the process have acquired an aura of wisdom and goodness."

Peter noticed that some of the older men had scars on their faces and he surmised there were scars all over their bodies. Alex picked up on Peter's quiet observation. He said; "Many of these men led dangerous lives and these scars were their 'stripes' of valor."

He was getting the message. Alex liked to talk, He gave Peter a chair and they sat down at a table on the outer edge of the patio. Alex had his teaching 'hat' on and he told Peter:

Aeschylus: "A Greek life was to be lived at the razor's edge was certainly their credo. For them, courage was all important. Death was bearable if done in an honorable way and they would lay down their lives for their families and for Greece. Given the history and suffering of the Greek people at the hands of the Ottoman Turks could the philosophy of these men and their ready willingness to face death for a good cause be any different?"

Alex was finally through for the day. He enjoyed his 'one-sided' conversations with Peter and Peter enjoyed it too. Living with Deme and Yaya taught him how to listen and, more importantly, how to enjoy listening and learning. Alex concluded Peter's first day of work with the words; "You'll be paid for today at the end of the week." Peter was elated with how his first day on the job went. The work arrangements made it possible for Peter to stay in school and worked at the kafenio part-time.

Peter enjoyed his job at the kafenio and was washing dishes and learning how to be a short-order cook. His work was interrupted when Alex came into the kitchen and told Peter to come with him. He wanted to introduce Peter to two mariners who spent time at the café when they came to port. He told Peter that they were two wise men, Costas and Yianni, who made a living traveling from port to port trading and smuggling goods. Peter asked, "Who is the third wise man? Alex replied, "I am."

He said; "They may be important to you someday if you want to leave or have to leave Lesbos. Think of them as men who can take you to a 'port in a storm' if you ever need one."

As they made their approach to two men sitting at a corner table away from the play of the cards, Peter noticed that they were younger than most of the patronage at the kafenio. For some unknown reason, he felt good about meeting them. He was fascinated by their leather hats and clothes. It gave him the feeling that they were adventurous.

Alex made the introductions. Costas seemed to be 'wily in nature'. He wasn't a big man and his long white hair and bronze skin gave him a unique look. Alex told Peter that they were Aegean travelers and was a dreamers and a poet.

Peter thought that was a very strange combination of a 'poet in a smuggler's body.'

Yianni was introduced as the helmsmen and he strove mightily to steer their ship to the shores and places that Costas dreamed about. He was a tall man, had wavy black hair which contrasted with his bronze skin tones. He was the navigator of their life, their relationship and their safety.

Alex asked them; "What's new in your world?" Yianni answered; "The upcoming war for independence. Preparations are being made all over Greece and the Islands for the war with the Turks. Peter overcame his shyness and dared to ask; "Do we have a chance?" Costas explained; "We have the important thing – the will to be free. Most of Greece is free but there are still large areas such as the outer island like Lesbos under the iron rule of the Ottoman Turks. We want to get rid of them and regain all of our lands, free all our people." A little more chatter and Costas and Yianni had finished lunch and left.

The next day, Costas and Yianni came to the kafenio for lunch. When he saw them, Peter rushed over to wait on them. They were getting fond of Peter and to entertain him they had a new story for him.

Yianni asked, "How old are you?" Peter hesitated and said, "I'm sixteen (which was an exaggeration). Yianni said, "Are you aware that Greece and our Balkans cousins are getting ready to fight for their independence from the Ottoman Turks?" Peter said, "I've heard some talk about it, but I thought it was just a dream." Costas added, "Yjr war has been an unresolved human disaster waiting to happen. It will be a bloody struggle and there will be extreme hardship for our people."

He went on, "The 'deals' and decisions by the so-called

Great Powers caused and created havoc for many people around the world. These tyrants carved up conquered territories in ways that separated tribes and peoples and they did it so that they could protect and maintain their power bases by 'divide and conquer' strategies. They usually imposed a king selected by the European Royal families to rule these war-torn territories. Looking back in time, their policies created the conditions for more wars and continued human suffering. Power politics and ill-conceived peace treaties have caused centuries of hatred, violence, destruction and the senseless loss of life in Greece and elsewhere."

Yianni said, "Actually, the war has already started. The klephts, roving bands of Greek guerillas, hide in the mountains and came out at night to kidnap, capture and kill the Ottoman Turks and their Greek collaborators. They explained that the word Klephtes means "thief" or "to steal" but these highwaymen changed. They turned themselves into a self-appointed Greek armatoloi or home guard military/police that defended their mountainous bases and territories from attacks by the Ottoman army.

Costas said, "They are fierce anti-Ottoman insurgents and warlike mountain-folk who lived in the countryside when Greece was a part of the Ottoman Empire. They were the descendants of Greeks who retreated into the mountains during the 15th century in order to avoid Ottoman rule. They carried on a continuous war against Ottoman rule and remained active as brigands until the 19th century."

Yianni added, "They are our 'modern day' Spartans. Some of them are somewhat bad characters, but they, never-the-less, are heroes fighting off the Ottoman Turks. Most of these klephtic bands will participated in one way or another in the Greek War of Independence. Costas said; "The klephts, along with the armatoloi, formed the nucleus of the Greek fighting forces, and played a prominent part throughout its duration. Yannis Makriyannis a famous Greek merchant, military officer, politician and author referred to the "klephtes and armatoloi" as the "yeast of liberty".

Costas chimed in and spoke to the Klephtic immortality as a brave fighting group. He said, "I've heard that there are Klephtic songs and poetry being written in mainland Greece, which are now part of the Greek folk music genre. There is also folk poetry and are thematically based upon the achievements and death of a single klephtic warrior and about the Klephts, as a group.

Costas said much of Southern Europe was prepared to go to war against the Ottomans." He told them about the Czech composer Antonín Dvořák, who wrote a song-cycle named 'Three Modern Greek Poems'. The first one was entitled 'Koljas – Klepht Song' and tells the story of Koljas, the Klepht who killed the famous Ali Pasha."

Yianni advised Costas that the tides were right and it was time for them to go. Costas' parting words were, "Get ready Peter. You are at the right age for military service. I have a feeling that we will soon be 'shoulder-to-shoulder' with the Klephts in the long deep trenches on the killing fields."

Peter heard Costas' words, but didn't react. He just stood there as they left the Kafenio. Costas' words 'rang a bell'. At some level of consciousness, he knew and feared Costas was right.

It was time to go back to the kitchen. He walked back with a big smile on his face. Peter loved the drama and the show at the kafenio and was enthralled by the play and power of the cards. He was attracted by the risk-taking, the challenge, the strategies and the unfolding of a players' hand. He watched as the old men would try to gain advantage in the play of the game by marking (bending or scratching) the cards in certain ways. When someone got caught 'marking' the cards, there was great and heated arguments; but no one real did anything about it because they were all doing it. This obsession with the cards fascinated Peter all the days of his life.

We all get shadow whispers from our subconscious and these whispers are usually heart-felt truths. Peter came to know there was something special about these men. They evoked the image of the 'loving father'. They were close to their end of their time. They worked hard all their days, suffered their pains, bore their sorrows bravely and in the process acquired a certain aura of bravery, wisdom and goodness.

He didn't realize, or didn't care that his mind was being shaped by his exposure to everyone he met there. At some level of consciousness, Peter knew that his time at the kafenio was preparing him for his Odyssey.

The spirited game of cards excited him. Peter felt the comrade bonded by love between the old men at the kafenio. They knew what Peter and other young men were facing. They gave him a broad preview of how different and dangerous the world was. There was a lesson in all this. Peter learned that the old men had one thing in common; they always stood ready to help fellow Greeks in trouble.

THE SECLUDED VIRGINS

"Socrates first observer of madness and blessings bestowed, viewed love as not for the advantage of the lovers; but the opposite, a form of madness, a gift from the gods fraught with the highest bliss."

It was Sunday morning and it was a day for home chores. Peter went into the hills to pick tjr "greens" for dinner and Greek salads. He learned how to distinguish between the poisonous 'greens' and the edible ones for their nightly Greek salad. Meat was not readily available. Exceptions were made for special occasions and holidays. Many Lesbos Greeks were almost 'full-time' vegetarians.

Peter enjoyed his moments in Nature's garden. From his vantage point on the hills he could hear the sounds of Aegean waves hitting the shores. He was fascinated by the Island's hot springs bubble to the surface throughout Lesbos. The intoxicating fresh air gave him a heady feeling. He reveled in Lesbos' beauty and its vast expanse of mountains covered with nature's painting of beautiful green hues rich with unrivaled scenic beauty.

As he made his way up and into the hills, he could look around and see the coast and the port. He remembered that one of the old men at the Kafenio told him that after Crete and Euboea, Lesbos was the largest of the Aegean Islands, as large as a small country. He also remembered hearing that the sailors could look over the side of a boat and see the bottom of the sea.

The climate of Lesbos made his trips into the hills refreshing. The Island has a temperate climate in winter and it was not too hot in the summer time. As he picked the kitchen greens, Peter remembered the stories about the invading horsemen from the North who were attracted to the climate and conditions of Lesbos. He was told stories about the herds of horses running wild throughout Lesbos.

These memories harken back to the horse breeding times of the Trojans when horsemen roamed and inhabited Lesbos and the Hellenistic settlements in the Biga peninsula.

That day he thought about his mother's spiritual stories. She told him that spirits haunted the fields and all the tortured souls from Troy roamed Anatolia and Lesbos. Their sadness filled the air and cast a spell of doom and tearful destruction over everything. Her stories had a great impact on him and made him a little scared; but Peter wasn't dominated by these fearful thoughts. He had a young spirit and wasn't dragged down by life, its problems, its heartaches and the nighttime fears.

He was learning how to deal with these psychological fears and issues. He was growing up quickly and waiting for his chance to see the world and experience the fullness of life, its agonies and its ecstasies.

His gardening excursions were not completely blissful. Peter hated walking into the fields which were dotted with 'shaped-beauty' olive trees. Although the area was beautiful, green and lush, and the views of the Aegean Sea were delightful; the walk was hazardous as excrement from the horses and other animals was everywhere. There was much to see in the field, much to smell, much to step on, and all too much to avoid. Being an old hand at working in these groves, he usually found a secluded place and went to sleep. When he woke up, he started to walk back home after what he termed a "hard" day's work.

Passage I

As he was walking down the long path to home, Peter met his friend Steve coming up toward him, Peter asked him where he was going. Steve smiled and said; "I found a part-time job working for a very wealthy Greek family and they live in a mansion at the top of the hill."

He told Peter, "They have a beautiful teenage daughter and I am really attracted to her. I have trouble keeping my eyes off her." Peter wanted him to tell him mor;, but Steve wouldn't say much more. He would only discuss his work and the odd jobs that he did for them, but nothing more about the young beautiful daughter - Cleis.

Steve asked Peter to change directions and go with him to see the grand estate. He was bragging a little when he said, "Sometimes when I work in the garden I can look into their living room window and see Cleis and her mother at a distance. They spend many hours together in their big room." A shy smile crossed his face when he told Peter, "Once in a while I get to work in the house and I can catch a close glimpses of Cleis. I think that she is taking shy looks at me too."

Peter asked, "Isn't she the quiet girl at the back of the class? The one you are always sending notes to? Are you starting to come on to girls?" Steve answered, "She is holding me off and making me crazy with desire? In fact, she has made me dumber than dumb. All I do is stare and lust after her. It is just crazy madness. I'm being driven out of my mind with wild thoughts about her."

Peter smiled. He was a little envious. All things considered, Peter thought he was fun to be around, had a happy-go-lucky personality which was enhanced by a continued and happy smile. People felt comfortable around him and everyone who knew him always enjoyed his company and his silly sense of humor.

As they were walking up the hill, Steve stopped walking and pointed out a spacious estate. Peter knew immediately that the father must be a very powerful man and that this was dangerous territory. Steve told him that he was engaged in the lucrative export/import business and maintained close ties with the Turkish authorities. Peter asked, "Is that like smuggling?" Steve response was, "It's not smuggling if the Turks let you get away with it."

Steve told Peter that he overheard the men at the kafenio saying that the father spent most of his time with a high-profile mistress. They called her a "hetaerae" and said that she was a beautiful woman, delightful, entertaining, classical and educated. She was a woman who could never be confined to the small spaces and restrictions imposed on wives and mothers and daughters.

Steve went quiet for a moment as his thoughts turned to what can only be described as a teen's main obsession – sex. He said; "I told my mother about Cleis and what I heard about her father. She told me that love demands many things, but one of them is to be true to your feelings. She also said that I should be careful. Her father is a very powerful man and you don't get that much power being a good man.

Steve felt a chill of fear talking about Cleis' dad. He quickly changed the subject. His discussions about his mother were getting a little embarrassing. He said, "I'm going there. Come with me. I'll knock on the door and ask them if they have any odd jobs for us." Peter was more than curious to see their estate and he readily agreed. When they got to the house Peter noticed that it was located on a secluded and private lot on the edge of town. He could see the

Aegean. He was excited just to be there. Beauty is always breathtaking.

Steve knocked on the door and they were let in by a maid. As they waited in the hallway, Cleis appeared from the living room. Peter never realized how beautiful she was. His thoughts began to wander in contemplation of this exquisite creature. He thought of her as a worthy subject for great poetry. Her beauty was "bright in chasten light" and a poetic delight. She was made in the image of a classic Greek goddess. Her fair complexion, white skin, blond streaked hair and blue eyes were of the early Greeks; perhaps of the Aeolian tribes that swept into Lesbos from Indo-Europe centuries ago.

After this brief 'breath-taking' moment, Peter remembered his mother's words, "Avoid beautiful women as they will drive you crazy." He thought that maybe his mother was right. Such unearthly beauty and strangeness that tempts and yet never allows it to be possessed will only torment. He now knew what Steve was going through. She was a truly maddening vision. These people and their vast estate, it all seemed so very remote and mysterious. Peter thought that it would be exquisite pain to be tortured by a women's beauty and the forbidden desires that such beauty inspired.

Peter was surprised when Cleis told her mother she was taking Steve with her to help pick and carry fresh flowers from the garden. Cleis mother said; "Okay. Hurry back."

He was upset that he was being left alone with her mother. She sensed his shyness and gave him a big smile to calm him down.

They talked a while and Peter mentioned that he has a part-time job at the kafenio in town. He wondered 'out loud'; "Why do so many Greek men have disdain for women?"

Cleis' mother mentioned the name Pandora. "Peter in Greek mythology her name means "All Gifts". All the mischief in the lives of men are her gifts. The myth goes:

"The Greek gods gave her a box and told her not to open it knowing full well that she would. When her maligned curiosity of a thief got the best of her, she opened it and all the human emotions, the blind desires and the tangled passions were released — the constructive, destructive and futile ones. Only hope remained in the jar and was not released so that men were forced to live without the relief and promise that it brings."

The gods made sure that she was a ravishing woman who led the whole race and tribe of woman. They became the scourge of mankind who quickly learned that they are only fit partners in times of plenty, but not in accursed poverty."

Peter asked; "How does the tale end? Why wasn't 'hope' released?" She responded to the question; "A typical Greek male answer, "Hope is a delusional state and works like a drug to dull the senses. The gods want us to feel the suffering and the pain of life and through these experiences we become wiser." Peter couldn't be sure whether she believed the myth or not, but the story served its purpose and gave young Pete a Greek male critique of women.

Greek poetry was way over Peter's head. He enjoyed it; but decided to change the subject and talk about more mundane matters. He said; "You have a beautiful home and you have security." She answered in a dejected tone; "Everything is not always as it appears. Sometime I feel trapped with only the illusion of hope that I could do more with my life. That's my interpretation of the myth."

Peter asked; "What is it that you want to do with your life?"

Cleis mother was quick to answer. "Sappho said it best. She was called a priestess of love who was inspired by Aphrodite, the goddess of love. Her poetry was so moving and beautiful that Plato described her as the tenth muse. She was fiery and was blessed with deep, abundant qualities of passion, bravery and fantasy.

This famous Lesbos princess has inspired generations of writers and poets and has left the world thinking of Lesbos and its women as strangely intoxicating, vivid in their contemplations, invitingly sensuous, whimsical, outrageous and, of course, so very overly dramatic.

"There are so many stories. Sappho's perfumed tales of love and the obscure melodies played by the flute girls of Lesbos still Athena throughout the Island. They linger on as intimate and pervasive aromas. The theme of her poetry was a timeless call to love."

She made the point that. "Life is love. Sappho's poetry is the poetry of love. She was the poetess of rapture, soul and love. Her few and only poetic fragments that still remain resonate through the ages. One fragment that I enjoy is "as long as there is breath in my lungs, I shall love —- and even after."

She added, "In fact, every kind act in life is an expression of love. The simple act of watering a flower can be done merely because the plant needs water to survive, but it can also be done as an act of love which transforms the moment from an ordinary activity into a spiritual reality within ourselves. We accomplish this by perpetual prayer and through inner concentration and attuning our soul and as we change the focus of our thoughts to the eternity of the moment, we rise to a higher state of reality."

After that moment, Steve and Cleis came running in the door. Cleis said; "Dad is coming up the hill. You have to leave righ away."

That was music to Peter. He had to get away from this lady who talks in riddles and poetry.

Cleis' mother made a last point to the conversation; "There is an important underlying truth contained in the myths and a reality that I want to share with you boys. Sappho merged her identity with Aphrodite. They became one unto each other. All life is like this. The Greek myths are part of our 'every day' lives and some of us have lives that emulate mythical lives – much like Sappho who took on Aphrodite's persona.

There is more to her story; "Sappho, the perfumed poetess of Lesbos wrote about women who never rang a bell. A short fragment from one of her poems reads:

You rang no bell. When you were living, never did you smell the roses by Olympus, where the Muses dwell. Now that you're dead, your faded ghost in hell is unremembered here on earth. Your fate is to ring no bell in life and to die alone, unremembered and unloved."

Sappho inspired many young ladies to become followers of Aphrodite. There were and are beautiful women who live together in the same house for economic reasons and for social reasons. They call themselves Hetaerae and many of them come from good families. They are educated, write poetry, are dreamers and are determined to make something of their lives. They want to 'ring a bell' in life. Find some up and coming young man and together do great things."

Cleis asked her mother; "Tell us a story about a Hetaerae

who did great things for Greece." Her mother said; "I have a lovely story;

"It is a true story about a beautiful young lady from a wealthy family in a Greek colony in Turkey. Highly educated she made her way to Athens to be in the center of power. She became a Hetaerae and was determine to devote her life to doing something great.

Long story short, she met the young handsome leader of Greece and he fell madly in love with her. Together they inspired the development of the Greek Parthenon high on a hill overlooking Athens. She convinced him to adopt Greek mythology as the Parthenon's motif. Many Greek mythological stories now adorned the top of the Parthenon and the statue of Athena stood tall in the center of the Parthenon's great hall. She rang a bell."

Peter asked; "What were their names?" Cleis mother answered; "That's for you to find out." Peter asked; "What ever happened to them?" She answered; "It is a very sad ending to a beautiful story. Time to go now. My husband will be home soon and he would not like to see you young men here."

With that last word, out the door they went. Peter felt a sigh of relief leaving Cleis house. How strange it all seemed to him. He had this thought that stayed with him all his life. They were two sweet, but pampered women who didn't know anything about the real struggles and passions of life. They had too high an opinion of themselves and they thought that they were so clever and smart with all their talk about Sappho.

As they walked down the hill, Peter said; "They have no idea of the suffering and the realities of the world and of the poor people of Lesbos. The father had protected and sheltered them, but he had denied them meaningful lives and treated them like they were 'dolls' and 'eternal' children.

On his way home, Peter picked a few wildflowers and green mint to give to his mother and to his grandmother, Yaya. The grand old lady would always put a sprig of mint behind his ears as a little Greek perfume. It was a small gesture of love.

He remembered the last poem that Cleis' mother read to him. It was an explanation of what she yearned for. She told Peter that it was the 'heart- brake' story of her life.

He realized what she was saying. Life isn't always about money and security, it is always about purpose and meaning. The sacrifice for others played a big role in achieving their purpose and meaning in life.

PASSAGE II

SOULFUL AGONIES

Choral Foreword: Whispers from Beyond

There is an ancient Greek proverb which opines: "We move forward into the past." One interpretation is that we move forward into the future and relive the past. Like all Greek proverbs, they lend themselves to different interpretations. Another interpretation is that life is cyclical, reality is an illusion and that we are reliving a past life. The themes are that our destinies cannot be changed and all things exist and are connected for all time.

A variation and another interpretation is that history is cyclical, that we incarnate, that we are doomed to repeat history, including the mistakes, cruelties and suffering (e.g. wars). "What goes around, comes around again until we get it right." Sophia favored this interpretation as it related to the Odyssey myth. She told her class that every journey was a spiritual one. This view resonated with Peter and he imagined that he too would take a spiritual journey, his own Odyssey. He would be the hero of his Odyssey and he imagined that he could be Odysseus reincarnated. He said to himself; "Why not throw it out there?"

Peter was now a teenager and about to experience and learn how quickly the trajectory of a life can change and that changes can create and come with danger. He was about to learn how some things in life can be right and wrong at the same time. Traditions make honorable people do harmful acts under the guise of honor. He would struggle to make sense of the workings of his world.

The events in this passage of his life made him aware that he (and we) are not in control. And there are unknown powers driving and shaping our lives. He would come to know that the universe is alive with the machinations of mystical forces. Everything gives off and receives energy impulses and these energy waves can be heard as heavenly chants which resonate with the heart. This other brain (the heart) can recognize these feelings as impulses that can change the sway and direction of a life.

These whispers from beyond were accessed by ancient Tribal people. From time immemorial, they 'sung and hummed' the eternal chants as a way to connect with their ancestors and spiritual guides. They believed by chanting and dancing they were able to release the healing power of the universe. It was a power that was felt at a deep level of consciousness and was released when the chants began. The chanting and dancing can induce a trance or spell that inspires and change for the better the play of destiny and fate.

Peter was entering a phase in his life where he was challenged by dangerous events. Many of these events were beyond his control. He would eventually experience and understand 'salvation', not in its religious context, but through the workings of silent, unknown forces that influence and navigate his life trajectory.

The chapters comprising Passage II have this common theme. Peter would learn, the hard way that he (we) was not completely in control of his own life. He had much to learn about destiny and free will. At times, it seemed that he had little or no control over what happened to him and that there are unseen forces that 'push, pull, direct and chisel' everyone's life to achieve the purpose and meaning of destiny's calling.

THE CHOKING SHREDS OF TRADITION

"Straightway may I die, after doing vengeance upon the wrongdoer, that I may not stay here, jeered at as cowards?" Socrates

There is a stage in life which could be described as the 'agony of becoming. It is usually early in life when we become conscious of the many dangers of life' and become suddenly aware that everyone has their agonizing moments in life.

Peter was at that stage. He was about to enter a new and challenging phase in his life. Before he even knew what was happening events seemed to take control of his life and everything came crashing down on and around him. These events just seemed to happen and seemed to be beyond his control. These were one of those times that would presently shape his mind and ultimately his future.

He went to work at the kafenio and was feeling refreshingly bored. As he entered the patio area in front of the kafenio, he saw four or five men huddled around Christos, all of whom were talking to him at once. Alex seemed to be driving the narrative and poor Christos was seated in the middle listening and being overwhelmed by the conversations.

Alex gained control over the discourse and said loud and clear; "It is all about the Greek traditions of honor. To kill and die for love and honor is very Greek in origin. Not surprisingly, there is pathos at the heart of many tender Greek poems and songs. The Greek myths and history are replete with stories that express and promote this divine code of honor at any cost."

Christos seemed confused. Alex continued; "There is an epitaph in the third century by the poet Amte that records a very solemn event. There was a number of sweet maidens who committed suicide rather than face the dishonor of rape or enslavement. Their epitaph reads:

"We leave you, Miletus, dear homeland, because we rejected thee lawless insolence f impious Gaul's {277 B.C.}. We were three maidens, your citizens. The violent aggression of the Celts brought us to this fate. We did not wait for unholy union or marriage, but we found ourselves a protector in death."

A man named Stratios, a stately old Greek, chimed in; "We Greeks are distinguished by this emphasis on honor in love and all the many forms and permutations that it takes. Lives had been ruled by love and ruined by the unyielding tradition. Add in the moral judgment of 'good and evil' and the pathos of Greek life cannot help overwhelm our thoughts and rational.

Remember, you may feel 'faint at heart' by what you must do. The underlying emotional currents and the ethical foundations of Greek drama and tragedy were born out of this emphasis on honor, more sacred than life and Kleos, dying the right death. The Greeks are bound by their traditions and they drown in their sea of emotions from the consequences of their actions to defend honor at any cost. "

Christos finally stood up and said he would confront Dmitri and defend his sister and his family's honor. At that moment, Alex took Peter aside and told him to go with Christos and help him as much as he could. His head numb with the constant barrage of historic hysteria, Peter just nodded his head slowly 'okay'.

After they finished their shift at work, Christos and Peter were getting ready to leave when Alex came up to Christos and gave him a 'just in case' green bag and wished them both 'good luck'. He told them to check back with him when they were finished and if they needed anything.

They took a short-cut and walked up the hill toward Dimitri's home. Christos said; "What is unusual you would think that Dmitri would accept his responsibilities and would marry my sister. I'm upset and and 'pissed' that he took advantage of my young sister. She is really a sweet young girl and very pretty. He was willing to let her face the consequences of what they did alone while he ran around like a 'big' manga.

Peter felt that his responsibility was to be by Christos' side. Christos' father was overseas working in Australia and it was left for Christos to deal with Dmitri and protect the reputation of his younger sister and his family. Christos had no choice. He would have to force the issue of marriage or be viewed as a coward and his family forced to live in shame existing as dark shadows living without honor or respect.

Christos knew that his sister was in extreme distress and not thinking clearly. He was not sure what she would do to herself and to her baby. Would she commit suicide or would she have the baby and make her way in the world as best she could? He didn't think she would destroy herself; but he knew that he had to take effective action to keep her from taking drastic steps. They had to escape from destiny's trap, and it was up to him to find a solution and a way out of the mess.

They both knew that Dmitri was much stronger and bigger then both of them and that he would prevail in a fight. Christos would lose and be humiliated but he would have protected his family's honor by trying at great cost to himself. He would need Peter's help. Together, they could be more of a match for him and he might be forced to listen to them. Dmitri had to be convinced to do the right thing and marry her. Surely, he must have some tender feelings for her as she was a morally a good person and she risked everything for him and for love.

Peter asked Christos; "What are you going to do. You have no real plan and he is a 'hot-headed' jerk. Christos didn't really have a plan; but he thought that they would talk to him about doing the right thing." Peter thought Christos was crazy to think they could talk 'sense' to a 'hot head'.

Peter asked the next obvious question; "What were they

going to do if he wouldn't cooperate and even got belligerent?" Christos answered; "We'd have a fight on our hands. Tackle him low and pull his legs down. I'll jump on top of him."

They finally made it to the hill. Dmitri and his family had a home at the top of this high hill which slopped gently down in some places and steep in other areas. There was a vacant lot in the middle of the hill and they waited there for him. Not many houses were built near the empty lot and it was relatively remote area.

Christos knew that Dmitri was a creature of habit and he came this way on a regular basis as he made his way into the city for a good time. They would be able to confront Dmitri in a private and secluded spot. All the while, Peter was hoping that he would not come out that night and he could just go home without having to deal with all this craziness.

Of course, that was not to be. Dmitri was walking down from the top of the hill alone and at a relatively slow gait. They were hidden in the bushes waiting for the opportune time to come out and confront him. That moment came too soon for Peter. Christos jumped out and got right into his face. His 'pent up anger' got the best of both of them and they started hollering at each other. Neither one of them was making any sense. One thing was clear and that was Dmitri had no intention of marrying Christos' sister or helping to support the child. He even went so far as to deny he had any sex with her.

Dmitri then made an unpardonable comment – he called her a whore. The fight broke out immediately between Christos and Dmitri. Peter went for Dmitri's legs to get him on the ground but Dmitri started kicking him and keeping him away. He caught Peter in the stomach and knocked the wind out of him and sent him down the hill. While Dimitri was attacking Peter, Christos was throwing punches at him. But he didn't have the experience and the strength that Dmitri had and didn't know how to move his legs and body behind his punches for extra power.

All the while Dmitri who was much taller than Christos or Peter was raining hard blows down on Christos' head. All the while Peter was scrambling up the hill to help Christos.

Christos' fear was that Dmitri would soon be on top of him punching him in the face and doing head slams against the road. At that point, Peter made it to the lower top of the hill and was shocked to see Christos and Dimitri standing tall, 'eye to eye' and 'body to body'. Neither one of them was moving. Christos had his left hand on Dimitri's shoulder and seemed to be holding him close to him. They never moved and just stared at each other.

Then Dmitri legs seemed to give out on him and he dropped slowly to the ground. Peter saw him clutch the knife in his stomach. He felled down slowly to his knees and was holding the top of the knife that Christos had shoved into him. Blood was spurting all over. Dmitri was face up and was shaking all over trying to stem off death. Then he stopped. He was dead.

It was over. Peter couldn't believe his eyes and just stared at Dmitri. "What have you done?" he shouted at Christos who was stunned by what he did. Taking the knife from the green bag was a mistake and all he was going to do was threaten him with it, not use it. Peter was shaking all over as was Christos. They both were crying and Christos was shouting over and over again; "What have I done? I've ruined my sister's life, your life and mine. I've made a mess of everything."

Peter helped Christos to his feet. Christos had regained his senses. He took the knife from Dimitri's stomach and wiped it clean on Dimitri's clothes and then put it back in the green bag. The both of them pushed Dmitri down the hill and out of sight of morning walkers. The panic and the adrenalin kicked into hyper-gear and they were both ran down the hill and away from the scene.

They were both scared. They felt insignificant and guilty of a great crime. They were sick with the horror and darkness of what took place. They were in trouble and immersed in the gruesome reality of what took place. They heard stories about people getting killed all the time; but it was horrifying to be part of the scene, to have caused his death, to see him lying there and to watch as he bled to death. It made them sick to see the knife in his stomach and watch him try to say something before he died. That scene went on for about fifteen seconds before he rolled over and died.

Peter's worst fears and nightmares had come true .He muttered; "Christos, what are we going to do?" Christos was too shock up to talk; but he managed to tell Peter, "Go home and I'll come over early in the morning with a plan. I need to see someone." Peter was clearly panicked and in a shaky voice he told him; "You can't tell anyone what happened. We'll be in trouble."

Christos whispered; "Go inside and say nothing. I'll be back in the morning with a plan." There was no pushback. Peter went into the house. Fortunately, nobody was up and he went straight to the bathroom to wash up and hide his bloody clothes. It was a relief to be back in his bed again. All he could do was bury his head in his pillow and cry.

SHADOW WHISPERS

"Look to the things of God. Know that you are bound to help all who are wronged, bound to constrain all who would destroy the law. Honor is more sacred than life."
Anonymous Greek proverb

Peter couldn't get his mind clear of the events and couldn't get a restful night sleep. He tossed, turned, squirmed from one side of the bed to the other. He was trapped in a rim sleep; reliving the horrid events leading to Dmitri's death. Everything happened so fast that he still couldn't get his mind into and around the painful consequences of what took place.

He was caught in a time warp and couldn't get the wheels of time to move forward. He was held still, suffocating, and was reliving the scenes of that unfortunate reality over and over again.

His mother sensed his pain and went to him. She kissed him on his forehead and softly told him to wake up; but he didn't react to her kiss as he normally did. The kiss came at the same time as Peter was seeing Dmitri in his 'dream' state telling Peter that he forgave him for what happened. The kiss was given at the same time that the forgiveness came in his dream state. It confused Peter.

When he opened his eyes, he could see his mother leaning over him, concerned and asking him in soft gentle words, "Are you hurt? Why is there blood all over your clothes?"

Peter rose slowly. In a 'sleep-graveled' voice, he said; "Not me. It's not my blood." As soon as she heard that it was not his blood and that he had no injuries; the soft, loving voice changed. She started yelling at him and wanted to know what happened last night.

He tried to calm her down. The words 'It was an honor-killing' came pouring out first. He told his mother, Christos' sister was violated by Dimitri. He wouldn't marry her and protect her and her family's honor as tradition required."

Peter described the fight that resulted in Dmitri's death. She was quiet, and was momentarily paralyzed by the seriousness of the situation.

She concluded that it was what it was. There was nothing she could do to change the circumstances. Calmly, she told Peter, "Let me think about what happened and what we should do. We'll talk a little later after you get up."

She went into the kitchen where Yaya was waiting. She poured herself and Yaya strong cups of Turkish coffee and explained the situation to her. Yaya asked, "What are we to going to do?" Deme said, "My first reaction and thought were to get Peter away from Plomari; but where could he go? He was still very young and she didn't think he was ready to be on his own yet."

Peter smelled the coffee, woke up and came into the kitchen. He told them what happened last night and how everything went so wrong. "It was about tradition and his sister and his family's sacred honor. I don't understand how tradition is a good thing. It is supposed to give us moral guidance. How can anything be so good and bad at the same time?"

Yaya said; "Life can be complicated. Good intensions sometimes creates bad outcomes and bad actions sometimes creates good outcomes. Deme interceded; "Yaya don't go into the Greek myths. You made your point."

There was a pause and Yaya took up the conversation

where Deme left off; "The Greek people cherish 'tradition and protecting a family's sacred honor. Traditions make us who we are in the eyes of all who see."

Deme added; "Tradition is about protecting one's Kleos- their honor and how history would perceive them. The brave mothers would not let themselves and their children live lives and be known as the slaves of a vicious Turkish overlord."

Yaya nodded her head 'yes'. "It was and is an event in history-the early 1800's- still near and dear to the national hearts of the Greek people. She went on and rhapsodized; "It was called the dance of Zaloggou – the dance of death. I still remember the first line of a poem written in honor of the Greek mothers and their children who died that day:

"Farewell Spring. We must go and embrace and embrace our Fate."

The Greek people will never forget the tragic heroism of these women and children. It was called the Dance of Zaloggou. It was a sacred moment and event where brave Greek mothers and their children displayed the highest call to country, courage and honor, even above life."

Yaya stopped talking. She was holding back her tears and couldn't talk clearly. She asked Deme; "Please tell the story. I need a moment to calm down. I cry every time I talk or think about what happened to these brave souls. It is a very sad story."

Deme took over the conversation. "This all took place during the Souliote War back in the 1800's. The Souliotes lost a battle to a Ottoman Warlord named Ali Pasha and began evacuating Souli. When they evacuated they had to leave behind a group of mothers and their children who were trapped in a mountainous area.

The brave souls, the mothers and their children were left with a horrible choice. Do they surrender to a vicious Ottoman war lord and suffer the dishonor of slavery and other atrocities at the hands of these Ottoman Turks and their militia war lord and his men. Surrendering to the Ottoman Turks and seeking mercy was taking a big risk for them and their children. Or, do they take their own lives – preferring to die and do they put their Fate in the hands of God.

Deme paused for a moment. She said; "The last line of a 'Dance of Zaloggou' poem tells it all:

"*One moment, one short moment…..then forever sorrow.*"

They gathered at a clearing on the top of the mountain overlooking a steep rocky cliff and set up a picnic area. The Children ran around and played. The mothers and some olf men who were also left behind formed a circle to discuss what they were going to do. After some discussion, the mothers followed tradition and selected honorable deaths for the children and themselves.

They took their children to the edge of the cliff where they kneeled to God, prayed, hugged their children one last time and, in a moment of absolute agony, they wept as they let go of their babies and children. They disappeared off the cliff leaving the brave mothers in a deadly silence. Some of the mothers couldn't bear to throw their babies off the cliff and see them fall to their death. They jumped off the cliff clutching their children to their hearts.

The other remaining mothers gathered at the clearing. One of them started singing a Greek song as they started forming a line dance. They all cried, hugged each other and told one another of their love for them. They knelt down and prayed and asked God to take them and their children into His arms. One brave mother went to the head of the line.

She was selected by all the mothers because they knew she would not falter at the last minute and would lead them off the cliff to be with their babies.

Deme felt their pain and had to stop talking. She wiped the tears flowing down her cheeks. Yaya added one last thought about the mother and their children. She said; "They did what every Greek does when face such terrors, they defiantly sing and dance and, then, they comply with tradition and die honorable deaths."

Peter asked; "I don't mean to be disrespectful and I understand the pain and sacrifice of the brave mothers, but how does this tragic story justify 'traditions' and Dimitri's death?"

Deme answered; "Christos defended his honor and his family's honor. It is about his Kleos. How he wants the Greek people to see and remember him – not as a coward but as a Greek son and brother with the courage of his convictions." Peter shook his head 'yes' It 'kind of' makes sense."

Deme said; "Tradition most times requires the Christening blood of violence."

Yaya changed the dialogue and the mood. She said loudly; "It is time for the cups." Deme served some dark Turkish roast. They quietly drank their coffee and then turned them over and let the remaining coffee dry into prophetic pattern that they could read.

After a few moments, Deme read the streaks in her cup. She asked Yaya; "What are you seeing in your cup?" Yaya replied; "I see an abstract image of a cross and another image that I can't quite make out. They looked at each other and smiled. Their subconscious minds were calling out the same message – the steeple and sanctuary of a church.

Deme made the observation that; "A church is the only place where he would be safe from the Turkish authorities and the Greek police. This move had an advantage. Historically, the Greek police believed that honor killings should be tolerated. The Ottoman Turks were superstitious and would not raid a church of any denomination.

Peter asked; "What are we going to do?" She looked into his eyes and said, "The messages in the cups are clear. I have to see if we can get you into one of the churches. The authorities will accept that solution. This will protect and save you." He knew that she was right.

But he was curious about how the message came from the cups. He asked; "How can that possibly be? How do you know what you are seeing is true?"

His mother replied first; "It is my truth from within that I see. When I see an image or images their meaning comes to me as shadow whispers from my subconscious."

Yaya responded with another explanation; "Peter, it is what you feel when you see a pattern that makes sense. You will feel a sudden surge of energy overwhelm you. Deep insides, your mind think it and your heart feels it, you will know it to be true and you better act on the information as foretold." Peter accepted her explanation without comment.

He went back to bed thinking and knowing that the ancients made the Greek believers in the mysteries and the signs and voices that come from the other side. Reading the Turkish coffee cups was one of the ways to summon signs from beyond.

After Peter left the kitchen, in a whisper, Yaya said; "There was another image in my cup. It seemed to be a 'gun' that was next to the church steeple. I didn't say anything until we talked about it." Deme said, "He's upset enough.

Let's not say anything about a gun and all it signifies to him. He'll deal with it when it comes. He doesn't need to worry about it before it comes."

Early the next morning Christos came by and tapped quietly on his bedroom window. Peter went quietly through the house and met him outside. "Peter I've arranged for us to go to the mainland and get away from here. We can join the Greek army and no one can put the blame on us. Get ready as fast as you can so that we can get away before his body is discovered and they coming looking for us.

Peter told Christos, "I can't go. I have to stay." Christos said he understood, but he was disappointed as he really wanted Peter to go with him. Peter said, "No, I can't go and I can't give you a good reason why I can't go." Christos thanked Peter for trying to help him and hoped that someday he could repay him. They hugged each other and said goodbye.

Before he left, Peter asked him about his sister. He told Peter, "I told her what happened and she started crying and was upset with me for killing him. She kept hitting me on the chest."

Peter asked, "What did you tell her?" Christos answered, "What could I say but to tell her that I loved her. Then I told her that I had to leave and she stopped crying. She hugged me and held me tight for a long time. She told me that she loved me for trying to help."

Christos' eyes welled with tears and he tried to hold them back. He said; "Peter, I have never felt so bad. I finally thought about her and her pain. It was no longer about me. It was about her. She has lost both Dmitri and me" he said sadly. Christos could not say anything more about his sister's plight.

"Peter, I must go. There is one thing I need to tell you. I'm so sorry I got you into my problems. One more thing. I've come to love you like a brother. I know we'll met again. When we met again just know that I will be there for you if you need me. Oh yes. If you need to leave Lesbos, see Alex who will make the arrangements with Costas and Yianni."

There was a moment of silence while Peter released his anger toward Christos. He felt a comradeship with him and bonded with him when they went through the tragic experience with him. Peter said, "Bye brother. Till we meet again." A 'man hug' and Christos was gone, running down the road to the port.

KYRIE ELEISON — HAVE MERCY ON US

"God – the pathway of his purpose are hard to find. And yet it shines out through the gloom, in the dark chance of human life. Effortless and calm He works his perfect will." Aeschylus

Saint Nicholas Orthodox Church Plomari

Deme made breakfast early the next day to give them a little extra time to talk about the tumultuous events before they went to the Church. Deme discussed her plan to meet with the clergy. She asked; "Peter how do you feel about telling them that you wanted to join their religious order?" Peter said; "There doesn't seem to be any other choice."

She told Peter; "It makes no difference if you leave the church before your training is done and you were ordained. With Christos gone; there is a chance that the authorities will blame everything on you. You need to wait until the authorities are onto something else." Peter answered; "I understand."

To keep everything 'light' Deme changed the subject and asked Yaya; "What she would have done if she was one of the mothers that was trapped at the mountain in Zaloggou?" Yaya smiled. She knew it was a 'set up' question. "I would have cried and then tossed you over the cliff. Then I would have joined the dance line and joined you and everyone else down below."

Deme said; "Peter, you're lucky. Yaya is not in charge. We are not going to throw you away. We're going to run away and hid for a while." She reached out and everyone joined together in a family hug. Deme said; "Yaya, you know I was just kidding." Yaya answered; "Of course I did; but I wasn't." Everyone was smiling.

After breakfast, Deme and Peter left for the Church of St. Nicholas. They would try to get Peter into a training program to be a priest or arrange for the protection of the sanctuary program. All the while, Peter was dreading what was taking place.

When they arrived at the Church, they were greeted by Father Theodore. He met them at the entrance to the Church and listened quietly to Deme's reason for the visit. She told him that Peter was interested in becoming a priest and that he would make a wonderful priest. She wanted him to have an opportunity to answer his religious calling. She did not mention the honor killing of Dmitri.

Father Theodore admitted them to the Church and introduced them to a young priest named Father Paris. He told them that Father Paris would be their guide and provide for their needs. He told them that he would present their request to the Council that was currently in session. He excused himself and went into a room off to side of the magnificent alter.

Peter felt comfortable with Father Paris. He was young, handsome, had a close-cut beard and his hair was cut relatively short. Peter noticed that he was not wearing a ridiculous 'stove-pipe' hat. He believed that Father Paris was his own man and open to 'frank' discussions of circumstances.

Father Paris said; "There is a small group of tourists on a guided tour of the Church and it might be interesting to join the group and hear what the tour guide was saying. He told them that it would be a while before Father Theodore returned. Deme and Peter agreed and Father Paris waived down the tour guide.

Introductions were made. His name was George Parkas. They happily joined the group of tourists and listened intently to his presentation about the Church and the Greek Orthodox religion:

"It is a beautiful church with a three aisled basilica. The roof is made of wood and covered with tiles. When you go inside, you will see beautiful sights including the ceilings which are decorated with full size pictures of the twelve apostles and in the center of the vault, there is a painting of

Jesus Christ Pantocrater. He is displayed in full size coming out of the clouds surrounded by the cherubs."

At that point, the Choir high above on the second floor started singing. Parkas talked over them and said;

"The Religious chant is the art and means of restoring one's spirit and beliefs and the poetry of it goes back to Greece's archaic beginnings. Many of the Orthodox Church chants were originally composed and for centuries used in a society where the concept of time was profoundly different from our own. These chants are the cries and prayers of lonely souls looking to connect with the holy Mother and are sung as heavenly voices. They convey an existence of timelessness.

The chants inspire the men of the cloth and gave them a delightful escape from time. In their cathedral there is no past, there is only the time, place and history of their Lord which for them is the beginning and end of everything. Their beginning of time starts with the acknowledgement of a God which is above all and their everlasting form of reality. This is their eternal Presence. There are memories of past times before they made their commitment to God; yet the world for them was now sacred. They live the religious myths as spiritual and immanent realities.

The ancient Greeks believed the chants were the music of the spheres and the gods. They believed that the fates heard the music and determined the steps of everyone's dance. It was time for Peter's journey to begin."

The Choir then changed from a chant to a musical prayer. Parkas explained: "The song they are singing is entitled: "Ave Marie" with lyrics by Roggero:

"Ave Maria, listen to a lonely soul from this troubled earth,
My voice rises up and flies away in the night.
You, outside of time and space, a breath from heaven, guardian of
Secrets and truths; light as the wind before a silent world
You are truly the joy that sets us free.
Ave Maria, listen to a true soul, when I know I am at peace
Your light explodes insides me as a sun.
You outside of time and space, a breath
Secrets and truths; on its knee, the world has no way out.
You powerful as a song, lift my faith from delusion with dignity.
Ave Maria, I gaze at the expanse of stars, beyond sins and mysteries, to reach the center of my life."

Peter and Deme were enjoying the singing. Deme thought that Parkas' presentation was interesting; but Peter just wanted to hear the Choir. He felt that the heavenly singing diminish existence in a good way. The feelings and the inspiration of the chants were in sharp contrast to the joyous Greek folk dances and their rhythm.

As they left the tourist group, Peter whispered to his mother; "The chants made me feel like I was in another reality. It was as if I was sitting on a rock jetty at the port lost in my thoughts and in my own reality in the world."

He immediately understood how the meditative power of the chants moved one's soul and consciousness into a spiritual spell. Although Peter did not believe in a creator-God, he felt that there was a spiritual force that influences the physical world. When he heard the heavenly chants, he sensed that major changes in his young life were coming. He felt safe in the church and had the eerie feeling that he was there to be saved.

Father Paris came up to them and sat next to them on the Church bench facing the Church alter. He told them that Father Theodore would meet them shortly. As they were talking, Father Theodore entered the room and asked Peter to follow him. Both Deme and Peter stood up to go, but the priest told Deme that only Peter was to meet with the council.

This was the moment of moments for Peter. He told himself to use what he learned at the Kafenio. It was a moment of high anxiety that required a straight face. He went into the room ready to play his hand.

He couldn't tell how many priests were in the room, but there were a number of them sitting at a large long wooden table facing him. He assumed that this was the board of priests who were going to make the final decision.

Peter was more than a little tense, but he couldn't show it. This was the first time in his life that he was going to be judged and he wasn't sure what he should do and say to them. He didn't want to make a drastic error?

Deme was just as nervous waiting in another room. There was nothing she could do to help him and that feeling of helplessness was breaking down her composure. She could feel her eyes beginning to "well" with tears. Stoically, but gently, she wiped them away so as to not show any weakness.

Meanwhile, Father Theodore was talking to Peter with sensitive, almost caring words. He told Peter that he only had a few questions. The first being, "Do you know what an 'honor' killing is?" Peter answered, "I think so. It is when somebody brings shame on a family and he is killed for that by a family member or friend to protect the honor of the family"

"Yes Peter, We believe that it was the killing by a member of a family because of the belief that the victim was shamed and the family dishonored. The concept of family honor is extremely important in Greece. The family is viewed as the main source of honor and the community places a high value on the relationship between honor and the family. Acts by family members which may be considered inappropriate are seen as bringing shame to the family in the eyes of the community."

We want to know, "Were you there when Dmitri was killed? Peter was surprised by the question and for a moment he wasn't sure what to say. He wondered, "How did they find out about Dmitri and how did they find out that he was there." His mother did not say anything about Dimitri.

Peter learned how to maintain a 'poker face' watching the card games at the kafenio and that might be a way of avoiding the question and letting the stage play of the meeting go forward and give him some clues on how to conduct himself. He thought about it for a few seconds and ultimately, he decided that stalling wouldn't help him and that he should be truthful. He answered, "Yes."

"What happened that night?" Peter said, "I'm not sure. Everything was a blur." Father Theo asked, "Did you stab him?" Peter was visually disturbed and answered, "No, no, I did not. I thought we were there just to talk to him." Father Theo could see that he was nervous, almost scared, and decided to stop questioning him. Instead he asked, "Peter tell us what happened that night?"

Peter looked unsure and didn't know whether he would get in trouble by telling them what happened. He always believed that he would not and should not discuss that night with anyone other than his mother. He was a little confused because his mother didn't tell them about it.

Father Theodore reassured him, "Peter whatever we discuss here and now will not go outside this room." Peter didn't feel like he had a choice and told them what happened that night. He ended his dialogue with the words, "Dmitri kicked me in the stomach and I rolled over into the ditch. The next thing I knew he and Christos fell over and only Christos stood up. There was blood everywhere."

As soon as Peter stopped talking, the priests at the table immediately engaged in a heated debate over the concept of an honor killing or shame killing and whether such an act is excusable in the eyes of the Church. A point was raised whether sanctuary for someone involved in such a killing should be granted. At that moment Father excused Peter from the room because the decision could ultimately involve him.

After some discussion, a decision was reach. Father Theodore and Father Paris came out to tell Peter and his mother the good news. Peter would be admitted to the Church. They told her that Peter would be safe with them and that the church was a sanctuary where mercy, pity and love dwells and so dwells the presence and influence of God's spirit.

The suspense was over. Peter walked his mother to the front door of the Church. Both of them had tears in their eyes as they hugged each other and said their goodbyes. Deme asked him if he told them that he was there. He said that they already knew. She asked him, "How did they find out?"

"I don't know how they found out, but I had no choice but to admit I was there." Peter said, "I had to play out the hand." She asked him, "Where did you learn about playing out a hand? What kind of talk is that? He answered, "I learned it from the old Greeks at the kafenio. I watch them play cards and I study the moves they make. The play of the cards is really exciting."

Deme said, "My God! Don't tell me that your teachers are a bunch of old Greeks playing cards all day." He answered, "They are really smart. They know how to bluff, what cards to play, when to quit and leave the table, how to take your losses like a man and how to save some of your gains for the next game. You can't even tell if they have a good hand or not. They do all this with a 'straight' face."

There was nothing more she could say or do. Peter didn't say anything to his mother; but deep inside he was holding back a loud shout-out: "Yashooo… to the old Greek card players at the Kafenio."

Deme felt her sadness, but it was tempered with some relief. She wondered whether she did the right thing for Peter. As she leaving the Church, she looked back one more time. She could see her son still standing in the doorway. He seemed like a lost soul to her, but there were no other choices for them.

She now realizes that Peter was lost to her. Out of love and concern for her son, she had delivered him to the Church for salvation. It was her only choice. She believed that he would be safe there. She told herself that he was in God's hands now.

As she was leaving the Church, something deep inside told her to look back. Peter was in the doorway to the

Church watching her as she left. She felt her tears take control at the thought that her son was a poor lost son. His life had been transformed in a moment. She realized that she had lost him to his Fate.

Her time with Peter was almost over. It was a sacred moment for her. She felt the need for a short prayer for God to protect him. From deep in her being came an old prayer that her deceased father taught her.

She just let it flow. It was an ancient 'aboriginal' prayer; which later was adopted as a Christian prayer.

In what seemed to be a sudden burst of energy, the words came quickly to her…… "Kyrie Eleison" (Lord, have mercy). This Greek prayer was far more ancient than Christianity and was used through the ages. In times of danger, pain, suffering and despair "Kyrie Eleison" was and is an entreaty to God for mercy, relief and salvation.

THE TWIN LIES

"Mythology was born as early innocence, beauty, chants and poetry. Its merger with truth, custom and ceremony lead to religion and, ultimately, science."

Father Paris was assigned primary responsibility for Peter's 'welfare', which included defining Peter's responsibilities, introducing him to church life and policies and his indoctrination into the conceptual basis of Christian belief and religion.

Peter tried to make conversation in an effort to show his perceived interest in joining the Church. He initiated his convers by asking; "Why is everyone wearing the same black robes with the tall hats?" Father Paris had a broad smile when he answered; "We wear the black robe because it is the easiest and cheapest color to dye fabric and it doesn't show any stains." Peter smiled in appreciation for the silly remark to his silly question.

Father Paris ended the 'silly talk' by telling Peter; "I assume that your question was a serious one. It goes to our fundamental belief system. I'll give you a more serious answer tomorrow at study class. After class, I'll go over your work and study assignments.

The next morning Father Paris came by Peter's bedroom and he showed Peter the way to the study class. Introductions were made among the students and then it was class time.

Father Paris opened the class by referring Peter's question from the day before; "Peter had an interesting question regarding the black robes we all wear. The black robes and apparel are important symbols of our commitment to spiritual poverty."

Father Paris stopped for questions and then continued; "The color is identified with sorrow; but in the case of priestly robe this color has another symbolic meaning. A black cassock is to remind a priest that he 'dies to the world' every day and immerses in eternity. We live in a very secular world. The wearing of the cassock continues to be a visible sign of our belief and of the consecration of our lives to the service of the Lord and His Church."

There was a question from one of the students in the back of the room; "What does the cassock mean?"

Father Paris answered, "The symbolism of the cassock symbolizes humility, poverty and devotion. The Roman collar symbolizes obedience; the sash or cincture around the waist, chastity; and the color black, poverty.

He joked; "I guess it's time for a little irreverent humor. You could say that we are standard interchangeable parts." All the students appreciated his humor and gave him big smiles all around.

Another student rose and asked; "I've always wondered how Christ could return in "bodily form". How can that be?" Father Paris answered, "That's a Roman belief. We believe that He came back in spiritual form."

"Was he the only son of God?" Father Paris replied, "The short answer is that we are all spiritual beings. The wording in the Greek version of the bible had it as; "He was 'a' son of God; not 'the' only son of God. We are all children of God."

Father Paris announced; "We have time for one more question."

Peter raised his arm to speak. "There is something that always confused me. My Yaya says that the Greek myths and the Christian religion are twin lies. She also said that the story about the serpent in the garden and original sin was inconsistent with ancient Greek thinking. She said that the old Greeks believed that the serpent brought consciousness to humanity."

Father Paris couldn't wait to reply; "They are not "twin lies". They are based on similar belief systems. The ancient Greek myth makers and our religious fathers believed that everything is spiritual and that at the core of everything is a powerful spiritual consciousness.

They are different philosophies and movements in history; but this does not destroy the divine underpinnings of Christianity or the spiritual basis of Greek mythology. Christianity is a way of living and thanking God for his many blessing.

As to the myths, it's said that they convey encoded wisdoms for humanity. They tell of the experiences, history and existence which provide the insights and wisdom of past times and lives. The stories of the bible tell of eternal truths of a higher order and holy divinity.

Father Paris continued to talk about his favorite subjects. "Of course, the religion and Greek mythology are not twin lies. Think of them as truthful expressions in poetic form. They express the ultimate realities that our ancestors tried to convey to us in words that we can understand. They elevates the mind beyond the rim of the eternal to what can be known; but not adequately told. They deal with ultimate truths."

Class was over. Father Paris said; "Peter you stay after class so that I can give you your assignments and schedule."

After everyone left, he told Peter; "I have a gift for you." He handed Peter a plain and simple black pant suit and shoes. It was a bright shinny moment in Peter's life. He felt like a man of the cloth. He did feel good about it, but deep in his heart he couldn't convince himself that he was a believer. He didn't believe that there is a creator-God and that death was final. As much as he wanted to believe in a God; he couldn't love God into existence.

Father Paris said; "Peter you have three primary tasks and responsibilities and they are to work at the Charity Dinners twice a week, attend study class every as scheduled and work on the clean-up crew as needed." Peter answered; "Yes. I understand. But I have one request and that is to be able to listen to the Choir practice." Father Paris said. "Of course. What is it that draws you there?"

"It puts me near the Port and the crashing waves. I remember the tour guide – George Parkas said that the chants and Church music dimities reality. I think that he is wrong. It elevates reality." Father Paris added; "It also connects us to our spiritual origins."

Peter asked; "What is the relationship between mythology and religion?

Father Paris answered; "It is my view that the ancient Greek myths and Christianity are not twin lies. He became aware that the ancient Greek myths and rituals gave rise to religion, which in turn spawned science."

Peter was slowly acquiring a degree of respect for the Greek Orthodox Church. Father Paris had fostered that belief. He learned that through the centuries, the Church and its priests proved themselves worthy by deeds and personal sacrifices for the people of Greece. They were always there to help individual Greeks in need. He believe that the Church and its leaders earned their crosses of courage and he always accorded the fathers of the Church the dignity that they deserved.

Father Paris took Peter by the hand and gave him a tour of the Church and onto his room. His time at the Church had begun in earnest.

When he was alone in his room, he thought about everything that Father Paris told him. However, Peter couldn't embrace the teaching and belief of Christianity. Peter did embrace the reality of a spiritual existence, but he was of the mind that there was no God and that we are on our own. He couldn't love God into existence.

HIS PERFECT WILL

Achelous provided a possible explanation of why unintended con-

sequences occur when he wrote: "In the dark chance of human life, God works his perfect will."

Peter spent the better part of four months working his assignments. His experience at the Kafenio made him a standout at the Church's charity events for the poor and homeless people of Lesbos. He was an excellent short order cook and handled the flow of people into his service area.

The misery of the poor and homeless people broke his heart. He didn't even realize the extent of the pain and suffering. He valued these people and wished he could do more to help them

He accepted his janitorial duties as it gave him a chance to see all the nooks and crannies of this beautiful Church. He was fascinated by the size, grandeur, beauty of this glorious institution. The choir music had a meditative effect on him.

Study class was another matter. Peter couldn't accept the teachings and couldn't accept everything on faith. Father Paris was aware of what was happening and was quickly coming to the conclusion that Peter was not meant to be a priest. He scheduled a personal counseling session with Peter to discuss the issue of whether Peter should stay or leave the church.

Father Paris knew Peter's dilemma for he too had struggled with the same issues before making his commitment to the Church and to God.

After some confusing discussion between them on the subject, he told Peter that all he had to do was pray for guidance and revelation. He told Peter to look for a sign from God. Father Paris said; "God will send you a sign and will show you the way."

Peter was lost in thought. He couldn't go to the Port to do his thinking and the choir wasn't singing. So he developed a new habit. He wandered from place to place in the Church looking for a quiet place to think and try to determine what he should do. He wandered around the the church grounds and the various floors. There were rooms that were empty and didn't seem to serve any useful purpose. They functioned more like storage spaces.

Peter wandered into a room, which was a re-created Lesvian (saloni) (sitting room). There was an attached room which was crammed with a mix of kitsch; but priceless objects from Ottoman copper trays to badly stuffed rotting egrets. There were many brightly painted trunks that were donated by the people living in the surrounding villages.

As he was leaving the room; he saw a large old Greek gold cross and temptation got the better of him. He took the cross thinking that they would never miss it and hid it on the roof of the Church. In all the "junk" it would never be missed. He was excited and scared. Once he left the Church, he could eventually sell it and get money to help the poor, hungry and homeless of his hometown. He knew that Christianity is replete with divine signs and revelation. He believed that the story of this gold cross may eventually fall into this category.

It was not long before the priests discovered that the gold cross was missing, perhaps it was a matter of divine destiny and revelation. They knew where to look. They wandering, wild child – Peter – must have it and, of course, they were right.

Peter was called to Father Paris' office. He knew immediately what was going on and he was surprised that they found out that it was missing and that he had taken it.

Father Paris started by telling Peter what the cross meant to the Church; "We believe that the cross is a symbol of the eternal affirmation of all that ever was or shall ever be. It symbolizes not only the one historic moment on Calvary but the divine mystery through all time. It signifies God's presence and participation in the agony and suffering of all living things. The gold cross had both material and spiritual value and, for the Church and its priests, it was a priceless relic."

Peter realized that there was no escape. He was trapped and couldn't refute their accusations. Peter saw the light of reason.

He finally confessed and told them that he hid it on the lower roof of the church. They told him to bring it back. He was trembling as he crawled out on the roof to retrieve the cross. "Would God punish him and make him fall to the ground were his only thoughts?"

After he returned the cross to Father Paris, he was asked why he took it. At first he hesitated, but ultimately he blurted out his truth, "The gold crosses belong to the people, not the church. Too many people are suffering in Lesbos and the gold cross would help them and ease their suffering. The church should work with elegant wooden crosses." Father Paris answered, "That is not your decision or even mine to make."

Peter wondered; "Was taking the gold cross meant to be? Was there any purpose and meaning to it all?" In the moment, he justified the act as a sincere effort to help the poor and, possibly, it was. However, he couldn't get rid of his doubts about why he took it. Was it just a stupid and greedy act?

He asked himself; "Was there another purpose? It may

have been that the taking and the forced return of the gold cross was part of an inspired plan. Perhaps; even the launch of his personal Odysseys. That all that transpired was a different destiny and that he was not meant to be a priest?

Long before this incident, Peter came to the conclusion that there was no God; and if there was, He could not be forgiven for allowing all the suffering and pain to take place. Peter wondered; "If He has made the world the way it is, then where is His goodness?"

He recalled his Yaya's discussion about the subject. She told him; "Greek literature is replete with discussions of these issues. There was only doubts throughout the literature. The great Greek poet Euripides did in times past, say it was the most tragic subject in Greek literature."

Not surprisingly, Peter came to the same conclusion. It was as if the poets were whispering in Peter's ears: "If gods do evil then they are not gods." Listen to my words:

"Long since my heart has known it false.

God if he be God lacks in nothing

All these are dead unhappy tales"

Father Paris finished what he needed to do to return the cross to a rightful place and joined Peter again. He said; "Peter, life has the blessings of painful experiences. These life's lessons come with divine love and through awareness and acceptance we are able to embrace and endure. We learn to conduct ourselves like men. But always remember that you are not facing the hardships of life alone.

As you go through life, you will experience unforeseen coincidences and events. You will discover that everything is the result of a divine energy. If you are able to lift yourself to a higher level of consciousness, you will experience a divine transformation that will help you find the purposes and meaning of life."

It was not long before Peter's mother was notified and summoned. She came to take him home. She knew that she would have to let him go and find his own way in the world.

What she feared had come to pass. She would suffer another loss in her life and it was another reminder that life is learning how to let go of everything. She knew and had experienced that, as we go through life, we lose our health, our vitality, our looks, even our loved ones and eventually ourselves.

It was time for them to go. As they were leaving the courtyard, Peter heard the hypnotic chants of the priests. He had come to love these chants, the religious poetry, the litany sung by priests on special occasions: "Hear us, we beg you." They were usually chants to the long lists of saints and, at times, it could be an appeal to parents, friends, and ancestors. It was a spiritual appeal to whoever needed to be reached.

Father Paris did not disagree and told Peter, "These are not our decisions to make. There are higher powers involved." It was clear to Father Paris that Peter was not meant to be a priest and his journey and ultimate destiny were elsewhere to be experienced.

There was a 'heart-felt' pause in the conversation. Father Paris broke the silence and said; "You will see God's hand in your life. There are divine moments in everyone's life. The New Testament refers to *'Karios'* which means "the appointed time in the purpose of God; the time when God acts. This guidance is found in *'Mark1.15, the karios is fulfilled.'* Look for these moments in your life.

As Peter and his mother were leaving the Church, Father Paris came to him and took him aside. He offered him forgiveness. He wished him good fortune and a happy life. He told Peter that he would pray for him and he hoped that Peter would one day find God and be saved. "If you cannot accept a God; at least know that there is a higher energy and purpose to life and that we are in His hands and care."

Father Paris and Peter could not know that one day they would meet again. It would be God's will and Peter's life would be at stake. It would be their *'Kairos'* moment: when God shows his love and guidance.

God had worked His Perfect Will. Peter continued on a new direction of his destined life journey.

PASSAGE III

LOVE CHANGES EVERYTHING

Choral Forward: The Madness of Love

The ancient Greek poets recognized there is the loss of will and personal control that is engendered by a love affair. Sappho's words mystically echoed through the air as she describes the epic helplessness of the lover in one of her myths:

"…..are you not amazed how at one and the same moment she seeks out soul, body, hearing, tongue, sight, complexion as though they had all left her and were external, and how in contradiction she both freezes and burns, is irrational and sane, is afraid and nearly dead, so that we observe in her not one single emotion but a concourse of emotions? All of this of course happens to people in love ……"

Socrates first observer of madness and blessings bestowed, viewed love as not for the advantage of the lovers; but the opposite, a form of madness, a gift from the gods fraught with the highest bliss.

This theme "the madness of love" is encoded in many Greek myths. It is embodied in the myth of Eros and Psyche, which is one of the great love stories in classical mythology. Eros, son of Aphrodite, was the personification of intense love, desire, and he was depicted shooting arrows at people in order to hit their hearts and make them fall in love. Psyche, a beautiful maiden, personifies the human soul. In fact, she is the symbol of the soul purified of unbridled desires, aches, lust, hungers, and thirst which in their indulgence always leads to misfortunes and madness.

Love and unbridled desire were viewed as tools of the Greek Fates. They were used to cause destiny to unfold. They serve as catalyst to help people on their life journey to become who they were meant to be. For many people, what was perceived as a disaster was a necessary event and step to fulfill one's life plan. Most important, they help many souls to experience, discover and learn the true meaning of love.

After he returned home Peter did a little "soul searching". He did benefit from his trip to the Church and he acquired a new way of looking at the world. He gained even a little wisdom and the experience caused him to think about where he was going in life. It was a defining life moment. He was 14 years old and he felt external and internal pressures to move on with his life; but like most young men, he was confused about what his next steps should be.

Young Peter was emerging through the phase in life described as the innocence of becoming. He would observe how the madness of love and desire changes lives.

EPIC HELPNESSESS

The encoded wisdom of the proverbs: Be aware of the destructive tides of life.

"O heart, my heart, no public weeping will you win; no solitude nor weeping when you fail to prove. Rejoice at the simple things; and be but vexed by sin and evil slightly. Know the tides through which we move."

Passage III

"With the passion of lust comes the agony of unbridled desire, constant heart ache, suffering and depression and other false harbingers of love." Greek proverbs

Peter was in for a surprise when he got home. He learned that Steve was in trouble and that the Greek police were looking for him. Deme told Peter to keep his head down and avoid the Greek and Turkish authorities. She warned him to stay away from Steve and the Kafenio.

She gave him a long lecture on the need to stay out of sight. It was important to give her time to work out another escape plan. Realistically, her inner 'gut' was telling her that it most likely meant that Peter would have to leave Greece and escape to another country.

After their discussion, Peter went to their small backyard to think about his situation. He was enjoying the peace and quiet. Before long he fell asleep.

When he woke up, he was startled to see Steve standing in the doorway. They started at each other for a couple seconds before Peter asked; "How did you get into the house?"

Steve answered, "Your Yaya let me and told me where you were."

Peter was surprised. "How did you know I was home?" Steve said; "It is all over town. Some of the rumors are that you have started on an Odyssey. The rumor came from the Church. The men at the Kafenio were whispering the same thing. I came because I am in trouble and you are too."

"So what happened to you?"

Steve had a smile on his face when he said; "I was having sex with Cleis when the maid opened the door and saw us. The maid screamed and I grabbed my pants and jumped out of the bedroom window."

"Did the maid see your face and recognize you?"

Steve smile changed to a 'smirked' and he answered; "All she saw was 'elbows and my butt' and a crazy person running down the hill waving his pants in the air." Peter laughed; "That must have been enough to recognize you.

Peter was visualizing Cleis' beautiful body. Her blond hair, blue eyes and her smooth white skin were captivating thoughts. His thoughts changed to Mr. Samson. He was reputed to be 'one mean bastard' with Turkish connections. Peter said; "I don't if you are lucky or not. Remember, the Greek saying 'the devil always comes with a 'pretty face. She is beautiful, but she comes with a devil."

There was a sudden noise from the kitchen. Seems, Yaya and Deme were arguing. Peter assumed it was about Steve being let into the house. They both listened to their conversation. Suddenly, both Yaya and Deme came out of the house and told them to come into the kitchen. Peter thought that 'It seems that Yaya had prevailed'.

When they came to the kitchen, they were shocked to see Steve's mother. The women got right to the point. Deme said; "We love you both, but you two boys needed to leave Lesbos as soon as possible. Peter you and Steve need to go to the Kafenio and see Alex for help."

Peter asked; "Do you think he will get involved? Do you think he can help?"   Deme with a determined look on her face said; "I've already talked to him. You are to go to him right away. His words were; the sooner the better."

Deme said; "The harshness of rumors had started. Cleis and her family are embarrassed by the talk. Word is that Steve had raped and violated the young helpless girl. Mr. Samson is saying that you ruined her life." Steve's mother added; "He has filed a rape charge with the Greek police and has vowed revenge." Yaya said, "Under the more extreme traditions of chastity in Greece, both real and perceived, Steve has ruined her life."

Steve said, "Her father has already filed charges against me for rape. He was incensed when he found out that I had sex with his young, favorite daughter. He didn't believe that it was consensual sex; he chose to believe that I raped her. He was using his power to have me tried and convicted of rape. If he can't get the courts to convict me then he will have the Turks get rid of me.

I feel like everyone is looking at me and blaming me. Truth is I am to blame I didn't do right by Cleis. This mess is all my fault."

Yaya said; "Don't be so hard on yourself. She said; "There is an old quote by Sappho which tells it all for all time: "Who can resist love - Irrational and Sane". Steve needed some sympathy and kind words. He came over and kissed her hand.

The mothers kissed their sons, hugged them and wished them 'God speed'.

Peter and Steve left and were turning to the only to the only men in Lesbos who that they thought had the courage to help them.

They went right to Alex, who escorted them to Costas and Yianni. Steve described his dilemma and asked them for their help. Peter brought them up to date on his situation. Costas and Yianni expressed no emotion and made no judgements. They had seen it all. Nothing surprised them anymore. It was what it was. It was life, love and the usual youthful disasters.

Costas invited a couple old timers who knew the hazards

of defying power and, in particular the ever dangerous Samson. One of them shared a poem with Costas which gave them a warning and to avoid getting in over their heads. The tides was a 'be careful' word.

After some 'what –to-do' discussions Costas pointed to an old man sitting in the corner and said, "He is the only one who can help you. His parents were of the tribe of Benjamin and very strict in his upbringing. His mother was a pious woman and she exercised all of a mother's influence in molding the character of her son Saul to be righteous."

Yianni came forward and added; "He was a great lawyer before he gave up his profession for his mistress — the bottle. It's said that he couldn't handle the guilt of being a lawyer. Probably, why he drinks." Costas said; "He's still a giant, a great lawyer". Steve needs him.

They decided that Saul, or Paul as he was known, was the only person who could save Steve. Costas walked to his table, explain the circumstances and asked if he could help. The lawyer listened intently and when Costas was done, he just shook his head 'no'. "I'm too old, retired and, frankly, I don't think that I can represent him."

Paul said; "I understood the consequences of Steve's predicament. It was clear that his life was in danger. He is up against a powerful man and he had little or no chance to extract and save himself from the powerful forces that the father could unleash.

Paul knew that Steve had no way of paying him and there was nothing for the old lawyer to gain by representing him. He knew that if he was successful he would always have to deal with the fury of the father.

Complicating his decision was his compassion for the girl and his admiration for the father and his attempts to protect his daughter's honor. He understood the father's strategy. The father could only do this by having her be a victim and to do that he needed Steve to be the villain.

Paul knew that it would be a tough case to defend. He could not attack her and he didn't want to call her to testify and embarrass her. There was no apparent defense for what happened. The old lawyer said, "I will have to think about whether I can defend you against the chare of forcible rape." He had much to think about and there was no answer given to Steve.

Once Peter and Steve emerged from the Kafenio, the Greek police arrived to arrest Steve. They grab and were dragging him away.

And then Steve's mother, Deme and Yaya appeared and confronted the police. They followed the boys to protect them. They pulled Steve away from the police and were screaming at them when they tried to get him back under custody.

Tears streamed down Steve's mother face as she held him tight and hit any policemen who tried to pry Steve from her. The three women stood 'shoulder-to-shoulder' between the police and Steve. They were fearful that the police would turn him over to the Turkish Authorities. The Greek people were aware that people who fell into their hands disappeared.

Peter was fascinated and thought to himself; "Ah! Is it only Greek women that can cry out of love and holler out of anger at the same time? He thought it a little bewildering for rational people."

The police were very patient with the women and seemed used to the histrionics and grief of women when they were helpless and could not defend their children. All the while, Steve was under a table terrified and helpless with fear.

Costas and Yianni and some customers joined the ladies and were pushing the police back out of the Kafenio. More police came out of the patrol car and engaged in the yelling and pushing.

After seeing this crazy scene and after much soul searching, Paul felt compelled to defend Steve. He went up to the police and told them that he was Steve's attorney and an officer of the court. He said; "I'll take custody of my client." The police were relieved and couldn't wait to extract themselves from the small mob's pushing, shoving, crying, yelling and all the madness taking place.

Alex came forward and asked the police to join him for a cup pf coffee and some 'sweets'. The police were aware what the word 'sweets' meant and willingly went with him.

Paul and Steve went off before anyone could change their mind.

Why he made that decision surprised everyone. It may have been that he didn't want to feel and appear as a coward to his friends at the Kafenio. He was an educated man and knew Greek history. He knew that Greeks are passionate people, taught to live heroic lives and not be cowards in the face of adversity.

Likely, Paul also acted out of pity. And it is possible that there was a more mystical explanation. Paul looked into Steve's eyes and saw his terror. The moment he looked into Steve's eyes – the windows to his soul - he knew that he needed to defend him to save his own soul.

Perhaps, the ancient Greeks were right when they said, "To have a soul you must be able to look into the heart of another person and reach out with love and compassion." Paul was captured by the universal love that connects us all at a soul level.

Attorney Paul knew that he would be up against the best lawyers in Greece. His deep-seated fears were that he would not be able to help Steve and that he would play the part of the 'old drunken fool'.

Paul knew one thing. Two terrified people would walk into the court room — Steve and his lawyer.

THE INNOCENCE OF YOUNG LOVE

In ancient Greece, large institutions and judges did not govern the affairs of people: *Greek law provides for People's Courts and trials are held in these Courts. It is an expression of Greek democracy and justice. The court is a Lesbos Popular or People's Court - no judge - only people from the town who were both jury and judge.*

Steve was remanded to the custody of Paul. The trial was scheduled for the next day and Paul had him spend that night at his home. He wanted time to prepare him for trial and to make sure that he did not run away and make matters worse for both of them.

This gave Paul a chance to get briefed on what happened between Steve and Cleis. Paul explained that Steve should tell him everything truthfully and that nothing should be held back. It was important that he had knowledge and command of the facts so that he could build an adequate defense. He did not want to be surprised in the courtroom.

This was also a chance for Steve to unload his

frustrations. He trusted Paul and he gave him a chance to express his repressed feelings. He told Paul that he was depressed and was scared. And, he was resigned to whatever happened.

Steve said, "I love Cleis. I dream of her, I want to marry her or run away with her. If I can't be with her, I don't care what happens."

Paul told him to concentrate on what they were doing. His life was at stake.

Paul asked; "What happened?" Steve said; "It was an exciting moment when I tasted the sweetness of her passions mixed with the terrifying fears of her father's punishment. We opened our hearts to each other. We believed that we were meant to be together. I believe that she truly loves me. We were overwhelmed with passion and we could not control it.

If we were separated from each other for some abstract reason called 'honor'; then this Greek 'tradition' has no worth to me."

Paul Asked; "Just to confirm, as far as you know, she feels the same way?" Steve answered; "Yes." The rest of the day was spent with 'Q & A' and prepping for the trial.

Steve was in agony over his situation and the possible consequences of his forbidden love affair. He was fearful and anxious and wasn't sure if he was in good hands or not. His mother gave him doubts. Before she left him at the Kafenio the night before, his mother told him; "He had a drunken old fool for a lawyer and, worse still, the lawyer was stuck with a 'love sick' fool for a client.

The next morning they woke up early. Paul told Steve what he could expect that day in court:

"One thing I'm counting on is that the jury will be composed of local people who may know you and have some compassion for you. There is a chance that some people are aware of any weakness of character you may have and hold that against you.

We must face the father and his team of lawyers. They will do their best to make you out as a 'bad' guy. You will need the jury's forgiveness for robbing her of her prime. I know that it was in a moment of weakness for both of you. I know that you love each other. But, he has tradition behind him. You have something too. Most Greeks have liberal philosophies and are pretty tolerant about young love. They believe that what happened is 'natural'. I'm hoping that 'natural' will mean "innocence."

Paul went over facts and tactics and attacks that Samson's lawyers may level on him. "They will try to get you so upset that you will be confused in your testimony. "Stay calm. Your life may depend on how you react."

"One last thing. The courts have an unusual rule. If found guilty; the convicted could request a lesser sentence such as exile and suffer the loss of identity to all the people who knew and loved him. The ancient Greeks believed that exile was a sentence as drastic as death which was also a loss of identity. I'm not sure this sentence will be available to you.

Let's stop for the day. I want you fresh for tomorrow. It will be the hardest thing you will ever face.

The next day, Paul was dressed conservatively and looked the part of an attorney. But he surprised everyone. He entered carrying a bowl of lemons cut into slices. He placed the bowl on his table in front of him. He made sure that it was in plain sight of everyone. It was an amusing scene.

Steve was scared to death and he showed it. He was looking side to side as he was walking. He couldn't look anyone in the eye as he made his way to the chair next to Paul.

When he sat down, Steve's mother and his Yaya came into the courtroom and they went straight to Steve. They hugged and kissed him. Tears added a sense of pathos to the moment. Everyone was surprised and somewhat amused.

The courtroom was beginning to think that the defense was on the verge of becoming a comedy act.

Paul thought that it was great theater and that it was good for the jury/judges to see that Steve was an ordinary young man and not the monster Samson's attorneys will make him out to be.

Everyone's attention turned to the door of the court room. As expected, the girl's father entered the room with four lawyers, two of whom came from Athens and were reputed to be brilliant. One was conversant with ancient traditions and the other in court presence and ligating tactics. By the rules of the People's Court, they were to present their charges first and then the defendant would enter a plea after he heard the recitation of charges.

Cleis was left at home. The revelation was clear. The so-called young victim, was not with her father because she couldn't be trusted on the stand. His attorneys believed that she would not make a good witness and her tears would free him.

Even Paul chose not to force her to be a witness. He wanted to spare her any embarrassment. Steve was happy with that decision as he cared for her and wanted her to remember him in a kind way. It was a decision that carried no small risk to Steve as she may have defended him and might have said that she was not forced and that it was consensual and a loving moment.

Under the rules of this court, once the defendant entered his plea, the parties and the jury members could interrupt and ask questions of anyone in the court room. More often than not, everyone was civil but it was not unusual for a Greek court like this to get out of control. This would usually work against the party that was causing the uproar and so the lawyers on both sides usually tried to keep everyone civil.

The plaintiff's lead attorney went first. He move to recite and establish the duty of the jury. He chose to open the proceedings by quoting from one of Euripides early plays – 'Suppliants'. In a commanding voice, he explained; "It is your duty to honor the great laws of tradition. Your city's honor is at stake as well as your own to find the defendant guilty of rape. We can find guidance in the thoughts and words of Euripides, the great Greek writer of tragedy. He cautioned that punishing crime was a matter of preserving 'honor' and our actions and judgements will be witnessed by the gods.

Euripides guidance is clear about matters of honor:

"Look to the things of God, Know you are bound to help all who are wronged.

Bound to constrain all who destroyed the law. What else holds state to state save this alone. That each one honors the great laws of right."

The attorney added; "This young man planned and committed a crime and he must be punished to right the wrong. He did great harm to an innocent young girl. He ruined her life and robbed her of the chance for a happy marriage and family. He took that life away from her and he should be sent to prison for his crime. The correct punishment is to take his miserable life away from him. There are no justifiable defenses for his evil actions."

While the attorney was talking and presenting his case, the old lawyer Paul was busy sucking on lemon slices. It was a major distraction and to some extent it undermined the attorney's presentation. The old lawyer did not interrupt. He said nothing in Steve's defense. He just sucked on the lemon slices and listened intently to the opposing attorney's case.

The attorney did not extend his arguments to include other possible damages to the young girl. His main attack was on how evil Steve was. It was clear that the girl's father had put some constraints on his lawyers and he did not want them to question her role and motivations. Further they were not allowed to say that she lost her chastity and, more importantly, her honor.

One of the jury members asked the attorney why the young girl was not there to testify. His answer was, "The case against Steve is clear and we did not want to cause her more damage and grief in court by having to face this villain in court." Another jury member asked the attorney, "Was she forced and beaten in the attack."

His answer was quick and to the point, "He overpowered her with his strength and may have inflicted some bodily harm and bruises to get his way, but we were not able to determine the extent of her injuries as this was treated as a personal matter and we did not want to cause her anymore pain and embarrassment with a public revelation of her condition."

The attorney then called his first witness. It was an elderly lady, one of the senior servants in the house. She testified, "When I heard the noises in the girl's room, I went in and saw him on top of her with his pants down around his knees."

Paul interrupted her and asked, "Did you see anything else? Did you see them making love?" She said, "No". He asked, "What did Steve do when you came into the room?" She answered, "He pulled his pants up and jump out of her bedroom window. What condition was the girl in? She was hiding under the bed covers and wouldn't come out or talk to me."

Paul continued; "Did you see him having sex? Did the young girl scream or resist or admit to having sex?" She said, "No." Paul said, "No more questions." He went back to his chair, sat down, pulled out another lemon slice from his bowl and proceeded to suck on it.

The father's attorney called another witness – a neighbor – and her response to his questions about what she saw. She testified, "I saw him jump out of her bedroom window, pulling up his pants and running away." Paul got up, came before her, and asked if she saw him having sex with the young girl. She answered, "No!"

Another jury member asked the father's attorney if she had attempted suicide because of the public shame. The attorney answered, "She knew that he had ruined her life. We are watching her and every effort is being made to keep her from taking her own life."

The jury members were now wondering why Paul was not more aggressive. They were watching him intently. He was not saying much of anything. He just continued to suck on the lemon slices.

The father's attorney pressed forward with his case against Steve. He made an impassioned argument that Steve was a villain and that she was an innocent victim. He argued that the Lesbos Popular Court was set up to operate in the same manner as the Athenian Popular Court and that court had held that it was against the law to corrupt the youth.

He called the jury's attention to that famous case involving Socrates who was brought before the court to answer charges of impiety and corrupting the youth of the city. His argument seemed to have a ring of truth. Socrates was convicted of corrupting the youth of the city and the death penalty imposed.

The attorney then gave the Lesbos jury an 'out' from imposing a death penalty. He noted that Socrates, now a convict, was allowed by custom to request a lesser sentence –such as exile — which they no doubt would have given him.

He could have concluded his argument; but like other lawyers who like to talk and do so for a living, the attorney had to impress and so continued to finish the precedent story. He asked a hypothetical question of the jury; "Did Socrates chose a high minded end? Exile, imprisonment, fines these would all be punishment; whereas death; well is death too severe a punishment?"

In the famous last scene of Plato's *Phadro,* before he drinks the hemlock Socrates comforts his friends assuring them that death – which is either a dreamless sleep or a passage to a place of true justice – is nothing to fear.

He concluded by saying that Steve was guilty of a heinous crime. As was the case of Socrates, the Defendant is also guilty of corrupting a young innocent girl and he should be found guilty and punished. He should face the same charges that Socrates did 'corrupting an innocent youth'. He needs to be punished and made an example to other 'would be' rapist." Then he sat down and gave Paul a chance to present his case.

Being perceived as an old lawyer worked for Paul. White hair was the sign of wisdom. He rose, took one last bitter lemon to his mouth and sucked hard and then went before the jury to present his closing arguments.

He opened his defense by saying, "I can't believe that we are trying him for being in love. When did we say that 'young love' was a crime? When did it become evil?"

He paused and said; "Love is a gift of God. When did we start trying our youth for their passions and for being in love? Lawyers, when they have no case, try to confuse the issue with skillful arguments. They make arguments that are sometimes guilty of the same crime Socrates was accused of and that is they corrupt people with their legalese and their artful words. They peddle sweetly designed concepts that distort the facts, confuse the mind, misstate the evidence and events and concoct vast fantasies.

As to Socrates, he taught the youth the 'love of truth'. Steve had both love and truth. There is no crime to teaching or believing in the truth of love.

Let me speak in plain terms and bring us back to reality. Steve is not a Socrates. He is a young innocent boy in love. There cannot be rape if there is blossoming and consensual love between a boy and a girl. The Socrates' precedent does not apply in Steve's case. He corrupted no one.

There are precedents in Greek history and literature which support my contention that their passion for each other was beyond their reason or control. Hector, the great Trojan prince, made a speech to Andromache where he discusses the concept of fate:

"And Fate? No one alive has ever escaped it, neither brave man or coward, I tell you – it's born with us the day that we are born."

These two young souls were born to the same destiny and that is by the Will of God. They could not change their destinies or escape destiny's chains." And their destiny and Fate were sealed at birth.

We can also look to the myth of Eros and Psyche for meaning. Like Psyche the fair young girl was an irresistible object of desire and he was possessed by his natural passions and the drive instilled in all humans by the gods. Their efforts were about lovers trying to overcome the obstacles of youth in order to achieve the divine happiness of love."

He went on to describe love as a spiritual state of being. "Plato has described love and attraction as a spiritual form, a pattern of thought and an image within us all that embodies the soul of love. Psyche, a beautiful maiden, personifies the human soul. In fact, she is the symbol of the soul purified of unbridled desires, aches, lust, hungers, and thirst which in their indulgence always leads to misfortunes."

This is a relevant historical myth and a precedent to be guided by. The lessons apply to Steve and Cleis. It is a most beautiful Greek myth that has been told and retold in several different versions and it has inspired lovers and artists all over the world.

Cleis is a young lady gifted with extreme beauty and grace; a mortal woman whose love and sacrifice for her beloved Steve should earn her admiration. As in the myth of Psyche, their story symbolizes a search, a reflection and personal growth through learning, suffering and ultimately saving the immortality of their true love by declaring it to each other. Who are we to challenge the purposes of the gods?"

He started his closing argument and tried to discredit the

learned and esteemed attorney for the girl's father by making a subtle point. He noted that the esteemed attorney for the girl's father presented many irrelevant arguments and he too had invoked the laws and precedents of historical myths. His conclusion of gilt was demanded by tradition, imposed by custom, required by court rulings.

Paul made a sage observation that all Greeks can take to their heads and hearts, "There is one law that supersedes them all and that is ...... the laws of nature which absolves people in love."

He paused and thought for a moment. "This situation is not just a case of the epic helplessness of young lovers. As in all matters of the heart, we are inspired, torn, forced, guided and motivated by the gods who look over us. This is case about the purposes of the gods who provide definition, meaning and purpose of life. We found the encoded wisdoms in the Greek myths and they provided guidance and, in this case, justification for a sentence of innocence for Steve and Cleis.

You saw me sucking on the lemons I brought to court. You had to drool and you were helpless and could not stop your juices from bubbling up in your mouths. You swallowed hard, but it kept on coming. That is our natural condition. It is a law of nature which man cannot change.

They were drawn to each other and at a time when love and its physical expression sex was blossoming. It was their Fate to be together. It was the law of the gods and nature that they were forced beyond their control to be together and to unite in a soulful embraces.

Did they have sex? No one really knows. He called their attention to the fact, "No one has testified that the alleged act was committed; nor has any evidence been presented to support and prove the facts of the complaint. In the eyes of the court, she must be found pure and not violated and he must be found innocent."

The jury convened to a room for deliberations and to come up with a decision. After a relatively short recess, the jury in their capacity and responsibility came back with a 'not guilty' verdict.

Paul was elated with their decision. He believed that it was the concept of the divine nature of love that swayed them. Greeks are a supersites bunch. Maybe, it was just the lemons and the laws of nature that makes all the rules that swayed them? Whatever it was, the jury came back quickly with a 'not guilty' verdict.

After all was said and done, the father's attorney asked the foreman of the jury why they acquitted Steve. The answer was, "To judge him guilty we would have passed judgment on Cleis. She remains pure in the eyes of the court. If the allegations had been proved, we would have found their actions to be consensual and we would have again found him not guilty."

Steve was free to go. He hugged Paul for defending him and for staying by his side at the risk of Samson's ire. Paul told him, "It may be time for you to leave Lesbos as it was not over with Cleis' father. His last piece of advice was; "He may bring the Hemlock and force you to drink it? Perhaps, it is time for you to go and find safer ground."

TO LIFE, TO LOVE

"The ancient Greeks believed that the madness of lust, desire, sex and love was pure bliss sent by the gods to torment humanity."

Steve tossed and turned in his bed most of the night. He couldn't wait to get up and celebrate the great victory in court. They stood up to Cleis' powerful dad, Samson, and they took him 'down'. Paul taught Samson's high-priced attorneys a lesson or two. Yashoo!!!

He usually slept late, but today was an exception. He had some 'bragging' rights to 'yell' about. It was time to enjoy breakfast with his mother and his Yaya and go over the great victory.

Feeling like a great conqueror, he stretched both arms high above his head and strolled casually into the kitchen. He was greeted by smiles. His mother Cleo and Yaya, his grandmother, Essie who were noticeably relieved and were ready to celebrate the outcome with him.

"Wow! Wow! Wow!" He shouted. And then he calmed down.

Cleo asked, "You didn't win. You were saved. Tell me, why do you think you were saved?"

"Because you and Yaya came and hugged me. Just kidding, but I think that it did help. But the power in the courtroom was Paul. He outsmarted that hairy monster Samson's high-priced attorneys." Essie chimed in; "He's really bald. He is wearing a wig. You are right, he is a monster. When we drive the Turks out of Lesbos, he'll pay a price for being a traitor and working with them against his people."

Steve continued; "Paul talked about the innocence of love and I think that hit a soft spot in everyone's heart. He also talked about the 'truth of love' and had all those quotes about the 'love of truth' by Socrates. But the most brilliant move was the 'slices of lemon, he was sucking on during the trial."

He paused for a reaction. Essie took a turn and said;

"Paul was great and he didn't charge you for his services. You should be grateful because we couldn't have paid him." Steve shook his head 'yes'. Essie continued; "The jury's verdict was appropriate: 'there was no real proof that the act was committed. The verdict of innocent protected everyone."

Cleo said; "I don't want you to forget you're facing. There is a downside to this victory in court. Paul warned you that it wasn't over. Samson wasn't done with you. Remember his words. 'He'll come after you with the hemlock.' So, we better get ready to deal with that very real threat."

Steve was prone to sudden mood shifts and he went 'down' with her remarks. He knew immediately that she was right. It was clear that she was talking about leaving Lesbos and finding safe ground. Steve was going through the acute anguish of separation. He was feeling the agonizing thoughts of leaving the family nest.

He left the kitchen and went back to his room. His mother's words evoked deeply rooted fears that he had buried and emotions which were soon expressed as sobs and tears. Everything was coming too fast. The danger was real. Even what he had to do to protect himself was scary. He had to rip deep family ties to save himself.

As he relaxed a little, he had a sweet thought. He had some regrets about what happened; but one thing was certain. He would not regret his moments with Cleis. He would always remember and treasure his beautiful memories of his 'first' love.

He went back into the kitchen in time to hear Cleo and Essie talking about 'survival. They continued talking-probably for his benefit. They wanted Steve to start thinking about the conscious realities of what it takes to survive in a harsh world. Steve didn't show it, but he was feeling a little sick to his stomach with fear. They were talking about the many perils of life that he may have to face. It was all too real and all too scary to keep thinking about.

Cleo realized that they had gone too far with the warnings. She changed the subject and tried to give Steve some confidence and comfort in the future. Her soothing words seemed to calm him down a bit. She reminded Steve that many young Greek boys and men were leaving Greece for other lands. They found ways to survive and some to prosper in foreign lands.

She came over and hugged Steve. It was time for a break. They ate and then came back for more talk. By the end of the day, after much discussion, they were left with the fatigue of circular and almost meaningless conversation. They ultimately concluded, and it was clear to all of them, that Steve had to leave Lesbos and more talk and chatter could not change that.

Essie said; "It's a shame. This is all about money, money, money! The father is upset because he considers his daughter a commercial asset which was spoiled by a poor Greek boy. He's just like all those other rich greedy Greeks who live life as a commercial venture. They are only motivated by wealth and power. Cleis was a trading commodity to be dealt to another powerful family so that he could further consolidate his base of power."

She paused for a moment to think. Then said; "There may be something wonderful, something spiritual, happening to Steve."

Cleo said; "You go mom. Let's hear it. I had a feeling that we are missing something. Why is this happening?"

Essie said; "There is old Greek knowledge about time. It

may apply to Steve's situation. The ancient Greeks believed that there are two times periods in life. One is linear or human time and the other is spiritual time. Steve is in Kairos or spiritual time and is being guided by powerful spiritual forces. I think that when a person is in Kairos time they are being guided to achieve their life plan…. their destiny."

Cleo was excited. "Of course, that's what's going on. Steve's a good boy and they are helping him. Paul is an example of the help they are arranging. Now it's up to us to come up with a plan."

Essie said; "I have a feeling that Steve should talk to Peter."

Cleo was excited; "Yaya's right. Steve talk to Peter. Maybe he has a plan to leave and you can go with him. You both have reasons to leave. Who knows, he might be open to leaving Lesbos with you.

We're not talking about forever. You both leave until everything changes and forgotten. The world is always changing and nothing is permanent. Everyone in Lesbos will forget about these incidents and let go of the past. New problems are sure to come and they are the only certainty in life."

Steve's mood had changed. His spirits were up. He was excited. It felt like the right thing to do – the next step. "Okay, I'll talk to him. It will be a Kairos meeting. He shouted; "Opa !!!! Here's to life."

* * *

The war for independence started when the Greek Church made the supreme sacrifice. The Church led the war for independence:

"Of course, we are with the Greece people. We offer you the personal sacrifice of the Church leaders as proof of our heart, our loyalty and our deeds. Father Germanos of Patros raised the cross as the standard of sacrifice and dedication to the cause of Greek liberty. Greek Orthodox Patriarch Gregory V and fourteen other bishops gave their lives bravely at the hands of the Ottoman Turks, who thought that by killing them, the Greeks would cower in fear before them. This was the start of the revolution that freed mainland Greece."

Hail O'Liberty

Peter felt the longing of the Greek people for freedom. Like most Greeks, he was keenly aware that the hope for freedom never dies. Embedded deep in the consciousness of the Greek people was the crushing need for freedom.

Underneath the stoic grind of life, the impatience of the Greek people was smoldering. They were waiting for their chance to rise and free the outer Islands that were not released in the war of 1833 by the ill-negotiated Treaty between the European powers and the Ottoman Empire.

The Greek people in the outer Islands had exercised patience, but their patience was at an end and now they wanted freedom 'at any cost'.

Peter heard the underground whispers coming from the shadows. It was a homage to 'liberty'. The people were quoting the Greek National Anthem:

"Liberty; Oh Hail liberty"

Peter heard the whispers. *"Small fire smolder in the heart of all Greeks for their homeland Greece"* He felt a change in people's attitude – from fear and compliance to one of defiance. The mothers and their daughters seemed to be leading the call and movement for charge. He knew the influence of the mothers; i they are ready, the men and their sons would rise. Once they took up arms, for them, it would be 'liberty at any cost, even death'.

Peter went to the Kafenio to see and talk with Alex about leaving Lesbos. Alex told him that only Costas and Yianni had the means to help him escape from Lesbos. He told Peter that they were expected back tomorrow and to come back then.

Alex told Peter that there was the undercurrent talk of war. He heard that the war to free more areas of Greece, including Lesbos, was imminent. He said; "The will to fight and sacrifice was inspired in our people. "I want to have a party at the Kafenio and reach out to our friends, our neighbors and guests. We need a moment of bonding with one another before the actual fighting begins."

Peter heard some of the old Greeks eating breakfast at the Kafenio say that the crises and warnings of war were being issued by the Greek statesmen. The failed politics and the inevitable and anticipated war brings to mind the horrors, the terror and the mass casualties in the last war."

Alex believed that there was a need for people to pledge themselves to each other, to be ready to help without question or hesitation, and be as one in this moment of crises. He told Peter and some of the old men; "This war is going to be a momentous time in our history. It is important enough for the Kafenio to hold an 'all night' party. We will celebrate life and enjoy music, song and dance and express our heartfelt feelings for one another and for our homeland."

Peter relaxed. He knew that Alex like to talk. Alex was on his pedestal.

"This will be the end time for many, they will know that they were not alone. They will summoned their innate courage and will give their all for a worthy cause. We will be remember as heroes who had the will to resist, rise and fight and bear the agonies and sacrifices of war with courage and grace."

Alex wanted a celebration. He told anyone who would listen; "That's what we Greeks do in momentous times – we play Greek music, drink, sing, dance, and shout their love of God, country and family.

"Let the word go out. There is going to be a party at the Kafenio to celebrate a divine moment in history. We will dance and celebrate the fight for independence."

Peter went home excited about the celebration. After lunch with his mother, he got ready for the party. He told his mother that Alex told him he could work the floor and help keep order. 'Clean-ups' was understood. He dressed in his best attire and he was off to help Alex with the preparations for the celebrations. He tried to be helpful, but actually he was always in the way; but Alex loved him like he did his own sons and he was pleased to have Peter around.

The band showed up early to practice, play and sing the songs they liked and had composed. Then they took the first of many breaks. They ate a little, started drinking early and then began playing music again.

The music was heard throughout the City. People gof off their chairs, couches, and they started to make their way over to the Kafenio for the festivities. Peter was enthralled. Peter felt important. Alex had him watch over the festivities. Alex knew Peter loved hearing the Greek band playing all the old songs.

The old men started to show up one or two at a time. Costas and Yianni showed up early and were teasing Peter about how he was dressed and how handsome he looked.

They warned him to be careful. All the girls would chase him and he could get in trouble like Steve did.

Alex came out and told everyone what the agenda was and it was to start with an invocation by Father Paris and a poetry reading by a young student, singing by the church chorus and the rest of the night would be dedicated to eating – a large buffet table had been set against the front wall of the kafenio – listening to music, drinking, dancing, shouting, and some shows of affection between everyone.

After everything was prepared, Father Paris came out from the inside of the Kafenio to address everyone. Peter listened intently to his brief invocation and his 'ever-brief' sermon which focused on atonement for the horrific sins that would be committed in the pending war against the Ottoman Turks, the hostile acts against innocents.

He began his speech;

"I want to remind everyone that the Church and our religion are not bound by the limits of time, but the empires and the kingdoms of man are. The question that I want to answer is why did the Church cooperate with the Ottoman Empire?

The leaders of the Church knew that our time would come and that until that time came, they had to keep Christianity and the Greek culture alive. Yes, we collected the taxes for them; but only to keep the Ottoman Turks at bay and thereby insulate the Greek people from the corruption and harsh cruelties of the Turkish overlords.

There is more to know about this subject. Perhaps, the Ottoman Empire at the start was enlightened when it came to freedom of religion. It was established by the highly educated and elite people of Turkey, many of them Greeks, and the Empire was intended to be a union of diverse people, cultures and faiths. They helped to restore the Orthodox Christian Society, and under the Ottomans, the Greek Ecumenical Patriarch, gained ascendancy over other beliefs and religions and we came nearer to universal religious authority under the Ottomans than we ever did or could under the Byzantine Empire.

"Many people think that the Ottomans and the family of Osman, the Empire would stay a dynastic and multiracial empire. The varied populations, whether they were Turkish or other – Moslems or Christians or Jews — were members of a single body politic. It was an advanced form of government and for a time. It was tolerant of all religious faiths. But, when faith is lost that which is human eventually changes and common belief deteriorates."

His speech was interpreted by Costas who shouted, "The Greek people only care about 'liberty or death'. Where is the Church in the struggle against the Ottoman Turks?"

He was surprised by the interruption and was highly animated when he replied;

"The Church never abandoned the Greek people. God has given the sign that the time had come to free the Greek Islands from the Ottoman Turks. This holy war was started by sacrificing ourselves – God's own faithful servants. With the signs and the signals, the religious callings, and the human sacrifices, we are ringing the bells of the Church throughout Greece. We are the ones that are calling the Greek people to arms. We have raised the cross of Christ and the brave people will follow the lead of the Church in the bloody fight for freedom"

"We are one with the Greek people. The Church is the soul, the spirit and the inspiration for the battle for independence. The bishops of our church gave their lives leading the struggle for freedom. This was our "signal in blood" to the Greek people and to the world that Greece was ready to fight and claim its God-given right to freedom and liberty. Never doubt that the Greek Church: Is the embodiment of Christ and freedom is the core of our faith.

Father Paris was finished with his speech and sat down to applause.

Then something incredible happened. Peter couldn't believe his eyes. A group of women with their young daughters were walking up the street and were heading straight for the kafenio. Peter and some of the old men gathered up chairs and these lovely souls sat at the outer edge of the patio giving the old men some deference to the patio area. There was a lot of hushed chatter and they all found a place to sit, stare and listen.

The old men were still having trouble getting used to the presence of women with their daughters. When they saw their lovely, smiling faces; they felt a inner joy take over everything. They were not really upset and uncomfortable as these women were wives, mothers, sisters and daughters. Then it started - everyone was hugging one another.

Peter knew that if the mothers and daughters were prepared for a war that their men and sons would soon take up arms. The fight for independence was going to happen.

Another unusual event took place. As the party and celebration went on into the early evening, everyone was surprised to see four police cars pull up across from the Kafenio. All the policemen formed a line and just stood there looking at everyone dancing and having a good time. They made no move to disrupt the party.

The speeches were over. The music and the dancing began again. Peter was like most Greeks when it came to music. It was an essential element of his life. In fact, through all of its history, Greece has been a land of poetry, song, dance and music.

"Let me not live without music was the theme song of the dancing. From the chorus in Euripides' play Heracles. To be without music was, for the Greeks, to be already dead. In fact, the Greek word for music is 'musica' and it is said that the Greek language is meant to be sung not spoken."

Slowly, at first, then some of the old men got up and with arms out stretched danced to the slow beat of the very sad song the band was playing. One thing about Greek dancing whether music was played at a slow or a fast beat; the old men would always dance at a slow beat, actually off or no beat at all, which was their speed. The songs were the 'nostalgic songs that remind people of the hardships of Greek life. This was a moment that made them cry and reach out to each other for love.

As the tempo picked up, more men left their tables and came onto the patio, which was being used as a dance floor. With their arms clasped to each other's shoulders, they danced round and around in circles, after circles. It was life played out in dance. The dances reminded Peter of the change of seasons. Spring became summer and then fall into winter. These circles were like the seasons and the cycles of life.

After a number of dances, something unusual, something wonderful happened. Costas and Yianni went to the band and requested a slow dance and then they went over to the mothers who dared to come. They reached out to the women, took them by the hand to the dance area and started dancing slowly with them. A few hushed whispers and then many smiles. The protocols had been broken and other men rose and danced with the women. The sons were dancing with their mothers in the restricted area of the kafenio and everyone's hearts were opening up in joyous union.

Peter watched old woman dressed in tribal clothes or just in black walk to the Kafenio and then stop when they saw women dancing with the men. They were fascinated by the fact that women were allowed at the kafenio. Many took a table and hoped and waited for an opportunity to dance with the old men, and at times, just dances with one of the other women.

The pretty young girls, who were with their mothers, were excited by the opportunity to dance. They went on the make-shift dance floor and danced with anyone who would dance with them. It was a tender and sentimental moment. The young girls showered the dancers with flowers petals (not plates) they had prepared for the occasion. It was a tribute to life.

During this wonderful moment, the old men who were dancing fell back and formed a circle around the dance floor. It was their way of saying;

"We will hold you in our arms and our hearts. We will meet again after we all cross over to the other side."

Peter was captivated by the scene. He watched them until the p;d men slowly tired. These old souls slowly left the dance floor. Against their faltering wills, they had to sit down. Peter thought to himself; "This too is part of life. We must leave the dance of life. When our music stops, it is time to move on and disappear."

It was about this time that Alex interrupted the dancing. He wanted to close down the party with a few words; "Let us remember this time together. Let us hold each other in our hearts and our memories. Let us remember the times we loved, the times we cried, the times we disagreed, the times we laughed and the times we held each other close. Let us commit these moments to our hearts.

It is time for me to close the Kafenio for the night. I want to wish you all a good night."

Somebody started singing the Greek national anthem. Peter heard the words ring true as the rallying cry for Greece's upcoming struggle for freedom:

"From the sacred bones, of the Hellenes arisen, and valiant again as you once were…..hail, o hail, Liberty."

Once everyone started singing, the Greek police who were on the other side of the street took their hats off, held their arms and hats across their hearts. They started singing the Greek National Athena.

After the singing was over, the Greek policemen joined the party. The band captured the moment and started playing again. It was a circle dance. They held each other at the shoulder, shouted and sang as they danced. When the music stopped, they gave everyone a salute and left.

Most times, Peter didn't pay attention to speeches. Certainly not speeches by priests. But this time he was moved by something Father Paris said. "The church is the soul, the spirit and the inspiration for the battle for independence. The bishops of our church gave their lives for the struggle for freedom.

These moments and the call for freedom would always be in Peter's heart. "Liberty O' Liberty".

THE SPIRITUAL CARDS

"We only have the 'present' moment; the past is gone and the fu-

ture hasn't come yet. Your whole life is in this moment. Dance and shout while you can. For life will be over before you know it."

After the celebration was over, Alex told Peter to come in early the next day. He wanted to talk to him about his future. He told Peter that it was a defining moment in his life and he wanted to do what he could to help Peter get off to a good start. Alex called it a defining moment because some 'life altering' decisions had to be made.

Peter welcomed Alex' offer to help. Peter knew that he had to decide whether to leave Lesbos or stay and make the best of things. He was facing a big obstacle. Peter had no money, no way of making money and no real plan or idea of where to go.

As he was going to the Kafenio, he was pondering the many unknowns. He had serious questions such as: "What should he do? What were his choices? Should he go and, if so, where? How could he leave his mother and his Yaya? He knew that if he left that he would never see them again?" This was a devastating thought.

He was almost at the Kafenio and he saw Alex waving at him. Alex had a full pot of coffee at the table. Peter knew that meant Alex had a lot to say to him. For one fleeting moment, Peter wondered if Alex wanted to fire him in a friendly way. What the hell was this meeting about?

When he got to the table, Alex reached out and gave him a big hug. He never did that before. Strange?

Alex said; "You've been like a son to me. You fill the void I felt when my son left Lesbos for a better life. I want you to know that if you stay with me one day I will give the Kafenio to you. Peter was overwhelmed. He managed to get out the words: "That's very generous of you. I can't decide whether I should go, or try to make a go of it here in Lesbos."

Alex smiled and said, "I understand. The offer stands until you make a decision. I have one more thing for you. In life, you must have a 'trade' or 'skill' you can always fall back on. I want to teach you a skill that will help you no matter where you go. I will teach you how to manipulate the cards. Let's call it learning the 'play of the game'.

Peter was a little perplexed. Was he talking about 'cheating' at cards?

"Let's start with ancient wisdom. Our ancestors believed that 'everything is spiritual- even our planet and all things in, over and below the surface. The entire universe including all of the inhabitants. The first thing to know is that 'playing cards for money is a spiritual undertaking'.

Peter couldn't hold back. He had to ask; "Wait. Are you saying that playing and cheating at cards is a spiritual experience?"

"That's exactly what I'm saying. Let me explain. Every card has a spiritual nature. There are aces, Kings and Queens that have standing and power; but even the lowly cards like two and three have power if played right. The key ro winning is knowing how the game is played, the strategic nature of the game and most important marking the cards and knowing what's in everyone hand.

But there is an obligation that comes with marking the cards and winning the pot. When you win at cards you have an obligation to give some of your earnings to the poor. You take money from those that have it and you give a percentage to those who don't. It is this act that connects you to love, charity and goodness. Okay so far?"

Peter shook his head – yes.

Alex said; "Let's get into the techniques and the art of the game. It starts with the reading of the cards. You have to know how the cards are 'stacked up' before you can know how to bet. This involves knowing how to mark the cards. If the cards have a white border, you bend them with your thumb and forefinger at the edges. If the cards do not have a white border, you scrap them with sandpaper at the edges. Here is a ring and I will show you how to hide a small slip of sandpaper under the edge of the ring."

Peter was speechless. He finally blurted out; "Thank you' for the ring and what you are doing to help me."

They spent the good part of the day going over techniques. Alex opened a discussion on the art of the game. "Alex continued; "You are an actor. There is a costume involved. Always dress ordinary and don't look like a 'high roller'. Don't scare the other players away. Fumble the cards and act like an amateur. You are playing a 'time honored' script."

Alex was on a roll. He almost sang his closing words; "Hide your winnings in your shoes. At the end of play, lose a couple of hands. Oh yes, there is an etiquette involved in the art of the game. If you enter a game that was going and you see 'marked' cards already being played, get up and leave. The first player stays and other pros leave."

The lesson was over. Peter asked; "If this is a spiritual game, is destiny or the gods involved in the play?"

"Remember Peter, you cannot transact business with the gods. You can promise them anything. They'll get you every time. As to destiny it always poses as 'free will'. We make our choices and then we have to live with the consequences of these choices. That's how life works. One more concept. Life and existence offer us endless choices and possibilities.

Maybe this is why everything seems so big and confusing. These many possibilities are the 'gifts' of the gods. We are on our own, but we are blessed with many gifts to help us along."

Alex looked around and saw Costas and Yianni seated at one of his tables. He told Peter to follow him. He went up to their table and asked them if they could help Peter if he needed or decided to begin his Odyssey?

Costas said; "Of course we will. Is this related to the Christos matter?" Alex said; "Yes and no." That was a standard way of saying it might be. Please don't delve any further.

Yianni said; "Peter we leave in three days. If the tides are right we'll launch at 3pm on the third day. You are, of course, welcome to go with us. If you are there on or before three we'll help you aboard. If you are not there, we'll assume that you decided to stay."

Peter asked; "Where are you going?" Simple question simple answer.

Yianni said; "We're going to Istanbul and then over to Northern Greece. You'll be lost in the crowd in Istanbul and safe in Northern Greece with our people. They talked a while about the challenges involved.

It was getting dark. Peter thanked Alex for everything. Hugs took place between Alex and Peter. He left the Kafenio and began his walk home. He looked up at the stars and wondered what was in store for him. He passed a nightclub along the way and could hear the band practicing a song. It was a song that seemed to provide spiritual clues and guidance for him

The song was a popular one that had been played many times before as Greek men said their last goodbyes. The song told of the pleasure of the expected journey and the pain of leaving:

"Let me tell you again - About years gone by - About the sad songs I love - My pleasure, my pain. And yet if you come - I'll give it to you drop by drop - To quench your thirst. Bear with me when I ask - What the future will bring The sun and the thunder are lying in wait for me - My pleasure, my pain...."

Peter wondered if the song was from the spiritual world. A destiny call for change. He was excited about beginning his Odyssey, the adventure. But he was depressed about the pain of leaving his family and his life in Lesbos.

He wondered if life was a sad song played over and over again. And that lying in wait was pleasure and pain that would come to him 'drop by drop'.

PASSAGE IV

THE ODESSSEY BEGINS

Choral Foreword: The Journey

Every Odyssey is a journey of a soul. They have an element of boldness in its execution. Cavafy embraced the power of the goddess Soteria and this power engendered boldness as expressed in his most notable poem: "Ithaca". The construction of this poem rises to the heights and captures the elusive fear knowing that daring brings verve to life along with the protection of Soteria.

The poem is an unforgettable and unique statement of the value of life's journey. Nobody else but Cavafy could have written it:

> *"Then pray that the road is long.*
> *That the summer mornings are many,*
> *That you will enter ports seen for the first time*
> *With such pleasure, such joy!*
> *Always keep Ithaca fixed in your mind.*
> *To arrive there is your ultimate goal.*
> *But do not hurry the voyage at all.*
> *It is better to let it last for long years;*
> *And even to anchor at the isle when you are old,*
> *Rich with all that you have gained on the way,*
> *Not expecting that Ithaca will offer you riches.*
> *Ithaca has given you the beautiful voyage."*

Odysseys are journeys of souls and our lives are governed by spiritual life plans. There seems to be universal themes experienced in our life plans. We all fall in love, make the same mistakes, travel similar roads, have the same problems, and dream the same dreams, suffer, learn, get old, some evolve to wisdom and, ultimately, we all suffer in old get sick and die.

Through it all, similar story lines emerge. Common life patterns are stitched together. Whatever is happening, it is all governed by a sense that we should enjoy and celebrate the journey for it may be the last and only one we take

It was his singular task to navigate the rocky shoals of life and find a place for a safe landing. The goal was to find a place where he could live and enjoy his life and be able to handle more of the 'sad passions of life' that were sure to come. Peter will search and try to find his 'way of the path' to a place in the world where he would find love, harmony and contentment.

EVEN HEROES CRY

"From an old Greek song: Destiny is a smoldering flame, life is a moan and a grudge. And at the end, Fate is a pile of ashes."

Peter suddenly woke up from a deep sleep. He was agitated and in a state of panic. Costas parting words were resonating in his mind; "Finish your business, make your goodbyes, pack your bag – we launch Wednesday afternoon at 3pm. We wait for no one. There are tides to catch.

He could hardly believe what was happening. Oh my God! – I am really leaving Lesbos for somewhere. But then, a great sadness overwhelmed him. His heart hurt. He laid his head back in his pillow and cried. He felt like a little boy again.

The little boy in him moaned the loss of his family, all his friends and even the men at the Kafenio. He laid back on his bed. When he thought of leaving Lesbos and his life in Greece, he sunk into depression again. He wondered whether he would ever come back. But it was time to swallow the tears and grow up.

Peter dressed and went into the kitchen. His mother and his Yaya were already up and making breakfast. A feast for Peter before he left. His mother said; "I cried all night." Peter asked; "For Dad?" She answered; "No. For you. I'll miss you." Yaya was there and she said; "I cried all night too. For you and for my little girl, Deme."

Brother George came into the kitchen and asked; "Why is everyone crying?" Yaya said; "Because Peter is leaving us." George started crying too and said; "Don't go Peter." There was a moment of silence while everyone collected their breath. Peter rubbed George's head and said; "I may go on a big boat. I'll be back." That seemed to satisfy George.

The family conversation was interrupted by a knock on the door. It was Sophia, Peter's teacher and Deme's childhood friend. She heard some of the conversation and saw the tears of goodbye on everyone's face.

Sophia ever the 'soft-feeling and spoken' diplomat told Peter that he is more of a man if he feels his passions. She told him tp let his pain soak in his tears. In soothing words she said, "Peter, I know that you are fascinated by Odysseus and his trials, tribulations and adventures. He went through the same process you are going through. He didn't want to leave Ithaca, his kingdom and his wife, and sail away with his Greek allies to fight against the Trojans."

Peter asked, "What did he do?" Sophia answered, "Odysseus cried. He didn't want to leave home and couldn't wait to get back. He was placed in a position where it was morally imperative for him to leave; despite his deepest wish to remain at home with his family and his people. He cried when he left home and cried when he was away and he thought that he would never make it home again. Even heroes cry."

As was her habit to interrupt whenever she felt the urge to do so, Yaya said; "As I recall, he was gone for years and was with many women. Homer wrote; "He cried and he wanted to get back home. But that's not to say he wasn't enjoying himself.

He was delightfully trapped by the sirens on an enchanted Island in the Aegean. There was a beautiful Princess and many women he met on that Island. There were hardships, longing for home, tears and passionate pleasures on his Odyssey."

Sophia said, "That may be true; but their pain and tears were genuine. In the Odyssey, Homer describes the scene as, "Odysseus and his men are repeatedly overcome with tides of sorrow as they recall their lost homes and loved ones. They were consumed with grief and they too wept live tears."

Homer wrote; "He wept". Homer, the bard, sang the following words about him:

> *"But Odysseus, clutching his flaring sea-blue cape*
> *in both powerful hands, drew it over his head*
> *And buried his handsome face,*
> *ashamed that his hosts might see him shedding tears."*

Deme told Peter, "Everyone who has a heart sheds tears. Don't be ashamed. All the Greek heroes, including Achilles the great Greek warrior, cried because they cared about people and what was happening around them. I am proud of you for having those feelings and being man enough to cry about your pain. Tears are an expression of love."

Yaya couldn't wait to say something. She interrupted the conversations with Sophia and asked Peter; "What we want to talk to you about is whether you have any plans to leave Lesbos? Steve's mother Cleo talked to us about Steve leaving Lesbos with you."

Peter said, "I'm not sure what I should do. Steve wants me to leave with him, but I'm not sure I should go with him."

Yaya persisted; "Peter, I hope you know what you are doing. Steve will overwhelm you with his 'needy-ness'. He's not capable of taking care of himself. He needs someone to take him by the hand, lead him and take care of him."

Deme said; "Yaya is right. Steve is a young soul and he has a lot to learn. He has so many issues to resolve. Like a little kid, he no doubt is enthusiastic about a new life adventure; but he isn't ready or able to survive on his own. Right now, no doubt, his one major problem is: "Can he get you Peter to leave with him?"

Peter said; "I'm not sure what to do. I don't dare bring up the subject with him. My hope is that he finds another solution for his problem. Leaving home is going to be tough enough. Assuming the responsibility for his well-being and safety may be more than I can handle."

Sophia said; "Peter, some things are beyond our comprehension, beyond reason and our control. Oh yes, before I forget, Cleis gave me this letter. She wanted Peter to give it to Steve after you two boarded the boat tomorrow." Peter said; "She is assuming a lot about a boat and Steve and I going together."

Deme took the letter and said; "Peter, I'll hold it for you. Why don't you take a walk to the Port and get into touch with your inner feelings and thoughts about what you should do. "

Peter got up and left. He was relieved to get away from all the little voices. The conversations were painful and confusing. He knew that everyone was concerned about him, but now he needed some quiet time. He had to get in touch with his center point to make sense of everything.

Deme felt his need. Even though the 'cord' had been cut at birth, she still was spiritually connected to her son. She knew that he needed to find an inner peace as the first step in making a decision. Over the years, she felt his calm when he was near the water. When Peter needed to go, she always knew it. She had an inner vision of him at the Port.

Her young man would always be a young boy to her. The scene at the Port was her favorite vision of her little boy. He was sitting on a small hill overlooking the water. There was a shared joy between them and an inner peace when they visualized the Port and the boats coming in and going out. It was the movement of life.

Peter made his way to his favorite spot at the Port area. He felt the winds from the Aegean Sea. The winds brought sea water that had a salty taste. He laid down and thought about everything. It wasn't long before he drifted away into a dream state and started to hear the sounds of another world. Gulls, birds and large fishes jumping in and out of the water fascinated him. The sounds of the boats chugging in and out put him in another place. He fell into a deep sleep.

When he woke up, he remembered the words from his dream: 'Goodbye Greece, Hello World'. Peter had his answer. He was ready to go. He had to go.

WHEN DESTINY CALLS

"Aeschylus in his poem – Prometheus Unbound – makes the case for destiny's strength quite eloquently with his poem: So I must bear, as lightly as I can, the destiny that fate has given me; for I know well against necessity, against its strength, no one can fight and win."

Before he went to bed, Peter told his mother that he was experiencing small tugs of his heart and that unexpected tears appeared in his eyes. His legs started shaking on their own. He was waking up in the middle of the night to quiet whispers and, at other times, strange noises. He experience all these signs and more before and after suddenly waking up from a 'deeply disturbing' dream state.

These occurrences bothered him. She interrupted these signs as nervous energy and Destiny's call to change the directions of his young life. She realized that it was time for the next stage in his growth and a new start in life. Sadly, she told Peter; "It is nerves energy that is bothering you. It means that changes are coming fast and that these strange occurrences are Destiny's call that cannot be ignored. They are 'angel whispers' getting you ready for big changes."

Peter sensed that she was right. He hugged and kissed her good night and then he rolled over and went back to sleep.

He woke up the next morning feeling different. He laid

in bed thinking about what was before him. He was excited for no apparent reason at all. His thoughts turned to a new life adventure appearing before him. It was the boat trip scheduled for tomorrow that lifted his spirits. He was going to sail on the Aegean Sea. His fantasy was turning into a dream with clear visions of a reality.

Peter inhaled a deep breath of air, dressed and went to the kitchen. He was feeling the sublime spirit of Lesbos' courageous souls coming through him. In Lesbos, people whisper every night; "Out of the dry wells, the statues emerge cautiously and climb the trees." His Yaya use to say; "They come out to help the people of Lesbos."

He was gaining some mental resolve thinking that supernatural forces existed and that we are all governed by a preordained destiny. He remembered being told by his Yaya that; "We are powerless to resist our life plan, our destiny."

With all the spiritual talk, Peter wondered whether destiny was taking control of him and influencing his decisions. It didn't seem like he had any alternatives, but to leave Greece. He was hoping to make his way in a big, blue, green, wonderful world and not a dark, chaotic one. As the old Greeks at the Kafenio would say; "I hope Destiny dealt me a good hand."

Deme fed Peter breakfast. While he was eating she told him that Steve's mother talked to her about Steve having to leave Lesbos and she wondered if you had made any plans. Peter asked, "What did you say?"

Deme answered, "I told her 'no'. That we haven't discussed anything yet. I told her there was no reason to do so." She told me, "Steve will ask Peter that question tomorrow. He is feeling the pressure to get away for a short time until his circumstances change for the better in Lesbos."

Yaya in her usual blunt manner asked, "Peter, are you thinking about leaving?" He answered, "Yes." She went right back to him and asked, "What are you thinking about and why?" Peter was always amazed at his grandmother's fearlessness and her attitude about addressing everything with bluntness.

She must have Peter's mind about her being so blunt. She said; "I know that I am blunt; but please know that "I learned long ago that spirituality is found in living the truth about oneself. And since I'm getting into 'end times' the truth is the only thing I want to know. I don't have the luxury of time to deal with a bunch of needless conversations, alternatives, lies and deception."

Deme wanted to reassure Peter. Her words; "Peter, fear nothing. You are born of a race and a land that makes us live and survive on heroic terms. Because of our circumstances we are forced to live on a dangerous scale. You will find courage as you go forward. Go in a bold, but in a careful way. You will triumph over all obstacles if you are clever and brave like the hero and trickster Odysseus."

Peter said; "I decided last night that I was leaving. When I went to sleep I dreamed that I was on the high seas heading to somewhere, anywhere." Peter knew that he had played the part of the 'big man' and engaged in a lot of talk about going on his Odyssey. Now, he was going to live his dream and not just a fantasy.

Yaya was the first to speak; "Well, are you taking Steve with you?"

Before he could even answer her question, George came into the kitchen and said; "Look what I found at the front door." It was Steve.

He came in the kitchen and quickly asked; "Are we leaving Lesbos together?" Yaya asked again; "Well Peter, what did you learn and decide while you were meditating at the Port harbor."

"Yes. We'll be in the same boat heading for somewhere, anywhere.

Steve was elated. He added; "We'll follow the stars. Sail the high seas. Go anywhere the winds take us. Thanks Peter. I'm going home to tell my family the good news. True to form, Steve said; "Goodbye all." He left right after Peter agreed to take him along for a 'Destiny' ride to who knows 'where'. He left before Peter could change his mind."

Pete never thought that he would assume responsibility for Steve. He suspected that it was his Yaya's comment about Steve's 'young soul' caused some concerns and apprehension. And, of course, she told everyone that he should start his new life without Steve. She thought that it was going to be tough enough to change his life, sail the high seas, and follow his Destiny and, at the same, 'babysit' Steve.

Peter told everyone that he was going to the Kafenio to make sure everything was in good order for the trip. He was hoping that Costas and Yianni were there to confirm arrangements. He also wanted to tell them that Steve wanted to come along for the ride. And could he?

After Peter left, Yaya told Deme and George; "I'm surprised that he's taking Steve with him. But, he'll be all right with or without him. Peter is an old soul, wise beyond his years and, as an old soul, much can be expected of him. For some unknown reason, he feels responsible for Steve. He knows that Steve has no real choice; but to leave Lesbos for the safety of another land. I think that Peter feels compassion and even pity for Steve. He knows intuitively that Steve could not survive on his own."

Meanwhile, Peter walked to the Kafenio. He was thrilled to see Costas and Yianni eating lunch. Alex was there. He had all three of them. They greeted him with smiles. A good sign for Peter. They invited Peter to sit with them and talk 'some skata, some good shit'.

Peter asked them if his friend, Steve, could go with them tomorrow. He got a short answer – 'Sure'. "Remember, we wait for no one. We leave at 3pm."

Alex said; "This is all about Destiny. All our boys have to leave." Peter told them about the 'angel whispers' he was getting. And that his mother said "It was Destiny's whispers that change was coming."

Yianni said, "With all due respect to your mother, that's not how Destiny works. You'll get pushed, pulled, kicked in the butt, and involved in traditional killings, phony rape charges and so on. Destiny influences are not subtle. They are 'whacks across the back of the head' to get your attention and make you change your direction. This is called life."

Peter knew that it was time for diplomacy. "That seems to make some sense. If there is such a thing called Destiny; it would play 'rough' to force us on life's death march."

The more they talked and he thought about it ; "It had to be 'whacks across the back of our head' to get our attention." He began to think that all this talk about destiny was crazy talk. There is no such thing as life plans and destiny.

Peter realized that it was time for him to go. He did a 'Steve' and got what he needed and it was time to go. He knew that this conversation could go on all night. There is no end to crazy conversations between highly emotional people like the Greeks.

THE TRICKERS

"The gods are tricksters who play with us." A Greek Proverb

Peter was forming his own thoughts about the supernatural and all the talk about destiny. He wondered about 'free will' and how it interacts with destiny. He remembered Alex's offer to eventually givel him the Kafenio if he stayed. He thought that the gods were tempting him. This was his first conscious encounter with the interplay of his will power and his perceived destiny.

He wondered if he should defy the gods and, abandoned his destiny, and stay. Then he remembered Alex's warning. Don't try to defy or negotiate with the gods. Promises don't work either. They'll get you every time.

He heard the call to get out of bed. It was the chatter of little birds outside his window. They were saying; "Put the idle thoughts away and get going." He knew that there was no real way to change the course of events. The little birds were right. It was time to get going.

Alex was on point again. Life is a game of chance. We have to play the hand that we are dealt. After further reflection, Peter came to grips with the thought that there are mysteries in life that are baffling. There isn't much anyone can do about that. He remembered Alex's advice: "It's like playing cards. The trick is to learn how to control the risks."

But, realistically, he knew that controlling everything in life was an illusion. As they say in the Kafenio, "Can't mark those cards."

He was starting to believe that reincarnation, religion, mythology and destiny were useless chatter and a waste of time.

But that was what he needed to get clear in his mind; "Is destiny real or not?" Peter concluded; "Nobody knows the truths about what happens before or after death. The supernatural has its secrets. It is all a riddle and it is a waste of time to based your life on these mythologies."

A little later, he had second thoughts. Alex may be right. Destiny does pose as free will. Or was it, free will poses as destiny? Even Deme seemed to be 'right on'. Destiny does give out signs that changes are coming. Intuition, dreams, omens, angel whispers, readings may be some of the signs of major life changes.

"But no." he concluded; "These are tales. Farfetched fantasies. The talk about Destiny is not true to life. It is the belief of small minds."

Some more time passed. Then he had another swing of belief. "Maybe it's all free will and we are fooling ourselves with talk about Destiny. It may be that when we do something, there are always ramifications. We don't take the blame ourselves. We blame it on the gods.

He was near his home and was surprised to hear singing and noise coming from his home. It sounded like a party was taking place inside. He came in the front door and was greeted by his Yaya. She hugged him and shouted; "Let's sing! Let's shout! Let's dance! We'll cry later!"

A surge of excitement went through Peter. He reached out and hugged his Yaya and then followed her into the big room. Everyone was singing and dancing even his younger brother George. He joined in the festivities and danced and sang the night away. The last song had been sung many times before young man after young man left Lesbos for other lands and opportunities. The goodbyes had been put to song:

"The kids went to America *** waiters, cooks ***and tonight the nostalgic fire was lit in their hearts *** my dear sea, the civilizations that bore you are tired *** that's what the foreigners say, but even if the Mediterranean drowns there will still be the earth *** the kids went to America *** waiters, cooks ***and tonight the nostalgic fire was lit in their heart."

Eventually, fatigue took its toll and the party was soon over. Peter was tired. The joyous party and the stress of leaving family and country took a toll on him. There was no 'after party' conversations. He went right to bed and quickly fell asleep.

Early morning came and he woke up with a 'thunderclap' thought. 'Of course, Destiny is real. He lived it all his life. He came into this world knowing that he would be a 'modern-day' Odysseus and that he would have his own Odyssey. He couldn't know this unless he was getting Destiny's 'angel whispers'.

THE FAINT OF HEART

"Through what is perceived as mere chance; Destiny sets the beginning, outlines the life story, dictates the flow and timing of events, establishes the purpose and meaning of life and determines the eventual outcomes of life."

The sadness of saying goodbye – perhaps forever – was too much for Steve. Leaving his family, friends and Lesbos was traumatic. Leaving his mother was the hardest thing he ever faced and had to do.

From his bedroom, he could hear his mother singing. He

listened to the words before going into the kitchen.

"*You can never give too much love. And you know you may get nothing in return. Do give what there is to give, don't put your soul in a corner.*"

Steve enjoyed the moment. He put the thought of her quietly singing a song of love into the memory of his heart. The words of the song convinced him that love is an emotion of the soul.

Everything was getting spiritual for him. His Yaya and how old she was came to mind. He felt like he was abandoning her. He always thought that he would be there to hold her hand when she passed away. His heart hurt thinking about it.

Once she stopped singing, he went into the kitchen. Not unexpectedly and much beyond his control, he approached his mother in tears. Everything was difficult for him. He knew that his mother wanted him to act like a man in the tradition of the brave warriors that Greece had always produced, but Steve couldn't play that role in life. He was cast in a different mold.

He quietly 'slip walked' across the room, fell to his knees and put his head in her lap. She allowed him to be her small boy again; perhaps for the last time. After a while, during which they both felt the pain and loneliness of separation, she spoke softly – almost whispered:

"I know that it is time for you to go. We do not need to talk about it now. Let's quietly enjoy our last time together. We will both take away from this moment what we need and will treasure the memories."

As she 'cradled' his head in her lap, she whispered; "Steve, life is a series of dreams. This dream is over and it is time for you to reach for your new dreams. It's time for you to leave and find your rightful place in the world. Become the person you are meant to be. Dream new dreams and live and treasure all your dreams and memories."

This was their last moment of mother and child. The emotional decision to leave had been made. Minds could not be changed. Nothing more to be said. Steve's time had come. He would join the growing exodus of the Greek boys leaving the homeland.

This was his defining moment in life. Steve had to bury his fears. He had to leave as a man. It was a Kleos moment that would define his character. Like so many other young men, he would cast his fate into the powerful tides of other waters and other lands.

Meanwhile, Peter started his day by sleeping late. He too went to bed worrying about casting his fate into the winds of a large and dangerous world. He had a dream that he was entering the large, empty halls of a church. He thought the dream was preparing him. It was a trip into the loneliness of forever. Before he woke up he heard the heavenly chants which reassured him. It was the right move to make.

Peter dressed and made his way into the kitchen. His Yaya was there and she walked over and gave him a heartfelt hug. She said, "Peter, there are big moments in everyone's life that should be cherished. This is your big moment and ours. Saying goodbye, possibly forever, is very hard to do. You came to us as a baby and now you are leaving as a young man.

Deme heard the background noise and followed it into the kitchen. She saw Peter and Yaya hugging each other. Not to be left out of the loving, she went over and hugged both of them. She said; "Peter, "life gives us these Kleos moments. How we handle them defines us. They make us who we are born to be."

She said; "By the way, you two, we are invited tonight to a goodbye party at Cleo's."

Perter was excited about another party. But he had boring tasks ahead of him. He would spend a good part of the day going through his clothes. Shabby, but good enough to give to brother, George. He handle a lot of boring tasks, but finally he was packed and ready to take on the high seas. But now, it was party time.

The Zaloumis tribe made their way to Cleo's home. The party had already started and people were already celebrating. The younger members of the Zaloumis Tribe joined the line dance and the older ones went straight for the coffee, wine and food. The house 'rocked' with Greek singing and shouts of joy. The joys of the festivities had temporally overcome the sadness of the goodbyes.

The party went on for some time before Essie got everyone's attention. She had a coffee cup reading to announce. She said; "My cup shows Steve dancing with many dancing girls." A few AH's from everyone. It was Peter's Yaya turn. "My cup shows Peter dancing with only one lady. A few OH's reacting.

Just before everyone got ready to call it a night, Essie held her hand up and wanted to give some parting advice to Steve and Peter. She had the floor. She said; "A poetic fragment from one of Sappho's poem. We all know that the perfumed poetess of Lesbos, was an ancient Greek princess acquainted with the affairs of the heart. She wrote:

"…..are you not amazed how at one and the same moment she seeks out soul, body, hearing, tongue, sight, complexion as though they had all left her and were external, and how in contradiction she both freezes and burns, is irrational and sane, is afraid and nearly dead,

"……so that we observe in her not one single emotion, but a concourse of emotions? All of this of course happens to people in love ……"

Essie said; "Sappho makes the point that women can be irrational and sane at the same time. Over the centuries nothing has changed. If you boys fall in love with a woman, they will freeze you out and at the same time burn to have you back. My advice is that you must learn to ignore what can't be changed. Otherwise, they will drive you crazy all the days of your life." The two elder Yayas put their hands together and sang:

"If you love the wrong person, she will destroy you. The key is to find the right one for this lifetime. The beauty and passion of love will bring joy to your life."

Every one cheered and clapped their approval. Deme stood for her take; "Boys, another word of advice. Many Greek men and women believe that love can be destructive. If the situation occurs; you must let go. What can't be changed must be let go. She stopped talking to let Yaya have the last word. She said; "Boys, you will learn in time that life is learning how to let go. When your time has passed, you must leave everything go.

Whatever you decide; follow tradition and cry, sing and dance the pain of it away."

EXPECTATIONS

Cavafy *"Do not hurry the voyage at all and when you are old expect and have achieved and lived a rich and 'beautiful voyage."*

The night before the boat left for Istanbul, Costas and Yianni had some private conversations with their two young passengers. They meeting was about their expectations. Costas said; "If one of you had any doubts; I want you to pull out now."

He said; "Who are we? We been called mariners, traders and water creatures. Even water rats. Let me clarify who we are and what we do. We have always been adventurers. Yes. We live on the water and we never fail to have new adventures every time we pull out and go somewhere."

He went on to say; "We've lived our lives that way. After our wives died from the plague that devastated parts of Lesbos, we found that the open sea was a place where we could enjoy the excitement of change. Change was a place where ordinary events were meaningful. This is where we are able to live our lives to their fullest."

Steve said; "Ordinarily, a ride on a boat is exciting; but this trip is a bit different. I'm not looking at it as high adventure. I have to go. That moron Samson was chasing me with his Turkish goons. I have no choices."

Peter said; "We're not strangers to the seas. We actually enjoy being on the open waters. But this trip is more than going to a destination. We are passing from one reality to another. But, that's not to say we aren't open to new adventures. I am excited about seeing more of the world."

Costas knew they had different reasons for leaving. Peter seemed excited. Steve had his issues. Costas tried to reassure Steve. He said; "Steve, we are not in control. There are forces in the universe that are more powerful than mere human beings. The goal is to enjoy the time we have.

He talked to them about Cavafy's poem and told them that life was like a trip to Ithaca. It is all about finding one's rightful place in this great, big wonderful world. Costas said; "Cavafy is right about the meaning of life. It was his view that the search for life begins by visiting many ports yet unseen. Ports means trying to experience new adventures before your time runs out."

Costas quoted an old poet. He said; "The goal is to have a long life 'rich with all that you have gained on the way.' Riches could mean wealth. It could mean the richness of the wonderful experiences that are gained by taking great voyages or journeys. Yianni and I believe that by being adventurous, you will live life to its fullest."

Peter asked Costas, "What would we be seeing on this trip?" Costas said, "A great Church will appear as we enter the port. Hagia Sophia is the largest church in Constantinople, now named Istanbul by the Turks. It was built as a Christian church of great mysteries.

The Turks stole the Church from the Byzantine Christians; but they thread very lightly as they are very superstitious. They worry about stealing holy relics from other people and their God. They fear God's retribution for unholy acts against the Holy Church and thus God."

Costas was on a pulpit and continued his sermon. "Boys there are clues that are hidden in the Holy Church to warn infidels away. One sign is in the dome of the church where there is an engraved angel. One day when it is discovered by the Turks, it will elicit a dread among them. Their fear is that the God will punish them for taking the Church and that the avenging Orthodox Christian angels will rise up to plague them."

Peter asked, "Has this happened yet?" Costas replied, "Many of the Turks I know are fearful of the mysteries of Saint Sophia and all the hidden dangers to them in the Holy

Church. They believe that bad things will happen to them in the future."

Steve ever fearful of life's mysteries was fascinated by the discussion and asked, "What other things are hidden in the Holy Church?"

Costas again; "There are the hidden crosses. The Turks have an indescribable fear of the hidden crosses. These crosses are found on the interior of the Holy Church. There are other crosses that can only be seen on the Church from above.

By the way, there is an old man named Panos who claims to guards the spirits of the Church. I can get him to tell you more about the Church." Peter answered; "Yes. Let's do it." Costas said; "One more thing. Yianni has a favorite poem he wants to read it to you."

Yianni gave the wheel to Costas. He said; "No eternally happy and optimistic Zorba will be met; no scary Captain Lemoni. No other earthy and unforgettable characters as the ones found in the book entitled: Zorba the Greek will be encountered.

No rough seas and rain – only the joyful serenity of sun, mild winds and gentle clouds. To quote the great Greek writer Kazantzakis:

"Happy is the man who, before dying, has the great fortune to sail the Aegean Sea. Many are the pleasures of this world – women, fruit, and ideas. But to cleave that sea in the gentle autumnal season, murmuring the name of each islet is to my mind the joy most apt to transport the heart of man into paradise. Nowhere else can one pass so easily and serenely from reality to dream?"

Yianni took a bow and returned to the wheel. Peter and Steve clapped their approval of his reading. They were starting to believe that there is purpose to life and that the voyage was a gift. No negatives. They just listened to these wise old men. The poem helped. They were into the sense of adventure.

Costas took center stage. He said; "There is an old Greek proverb which illustrates the point we are trying to make. Life is not about waiting for the storms to pass. It is not waiting for a Samson to pass. It is about learning how to enjoy and dance in the rain until the storm passes."

THE LAUNCH

"Every wanderer is not lost." Greek proverb

Peter woke up with a feeling of joy in his heart. He laid in bed and let his thought wander; "Enough with the tears of goodbye. The adventure is before me. It's time to follow the stars, howl at the moon, sail the high seas and ride the tides of life."

He thought for a moment; "And there is more. "I'm not running away. I am running toward. I have an adventure to experience. It's time to cut the cords that binds, grab my freedom and capture the essence of life. Destiny is calling me."

He heard his mother call him from the kitchen. "Get up Peter and spend some waning moments with us before you leave."

It was good she called. He was enjoying his brave thoughts-his promises to himself. He dressed and went into the kitchen. "How fragile his mother and Yaya looked to him. He felt guilty leaving them. Breaking the bond and leaving would not be easy.

They were both sitting at the table drinking small cups of Turkish coffee. Peter went up to his mother and gave her a kiss on the cheek. He then kissed his Yaya on the forehead.

He told his mother; "I will always remember you and Yaya and, when I do, I will be close to you. Yaya said; "You better." Deme smiled through her tears and said, "As will I." She reached out to him and put some money in his hands. He looked at it, hesitated, and then put it on the table. "Thanks Mom; but I can't take it." He went back to his room to pack a few things for the trip.

Peter was back into his thoughts again. Like the fabled Odysseus, Peter knew that it was a hostile world and that he would face many dangers on his journey. He would have to navigate the rocky shoals of life and find a place for a safe landing.

Steve's thoughts about the trip were different. He was escaping. He didn't know what to make about a trip to Istanbul, the capital city of the enemy. The logic seemed flawed to him. They were fleeing their own country to get away from their own countrymen, in this case, the Greek authorities. The plan seemed like the lunatic ravings of a Greek comedy.

He remembered Peter saying; "We are getting lost in the crowd of a big city."

Cleo and Essie were what lead to Steve having to leave. His Yaya said; "He has to go. Love came too early." Cleo had a more pragmatic view of the situation. "It was sex that came too earl. If there was a fault, it was Steve's. He tried to take the stem and the bud before the flower had bloomed."

Time was pushing the goodbyes. Both familys were going with their loved ones. Not surprisingly, they caught up with each other as they were walking to the docks. The combined size of the families seemed like a small parade marching to the Port. They made Peter and Steve feel important and, more importantly loved.

When they arrived at the dock, they were greeted by a group of friends. It was a wonderful scene — so Greek in the happening – goodbyes with tears, kisses, hugs and sworn statements of love. The older family members were giving their blessings and prayers for their safety.

Alex made his way through the people gathered around Peter. He had a gift. It was a money belt filled with money – a contribution from everyone at the Kafenio. Peter was speechless. Alex said; "Go with God." And then he left before the goodbyes got too emotional.

It was time to go. Costas yelled at Peter and Steve to climb aboard. Both Peter and Steve had a big 'gulp'. Suddenly, reality was there. They were really going! One more clutch of goodbyes and they made their way into the boat.

They were helped by Costas and Yianni. Deep inside, Peter was relieved to have them. It was less scary. He was learning that the men of the Kafenio were there to protect them and help them get a safe start.

Once aboard, Steve looked up on the hill high above the bay and saw Cleis and her mother. Peter was shocked to see them; but Steve was not. He must have sent her a message somehow. It was that she had her mother's permission as she was her chaperone.

Cleis was waving a white linen handkerchief. No doubt soaked in tears. The Greek tradition is to send 'a tear in a white linen handkerchief' to a loved one who had to leave.

Peter gave her letter to Steve. He took it and quickly tore it open. He was speechless. It was a 'hand written' note from Cleis:

"My love,
I know that you must leave,
My heart yearns for you
Oh! That I may go with you
Come back to me"

Steve was swallowing his tears as best he could. Waving kisses to her as the boat left the dock. The two lovers were exchanging their sad goodbyes. Waving the white linen handkerchief was her gesture of undying love.

Their attention turned to Costas who was saying his mariner's prayer. "Let us ask the help of our ancestors. We place our fate in the hands of God." Yianni added; "And of the Devil." Costas disagreed; "There is always a steep price to pay when a deal is made with the devil. Let's stay with God."

Everyone was at the edge of the dock waving goodbye. The two Yayas were singing a little song of goodbye. They were expressing their love. It was an old Greek folk farewell song that captures the pathos of a son's farewell.

"My little bird, far away in a foreign land, sad and with a heavy heart, that foreign land rejoices in your presence."

And then it happened. Samson arrived to stop Steve from leaving. He pushed everyone aside, including the two Yayas who fell to the floor of the deck. He made his way to the edge of the dock followed by a contingent of four Greek policemen.

The boat was pulling away as Samson found his way to the edge of the dock. He was yelling at Costas to come back to the dock. And then another surprise was in store for everyone. The two Yayas pushed the police aside and together they pushed Samson off the dock into the water. The police didn't know what to make of it, except to laugh along with everyone else.

Samson was swimming and struggling underneath the dock to find his wig. It added some comic relief when he was pushed into the water and his wig came off. The idea of him forced to struggle underneath the docks was a good encore for everyone.

Samson made his way to the floor of the dock. Everyone had gone, including his police escort. The two Yayas were at the far edge of the dock and were amused to see him soaking wet, standing at the edge of the dock trying to adjust his wet wig on his wet head.

Samson's time was over. Once the war between the Greek army and the Ottoman Turks was declared; all the Greeks who colabored with the Turkish overlords would be rounded up and tried as traitors.

PASSAGE V

DESTINY'S LIFEPLAN UNFOLDS

Choral Forward: I Am Who I Am

Peter and Steve were immigrants trying to exist in a strange new land. They suffered the lament of loneliness. These feelings are conveyed by a poem written by John Clare entitled: "I am". It tells of the solitude and loneliness that people away from home feel. It is a dream state. They are like shadows in the light of day.

"I am – yet what I am, no one cares or knows;
my friends forsake me like a memory lost:
I am the self-consumer of my woes—
They rise and vanish in oblivion's host

Like shadows in love-frenzied stifle throes—
and yet I am and live –like vapors tossed
Into the nothingness of scorn and noise,
—into the living sea of waking dreams

Where there is neither sense of life or joys
but the vast shipwreck of my life's esteem;
Even the dearest that I love the best are strange
—nay, stranger than the rest.

I long for scenes where man hath never trod,

a place where woman never smiled or wept;
There to abide with my Creator, God,
and sleep as I in childhood sweetly slept,

Untroubling and untroubled where I lie,
the grass below — above, the vaulted sky."

They feel nothing. They are strangers in a strange new world. There is no sense of life or of joy. There is only the strong desire to sleep sweetly in the loving arms of the Creator:

GOODBYE GREECE, HELLO WORLD

In his poem entitled "Ithaca" Cavafy made a treasured statement: "You will enter Ports seen for the first time with such pleasure, such joy!

Peter sat on a bench at the rear of the boat, lost in his thoughts. He could see Lesbos fading out of sight. He remembered His dream: "Goodbye Greece, Hello World". He was living his fantasy. His destiny was coming into being. The moment was magic.

He stood at the end of the boat and stared at the wake and was reminded of Zorba's rhapsodies about sailing the Aegean Sea. He was trying to remember – what Zorba said? Ah yes, he recalled his precious words:

"Happy is the man who, before dying, has the great fortune to sail the Aegean Sea. And to cleave that sea in the gentle autumnal season, murmuring the name of each islet is to my mind the joy most apt to transport the heart of man into paradise. Nowhere else can one pass so easily and serenely from reality to dream?"

Peter smiled. They were on their way to new adventures; starting with the mystic land of Turkey. He looked around and saw Steve nervously walking in a tight circle at the center of the boat. Yianni was steering the boat and concentrating on his own thoughts. Costas was bored with the whole scene. It was time. Costas took out his ukulele.

He caught everyone's attention when he started to sing:

"Give me the courage to live my dreams
Let me spread my wings and fly to destiny
Guide me by the heavenly light of the stars
On my journey to become who I am to be
My dream, my destiny
My pleasure, my pain."

While Costas was playing his ukulele and singing his song, Peter and Steve were dancing. Peter felt like he was being inspired by the spirit of Zorba.

As the boat pulled into the busy port of Istanbul, Peter and Steve were overwhelmed by the sight. The Byzantium City of Istanbul is a great wonder of the world and a powerful sight to behold. Its skyline was rimmed with the Theodosian wall, which towered above the outskirts of the city.

They could see large spiraling and ornate mosques, richly decorate Byzantine churches, ruins marking the rich history of this ancient city, the historic "Hall of Silence" where decisions involving war and peace were made, the Hippodrome, the racing-stables – the Circus-factions of "Greens and Blues" – and the teaming ghettos and the many bazaars that lined the streets of Istanbul.

Peter made a passing comment; "Whatever happened to the Christians and why did they let go of the City to the muslins?"

Yianni picked up on his comment and said; "Nothing is eternal on earth. Everything dies. Even great and powerful nations and civilizations collapse and are no more. They all eventually tumble down and new ones rise to replace them. The loss of the city and the Holy Church symbolize the change of power between the Christians and the Muslins in Turkey. Yes, glorious even mighty Rome lost many of her crown jewels over time.

Costas had something to say and interrupted their conversations. "This is what we are going to do. I promised you a meeting with Panos He is the 'self-appointed' protector of the Christian spirits that occupy the Holy Church. It will be a fun start to your journey. You will learn a lot about the Greek and Turkish cultures. Many people of both cultures are supersites and fear the reality and power of the occult.

Yianni will contact some of our friends about temporary employment where it is safe for you young rascals. We will leave Istanbul as soon as we finish our business and can make the necessary arrangements to leave. Our next stop will be a small town in Northern Greece."

Yianni said; "Get ready. We are nearing the Istanbul port."

Peter and Steve were entering the great port of Istanbul. This was a symbolic event. Peter and Steve had started their journeys with much trepidation tempered by restrained joy.

They were mesmerized by the serenity of the 'wine-dark' Aegean Sea. It was captivating. They experienced a profound change in their lives and were looking forward to finding destiny's meaning and purpose for their journey to the mystic City of Istanbul.

THE CROSSROADS

"Know this, the immigrant's lament: But ever that man goes a stranger to strangers; he finds that who he is, no one cares to know".

Right off the boat, they went to the Kafenio, which was located near the wharfs. The old Greeks at the Kafenio used to say that were near their boats in case they had to make a quick 'get away'. The old saying seemed appropriate for the dangerous times in Istanbul and Turkey.

Costas and Yianni heard that the Turks destroyed some of the Greek communities and its leaders and bishops. When world events went against the Turks they went on periodic rampages killing and destroying the so-called infidels, especially Greeks, Jews and Armenians. Everyone was near their boats.

They took Peter and Steve with them to meet the old Greeks at the Kafenio and Nikos, an old friend of theirs who was well connected. He wasn't there. It was a little early in the day and they assumed that he was still working at his Greek deli.

Costas and Yianni told Peter and Steve to stay at the Kafenio. They had a little business to take care of and they would come back with Nikos. They promised to return soon. Before he left Costas found a table near the windows. He told them they could see the Port from there.

Peter was distracted by a scene taking place in the room. He saw an old disheveled Persian in the corner of the room who was talking to himself and to anyone crazy enough to listen to him. Apparently, he was a victim of the free flowing opium in the city. This bad stuff has the tendency to poison the brain.

He was rambling in his speech, but lucid enough to say that he was a religious follower of Zoroastrianism, an Iranian religion. His diatribe was about some old polemic of his religion: the legend of the three imposters – Moses, Christ and Muhammad. It wasn't long before the proprietor showed him to the door.

Peter wondered if the proprietor and some of his helpers would 'man handle' the bewildered man or not. He was relieved when he saw him put some money in his hands as they showed him to the door.

They were relieved when Costas came back sooner than expected. He said; "Yianni went to get Nikos. I wasn't able to finish my business so I came back. I have some old friends here who may be able to help you guys. It might not be so easy to find jobs with living accommodations."

Costas said; "A word of warning about the old timers. They like to tease and sometimes make fun of youngsters. Peter smiled; "I know. They kind of 'fathered' me when I worked in the Kafenio."

It was now a 'face time' moment and they went to the other side of the room to a large table. Costas 'rounded up' a number of old men who were just 'hanging' at other tables just doing what old Greek men do best — they talk a lot about the past.

The boys were a new diversion for this 'out-of-time' council of elders. They were somewhat qualified. During their younger years they learned what life was all about: 'life too hard, wisdom too late.'

An old man at the head of the table looked these two young men. It was a useless 'head game' and an attempt to establish 'presence'. He looked over them slowly, and then started asking questions. "Do you know how to cook?" Peter answered, "No. But I've done some 'short order' work at the Kafenio in Plomari."

"Do you know how to sail a boat?" Steve answered, "No." The old men asked, "Do you know how to tend bar?" It was Steve's turn to answer, "No, not really." The old men around the table were smiling. This was great fun questioning and teasing these young men.

Another one asked, "Can either of you read and write and can you keep a set of merchant books?" Steve answered sheepishly, "Yes, we can read and write, but we never finished school. We don't know how to keep a set of books."

Another asked; "Can either of you play any musical instruments? Peter answered; "No."

Do you have any skills?" Peter answered, "No. Not really. We are just starting to work." At this point, Costas came to the boy's defense and said, "None of us have any real talent, experience or training or we wouldn't be here."

Another old men quipped, "They are too much like us. They don't know how to do anything". He smiled; "In my mind, that makes them both qualified."

Yianni and Nikos showed up. Introductions were made. Nikos told everyone that he could make arrange for employment and housing for them. Meeting over.

Nikos said; "I have a warning. The times are bad. There is chaos throughout Istanbul. The Ottoman Turks are getting ready for a war with the Greeks and the countries of Eastern Europe. They are striking for freedom.

The Empire worked for the Turks when they occupied

countries. That's over. So much for a multicultural Empire. Now the Turks changed the word 'occupation' to 'genocide'. They are 'purifying' their country of all foreigners. They don't have the right blood (DNA). The Greeks in Turkey are an 'endangered target' of the Turks."

Timely reassurance. Costas interrupted; "If we find out that something is going to happen, we'll come back and get you and Steve out of here."

Nikos described one opportunity as a grocery store run by a widower named Antigone. The other one is a bar plus other businesses on the premises. There are lessons that come with these jobs. One teaches 'love without sex.' The other is 'sex without love'. Take your choice."

Steve chose quickly. "I'll take sex."

A SPIRITUAL CALLING

"When the Turks discovered that there was a casket buried in front, which is constructed of bronze gilded with gold, the Muslin builders didn't know what to do".
"Where might was tumbled down."

Peter was in an old mystic City and land. He believed that he was being guided by his destiny and living his Odyssey. It was the spiritual journey that he dreamed about. It wasn't romantic. He felt that the 'flow of his life' was upstream. It was exhausting to think about managing his circumstances and finding a 'proverbial' safe harbor.

He knew that it was dangerous to continue to swim against the tide. Survival was dependent on a constant struggle against the swirling currents of his life. He never thought that the unknowns would dominate his every walking moments.

He asked Costas; "Who is Panos and how did he learn all these things about the Holy Church?" He replied, "Panos is the wise old Greek in Istanbul. He thinks that he guards the Christian spirits in the Holy Church. The Turks believe he is mad and he probably is. But Greeks and Turks believe that crazy and mad people are in the hands of God and they don't bother them. They are religious scared. The worst kind of scared."

Panos played and acted out the role of the wise man. He was an old man with long, white hair. His beard went to his chest. He looked like a wise old man. He was who he was. The perfect image of someone who would be assigned by God to spend his life guarding dead Christian spirits. He was where Costas said he would be. On the Holy Church grounds. Wandering around searching for 'only God knows what.

He came over to Costas right away. They embraced. "What is it that brings you here?" Costas introduced him to Peter and Steve. He said; "My friends want to know the hidden secrets of the Holy Church." Panos said; *"You came to the right man.*

There is a surprising thing about the Holy Church of Constantinople. God protects me and Saint Andrews. The Turks don't know that there is a Cross of Saint Andrews on the roof of the Holy Church etched in a diagonal form. Even if they knew they wouldn't know what to do about it."

Costas asked; "The Turks seem to feel the power of the Christian cross. Are there any more hidden crosses?"

"Yes. For example, there is the Cross of Justinian. It is another cross which forebodes disasters for the Turks is the

Cross of Justinian. There are legends which refer to a very ancient jewel which is found mystically in Saint Sophia and in fact comes from Egypt that has great power."

Steve asked; "How did the Muslims deal with their fear of the occult?

There was a short silence. Panos thought for a moment and then said, "The Muslims assigned their own holy place on the Holy Church grounds. They turned the Holy Church into a museum. After the Holy Church was turned into a museum, the well-known Muslim Mihramp built the Muslim place of prayer, on the eastern side of the Church in the direction of Mecca.

And then there is the return. The construction of this great Orthodox Architectural Church is based on the Christian symbol of the Cross and this reality generates a sense of awe and fear about the future return of Saint Sophia to its traditional occupants, in other words, to Hellenic Orthodox worship.

"Queen Sophia lies in the casket and she is most likely Saint Sophia. According to legend, Queen Sophia and her casket are connected to a commandment that has existed for centuries up to the present day. This commandment directs that no one should ever disturb the casket."

It was a time of wonderment for Peter and Steve. Peter broke the silence and asked the question, "Are there other hidden objects in the Holy Church?"

Panos seemed a little nervous talking about the return. Nevertheless, he answered; "The Turkish workmen posed a question for the Muslin religious leaders. Should they remove it or just leave it where it was?' Peter asked, "Who is in that casket?" That gave rise to a serious moment. Panos almost seemed scared to talk about it.

He finally answered: There is an inscription which warns everyone away from damaging or destroying the casket:
"not even to touch it, and if something like that should happen; then according to the legend Queen Sophia will rise from the dead and make a frightful noise that will shake the whole structure of the Church to the ground. The Turks left the casket alone and it still lies buried underneath the Church."

Although he was a little hesitant about saying anything about God and Sophia, Peter was skeptical about the truth of the legend. He asked, "How could spirits rise from the dead?" Panos seemed a little irritated. Peter's question seemed to question everything that Panos had talked about. Panos said; "We all come back from the dead. We are all born again."

KNOWING YOU, KNOWING US

"Constantinople: Where great mysteries exist."

Nikos told them about an Istanbul legend: "Istanbul was and is an important city and one of those cities that has a rich history in mythological lore. It has been the scene of many historic battles, which have impacted the history of the world."

Yianni asked him, "Do you know how this City came to be?" Nikos answered, "I know a little. There is a legend about Istanbul which comes from classical mythology.

The legend is about a Greek settler named Byzas, who chose the spot after consulting the Oracle of Apollo at Delphi. He was told to settle across from the "land of the blind ones." Byzas was clever enough to interpret the Oracle's statement to mean that the earlier settlers in the region must have been deprived of the foresight to have overlooked this superb location at the mouth of the Bosporus Strait.

He was right. This proved an auspicious decision by Byzas. History showed that Istanbul's location was important; far beyond what these early Greek settlers could have conceived."

Yianni asked; "How did the Greeks lose the city?" Nikos said, "It is common knowledge that because of its strategic location, Constantinople was a hub of constant warfare throughout the ages. Finally, weakened by almost constant battle, the Ottoman Turks eventually conquered Constantinople in 1453. They renamed the city Istanbul and it became the third and last capital of the Ottoman Empire.

"ODD"

As they walked through the streets of Istanbul, Peter saw the strangeness of the moment. He thought it would be different. He was appalled to hear about all the violence taking place in Istanbul? Was the rest of the world any different?

He wondered if anything was real or was everything just an illusion. Was there any difference between his reality and his illusions? Was reality just an illusion that he called 'destiny'? He was so sure about the meaning and purpose of life when he left Lesbos. Now, he was confused by it all.

Nikos took them to a local bar and introduced them to the proprietor – a filthy, sweaty old man who could have been almost anything — a Greek, a Turk, an Arab, a Jew, a Persian or any bad combination of these tribes. He was a prototype of a satyr who was a clothed 'beastlike' specimen of a man. He introduced him as 'no name'.

Steve asked; "What is his real name?" Nikos replied; "No one in Turkey uses their real name. So, that's the name he chose for himself: 'No name."

He agreed to hire Steve for an 'odd job'. No Name gave Steve a smile of acceptance. Steve was reassured. No Name seemed to have a sense of humor. He described the job as a mixture of sex with work and calling it an 'Odd Job'. Steve thought that was funny. He also thought that having 'no name' as a name was also humorous. Steve made his choice. He would take the job. For the first time in his life, Steve would have to fend for himself; but, oh, what a wonderful trap it was.

ANTIGONE – THE VISION

"Antigone – "Every gift of beauty and of grace." Homer

Nikos, Costas and Peter left for the City. They were going to lunch at Niko's deli and brief Peter on what he could expect at his job interview. He told Peter that they were going to a beautiful remote area of the City to meet the owner of a grocery store. Peter's spirits improved as they walked through the outskirts of the city.

He said; "You are going to meet a lady named Antigone. She is a lovely lady; but a dangerous one. For centuries, Greek men have been possessed by these beautiful creatures. It is a fact that the gods put them on earth to torment mankind. Who can resist such beauty? The gods knew that there was nothing that could be done to quench the fires of hidden desire. Antigone is an unattainable beauty. One who can drop men to their knees just by looking at her."

Costas said; "Peter, we wanted to talk to you before you met Antigone. She is still very striking in appearance. There is a softness about her. When you see her you will want to hold her in your arms. She is of medium height, not too tall or too short. She was made that way so she can fit into a man's arms. She is slender. Her dark soft eyes will drive you mad. The gods gave her olive skin and long black shiny hair. She has no blemishes and no visible wrinkles. She is perfection.

This has been a problem for men ever since the gods put such creatures on earth. Sophocles of old, and all of the old poets and philosophers, knew that Antigone's beauty was powered by the "grip of attraction". They knew its power. The myths were right, not even the deathless gods can flee its onset. Whoever feels the grip of unattainable attraction will be driven mad with desire.

Costas added; "She wears the tight clothes of a very young woman, but still looks elegant. Her tight clothes betray a wonderful frame that enhances her look. I agree with Nikos. There is an air about her. She seemed to be a blissful spirit; not flighty, but instead slightly reserved.

He said; "She is a classic Greek beauty. A myth, untouchable. What a disaster for any man who lays eyes on her and falls in love. "

Peter said; "I can't wait to see her. My Yaya once told me a story about a lady named Medusa. She had snakes in her hair. I don't remember what she did if you looked at her; but it was bad."

When they came to the grocery store, which was quite large and filled with shoppers dressed in all kinds and varieties of clothes and attire – he was almost joyful.

Nikos took them to the back of the store and up the stairs where Antigone had her offices. Nikos introduced them to Antigone as the owner/manager of the grocery store. Peter couldn't take his eyes off her. He was mesmerized by her beauty.

After a lengthy interview, Antigone made her decision. She told Peter that she would hire him on a trial basis. There was a factor that persuaded her. She told them that she appreciated Peter's quiet energy and his humility. That was the quality she was looking for.

As soon as they knew that Peter was placed, Nikos and Costas told Peter to come with them to the picnic tables outside the grocery store. They excused themselves and nudged Peter out of the office. Nikos and Costas were smiling. They knew what Peter was going through. What joy he will have seeing a beautiful vision every day.

Nikos asked Peter; "What did you think? Is she your vision of beauty?"

Peter thought for a moment and said; "She is beautiful; but not devastatingly beautiful. I saw something more than just her physical beauty. There was a lightness, a warmth and a sweetness about her. I was taken by her smile and the inner lights that radiated from her eyes. She is timeless. A spiritual myth that came to life.

Nikos and Costas told him that; "You shouldn't think of women as 'angelic'.

Peter asked; "Why is that?" Nikos replied; "They want a man to be aggressive with them. They want a man to be wild about her and be a little of a 'bad boy'. Angels are for the eyes and hearts only. Not for the body. They can't be possessed."

They were right. Once Peter saw her and once he was in her company, he was immediately attracted to her. They knew that it would be sheer hell to be around her all the time. He would be tormented by temptation and, yet, know that he could never hold and have her.

Peter felt the 'grip' of desire and love that drives men crazy with desire. He didn't know whose fate was worse — his or Steve's. But Peter knew that he would be a 'love sick' fool for this lovely myth and seeing her vision every day would be worth it.

Nikos said; "Peter, you know that we were 'half serious' and kidding you about how helpless you will be around her – a captive of her beauty.

Peter told them; "I grew up with the old men at the Kafenio. They fathered me and used to tease me all the time. They always had a good laugh teasing me. That's what old Greek men do. It is a form of love."

It was a month before Antigone scheduled a meeting with Peter. She called him to her office and described the meeting as an opportunity to connect with him. There was a soft drink to relax him and, while he drank it, she started questioning him.

She asked; "What is your full name and where are you from?" Peter responded without a lot of emotion or detail. She asked, "Why did you leave your country, your home." He answered; "it was my time to go – he said no more. She knew much more could be said. His discomfort was apparent.

She was a little perplexed; "Why didn't he actively participate in the conversation? Then she got it. She was too aggressive and she came across as probing and questioning bitch."

She appreciated the fact that he didn't lie to her and give her some convoluted story to make it seem like he was conversing with her. In fact, she was greatly relieved at his discretion. It could be shyness, but probably not. She suspected that he had a major problem, but even with that suspicion she felt safe with him.

Antigone decided to take a less formal approach in their conversations. "I have an idea. Let's play a game. 'Tell me something I don't know'. We can call it 'tell and tell'. Peter used a Kafenio line; "Okay, I'm in. Let's play. You go first."

And so she did. "My 'birth- name' is Catherine, but my friends at Church gave me the name 'Antigone'. They thought that my life was a little like Antigone's life and they renamed me after the mythical lady."

She told me that most people in Istanbul used aliases to protect their family and friends from the Ottoman government agents. I kept the name 'Antigone' because it felt right."

My name is taken from the myth about Antigone, which is a Greek tragedy, a play that was written in 441B.C. by Sophocles and, of course, the setting of the play is ancient Greece. The theme of Sophocles' play is a classic conflict and portrayal of Divine Laws versus Man-made Laws. Your turn. The myth epitomizes the virtues of family loyalty and adherence to divine law. My adopted name can be defined as "unbending, opposed or against."

It was Peter's turn to talk. He knew enough to measure his response so as not to be the young 'fool.' He didn't want to talk just to impress. Sometimes, silence is golden. Knowing how to listen can be a virtue. Perhaps, he would be lucky to be thought of as a wise listening by not talking nonsense. He decided; "To relax and just be himself. Whatever that was."

So, it was game time. He said; "All in. Antigone, I've been to Mytilene and everybody thinks that is where I'm from. Lesbos is the largest Island in the Aegean. It is a beautiful island."

"Is Mytilene the City that you are from?" He answered, "No, I was born and raised in Plomari." She asked; "What is your last name?" Peter said, "Zaloumis." She smiled to relax him and asked, "Does the name mean anything?" Peter started to relax a little and said, "My mother used to say it meant "much light".

Peter asked; "May I ask you a question?" Antigone said; "Of course."

"What is the meaning of the Antigone myth?" She thought for a moment and said; "It conveys important encoded wisdom. At the heart of this most enduring legend is a hero. In this case, it is a woman who triumphs over 'death defying' obstacles. She said; "My personal story tracks the Antigone myth: "The main characters in the play are Antigone and King Creon. He is cast as the ruler of Thebes in the legend of Oedipus and the conflict between them had to do with the burial of her brother. Because King Creon perceived her brother to be a traitor to Thebes, he ordered his body left to rot in the streets and denied him a proper burial.

In Greek mythology and practice, the act of leaving a person's remains unburied and exposed to the elements was considered an affront to the Greek gods. At the risk of her life, Antigone decided to defy Creon's laws and give her brother a proper funeral. Antigone defied King Creon because she believed in a higher morality, that of the gods. It was her contention that the laws of Heaven overrule the laws of man. Of course, it did not end well for her or for

King Creon."

The legend makes the point that anyone can be a hero. Heroes are not all-powerful and immortal males. Instead, heroes represents the best of what it means to be human. In the conduct of our lives, we must demonstrate loyalty, courage, wisdom and devotion. These are values that the gods treasure and they will reward the hero with eternal life."

It was getting late in the day. Antigone said; "Peter, it's time to call it a day. Let's do it again. I feel like we connected in a simple, but beautiful way." Peter said; "I feel the same way." But, deep inside, he felt awkward. He still wasn't sure how to conduct himself when he was around her. His problem was: 'he was fascinated by her and he 'hung' on to her every word and gesture'. He was confused by his feelings and bewildered by his mixed thoughts about her.

He wanted more of her. In Greece, a conversation was real. "There is passion, shouting, laughing out loud and crying. They bang on tables to make a point. They dance and sing when they are tired of talking. People felt each other's pain. They suffer for one another.

Peter thought that she didn't care about having a real conversation. "She was so 'gentile'. So correct. She said such things as: "It is a pure heart that values goodness and loyalty." Peter wondered; "What the hell does that mean? Greeks are passionate, almost inarticulate when they love. They love each other and drive each other crazy. He realized that she can never be that. She is possessed by the past. A story from a myth."

LIVING THE DREAM

"When words have no meaning, silence is precious" Greek proverb

The grocery store was closed for the day and everyone who worked there went their merry way. Antigone went to take in the City and do her shopping. Peter was left to himself and he went walking, 'sight- seeing' and 'people-watching'. He spent most of the day around the parks and playgrounds watching kids play soccer. He stayed near the grocery store for security reasons.

They both arrived at the grocery store within minutes of each other. Smiles and hugs for each other. Antigone invited Peter to her office for a soft drink and for some chatter. She said; "I saw Nikos when I was in the City and I had lunch at his deli. Nikos loves to gossip and he told me something very interesting about you." Peter didn't say anything and didn't react in any way to what she said.

"He told me that you left Lesbos to follow your destiny. And that you believed that you were Odyssey reincarnate and that you were on a journey to somewhere, anywhere. That's so interesting. To have such a grand life plan at your young age?" She stopped talking for a moment to give him a chance to respond. Nothing from him.

She asked; "Peter, you seem awfully young for such an ambitious journey. How old are you?"

Peter replied; "Hard to know. In Lesbos, they hid the birth records in caves for security reasons. They lost my records. I could be any age between 15 and 21. My Yaya told me that I was 20 years old; but my mother wanted to keep me by her side for 4 or 5 years more."

She changed the subject and asked him, "Peter, what are your goals and plans?" He answered, "Short term, I want to go to America. Catch up with my father and, perhaps, together we'll return to Lesbos."

Antigone said; "Peter, I care for you. I want you to be successful like Odysseus. You are a very fine young man of some unknown age. But, to be like Odysseus, you must become a trickster like him to be able to outsmart the gods and monsters. Being realistic, you haven't yet encountered and survived the dangers, temptations, the anger and attacks of Poseidon, escaped from the loving arms of the beautiful Calypso and you are not a hero of the Trojan War."

He said, "Yes, I guess so." She smiled and said, "You have a long way to go. You left Lesbos with your comrades and your first stop and adventure, is a grocery store in Istanbul. I'm honored to be a stop along the way of your journey."

Peter didn't respond. It was clear that she hurt him with her remarks. He thought to himself, "As beautiful as she is, I can't be mad at her. Maybe she was just trying to tell me 'truth'."

Antigone felt his disappointment. She now felt bad and said, "Let me tell your story in a different way."

She put her right hand on his shoulder to comfort him. She started, "You left Lesbos because of a matter of honor. You sought the meaning of life in a church and refused the protective Cloak of Divinity. You followed Cavafy's advice and left for ports unknown for the first time – the start of your journey of life. You are young and you are just starting your Odyssey. Who knows you may meet your Calypso soon. Peter you have the makings of Odysseus and a chance to be a hero, my hero, for our time."

"I need to be honest with you. My leaving Lesbos was for a different reason. I was involved in a 'tradition' killing. It didn't have to be that way, I agreed to help my friend Christos right the wrong of Dimitri. We were just supposed to talk to him about marrying his sister. He got her pregnant and wouldn't marry her. We wanted him to follow tradition and do the right thing by her. Anyway, long story short, I didn't know that he had a knife in his bag and he killed him in a fight they had. It didn't have to be that way."

She could see that he was holding back his tears and she came to him. Hugged him until he was calm. She told Peter; "I feel your pain. I've had some 'difficult' times. My brother was killed by the Turks in a riot. The Turks issued a death order and wanted the bodies of her brother and the other protestors to rot in the streets as a lesson for all. Anyone who interfered with their order was to be put to death. I searched and found him lying dead in an alley.

Against the orders of the Turkish police and at great risk to herself, with the help of her friends from the Church, they defied the Turkish authorities. In the dead of the night, we moved his body to a gravesite and gave him a Christian burial."

Her courage and love of family renewed his feelings for her. He was wrong about her. She had a sense of loyalty to her loved ones and her courage to do what was in her heart and what she believed was God's will was redeeming. Now he could see her holding back her tears. He told her; "I feel your pain and love you for who you are."

She held out both of her hands and took his hands into hers. They cried together. She said; "Peter, there is more; but I can't go into it right now." Peter said; "There is no need for you to do so."

She took him by the hands and led him up the stairs to her room. She quietly closed the door. Peter couldn't believe what was happening. He 'dreamed the dream' and now he was 'living the dream."

PASSAGE VI

INTERLUDES: EARLY MORNING MOMENTS

Choral Foreword: Freedom's Sound

There is a 'back-stage' story about the war. It started with a Greek Island's call for freedom. The Greeks people were ready to sacrifice all. It would be a rehearsal for death. The Greeks knew that many dear souls would die before peace could be achieved. Angelos Sikelianos wrote a poem entitled: "Rehearsing for Death." His poem appears below:

> "And there, from my being's depths, from the depths
> Where a god lay hidden in my mind's shadow,
> The holy delirium was set free,
> And from the obscurity of my silences
> Powerful verses suddenly engulfed
> My brain, quick verses, and they spoke these words:
>
> Listen to your Freedom's sound; if all of You
> Was burning with fever but a while ago
> And if Your body flamed like pine kindling,
> It was so that you could find out how to burn.
> Because now You are coming near to the fire
>
> You are no longer with what the sun illumines

But in Your depths, you seem the burning life
Of the sun's soul, You seem inside the sun,
And the flames that light the other stars, that light
The world, are now outside, outside of You.
You see the stars; the stars do not see You.
You see the world; the world does not see You.

You seem all hidden in your passion's sun
And from there You aim Your arrows where
Creation's stubbornness has not yet dawned.
For You this passion is a rehearsal for death:
Rehearse it as is worthy of the holy fire
Deep inside You, that Your mind encloses
Not as created but as Creator."

This choral poem has many interpolations. One of its truths is that all things come into being in the fires of creation. And that creation takes place in a Holy Fire. The ancient Greeks believed that everything is spiritual and that we exist in God as a creator of ourselves. Another wisdom conveyed by the poem is that our passion for life is a rehearsal for death.

THE HETAERAE

"They have no choice. Sometimes they are forced into prostitution, other times they want enjoyment; and many times they prostitute themselves for love, attention, for money, for power and more often than not for survival."

Peter was in the back yard of the grocery store drinking his morning coffee when an image flashed through his mind. It was a picture of Steve standing outside the old 'run down' building where he worked. He wasn't sure what it meant; but he assumed that Steve was trying to reach him.

He settled back in his chair and dozed off. He dreamed that there was chaos all around Steve. Men, and mostly old men, were going into the building and others were coming out. He saw beautiful young women going into the building and 'half-dressed' women racing out. Everyone had the look of panic on their faces.

He heard some shuffling of feet and looked up to see a young messenger in front of him. Sure enough, Steve wanted to meet him today at the Istanbul Kafenio. Peter confirmed the meeting. He was anxious to find out what his 'rim sleep' dream meant, if anything.

Peter got dressed and went into the City. They met at the Kafenio in Istanbul and left immediately to find a quiet spot at the Port. Peter was curious to know how Steve was doing and Steve was anxious to tell him.

Once they were settled in a spot near the Wharfs, Steve told Peter, "I am 'kind a' happy and I'm glad that I took a chance on the odd job. In a way, I was promoted and put in charge of the Hetaerae. Satyr is pleased and everything is "good" between us. He increased my stable to four girls." Steve felt good telling Peter about his successes.

Peter put on his 'happy face' and said; "I'm really happy about your success." Underneath these kind words, Peter's really believed that Steve was getting too 'street-smart' for his own good and was losing his reliability as an innocence who doesn't lie and has honest intentions.

He believed that Steve was trapped in a distorted reality

and losing his sense of perspective. 'His common sense'. Peter didn't say it; but he believed; "This guy, Satyr will get him before it is all over."

Peter changed the subject and told Steve about his dream. He asked; "Do you know what it means? It seems to center around the Hetaerae." Steve said; "You must have 'tapped' into one of their dreams. The girls have the same dream that someone will come along and take them out of their dilemma.

They talk about young Greek men from good families having affairs with girls like them and then falling in love. Their mothers and fathers try to stop their sons from leaving with them; but many of them are caught in the web of beauty and first love. They dream a dream that they will find a young man who will take them away and that their man will become powerful and successful in life."

Peter said; "That may be why so many Greek men marry a girl from a powerful family to consolidate their standing and had a Hetaerae for love and sex."

Steve said; "One of the older Hetaerae told me that in Ancient Greece, the Hetaerae were a relatively powerful group of women. They were not only beautiful, but their situation made them cunning. They usually outsmart these young men with 'sweet talk. They make believe they are in love too, which made these beautiful women more appealing to them.

Peter you should sympathize with this. "All young men fantasize about having sex with a beautiful older woman. It is their first introduction to desire, lust, sex and love. All of us hungered for a beautiful woman. It is a "natural" thing. It's the lipstick, the eye shadow and the make-up that sets them apart from the natural look of an innocent teenage girl.

Our youthful fantasies got the juices flowing. The Hetaerae have this strange appeal to younger men."

He added; "They are beautiful ladies, dreamers and poets. They are trapped by circumstances; but they remain pure in heart. Many of them are bright. They are captives; taken prisoners in one of the endless wars that go on in this part of the world. Some are educated and come from good families. They are sweet and really innocent. Nobody volunteers for this type of work. They are defiant and protective and will not let anyone corrupt their mind."

He went on; "They don't think of sex as degrading. Sex is viewed as a dance, where they must change partners when the music stops. They write poetry to understand and add meaning to their lives. I found a fragment of a poem they wrote and brought it to you. They imagine themselves to be inspired by Aphrodite, the Greek goddess of love who emerged from the foam and waves of the sea.

They think that they are being protected and controlled by this goddess and that they are engaged in a spiritual act when they have sex with these different men. Aphrodite administers a 'small death' each time they have sex with a man. This keeps them safe and spirited away. They believe that they are protected from the dark passions and wanton energy that comes from their intimacy with a stranger.

I brought you a poem that they wrote for themselves. They tell their story in their poetry." Steve read from a torn page with the title 'Defiance' on it:

"We are the heart's celebration of love and beauty;
We give ourselves willingly over and over again.
We find the glory that is love in the moment;
Slowly we surrender.

We have no fear of losing ourselves to others.
We give ourselves, yet we belong to no other.
We belong to ourselves. This our inner strength;
This our chosen destiny.

We are free, we are brave; we are beautiful,
We contrive and indulge each erotic moment.
We embrace our Fate; we fear not dark death;
We are Hetaerae."

After he finished reading the poem, Steve waited for Peter to respond. He wanted Peter to respect his girls. He offered to give Peter a beautiful girl as a way of freeing him from Antigone's spell. Steve wanted him to take advantage of the wonderful opportunity he was offering him. Steve was losing respect for Peter because he didn't want to do what Steve wanted him to do. He now thought himself as 'head and shoulders' above Peter.

He told Steve, "It is true that Antigone is my first love. That's all there is between us. My mother used to say the same thing about my Dad who was away working in the United States. All we have is love.

There was no way he was going to tell Steve or anyone else, Antigone and his private business. He told Steve; "I can't have sex with one of your girls. It is out of the question. I don't want to fall in love with one of them; even worse, I don't want to need one of them. It would be a horrible fate."

Steve said; "You are fatally possessed by Antigone. You're not able to see clearly and enjoy the delights and pleasures of another beauty. My girls know how to race your heart and numb your senses. They will take you places you can't know or imagine."

Bad energy was taking hold of them. Peter had negative feelings about Steve's attitude as a so- called 'power broker' whose specialty was selling sex. He felt that Steve needed help to escape from his job, his fantasies and his obsession and 'love-sick' admiration of the girls. They both wanted to free their friend from their self-imposed obsessions and their debilitating captivity'.

They were both quiet for a while. Peter finally broke the silence; "I don't know who is more pathetic – me, a love-sick fool or you, a dandy working your girls?" They were quiet for a moment and then they both rose to leave. Steve had a pained expression on his face and Peter left in a state of depression. They were both wounded by words and by a lack of respect for one another.

Peter came over to Steve and put his hand on his shoulder. He said; "We started this journey together. Let's finish it together." Steve back to Peter; "We are on our way to somewhere, anywhere together." All smiles.

THE GOLDEN ARROWS

"Love is a form of madness sent by the gods with the highest state of bliss." Socrates

Steve was seething. Things were going so bad for him that he needed Peter's calmness and advice. He knew that Peter wouldn't come just to listen to him rant and rave. So, Steve being Steve he made up some good reasons to have another meeting so soon after the last one. He sent a runner with a note telling Peter he had something important to tell him about Costas and Yianni. He also told Peter that time is running out and they could make it an opportunity to take in the sights of Istanbul.

The great conniver sold the meeting to Peter. "It was a new land, with new people, new sights and different possibilities. Word was that Costas and Yianni were coming to the City with important news. The meeting will also be fun. It will feature sight-seeing."

He hit a 'hot spot'. Peter talked about seeing some of Istanbul's tourist attractions. And, of course, meeting their mariner friends was critical. All part of the Odyssey.

They met at their usual place, the Istanbul Kafenio. They had a couple very necessary cups of coffee at the Kafenio coffee bar. After that, off they went to see a fascinated sight, the Basilica Cistern. This attraction featured a look at the complicated system that once brought drinking water into Istanbul from Thrace (an area of the south-east Balkans) constituting Turkish land and part of the European mainland. Mostly, it was a chunk of Bulgaria.

Antigone told Peter about the Aya Sofya, which was next on the list. It was Emperor Justinian's sixth-century Byzantine masterpiece, which they thought was thrilling. It was an opportunity to enjoy the extraordinary spaciousness of this famous church-turned-mosque-turned museum. More important, Peter wanted to tell Antigone about it. She would be impressed that Peter had an interest in such an attraction and, in fact, he enjoyed it.

They wandered over to the Blue Mosque, which is one of the few mosques in the world that has six minarets. It took a while; but Peter eventually noticed that the Blue Mosque was not blue at all. The walls were covered with fine Iznik tiles which gave off a blue hue.

Steve was getting anxious. He wanted to talk 'real' before his time with Peter ran out. Peter was unsure of what he should do and what he should say. He remained non-committal.

As the day progressed into the afternoon, at Peter's urging, they made their way to the port before going home. The Port dominated the water front so it was it was easy to make their way to the Port's exterior area. From there they made their way down to the wharfs and the moored boats. After a little exploring and searching, they found a remote site to rest and view the intriguing nautical sights.

Steve said; "I have some good news. I'm in love with a beautiful Russian girl and we plan on running away to her home in Russia." Peter was shocked to hear what he was saying. He said; "We just talked yesterday about how the Hetaerae operate and fool young men into marrying them to get away."

Peter asked; "Let's suppose that you marry her and one day you are walking down a street and Cleis is walking up. What would you do?" Steve said; "I'd cry. I'd cry with regret." Steve got the message and told Peter; "You are right. I'll call it off."

Once they were settled, Steve couldn't hold back his erupting anxieties. He blurted, "Peter, I'm upset with the damn arrangement that I'm stuck in. Peter thought that it was time for 'Steve to be Steve'. It was clear that he was in over his head with something or other and over-reacting as usual.

Steve left Peter alone for a few minutes so that he could enjoy his moment by the water. They both listened to the swirling water surging under the wharfs.

Steve finally had enough with this frustrating thing

called 'patience'. He blurted out again; "He made me a clown pimp. He said that I was his Eros." Peter asked, "Who did what to you?" Steve answered, "Satyr, that ugly shit, has me dressed like a clown. I'm no longer a janitor. I'm now a clown pimp. It is my job to get customers for these poor young girls. So, he made me dress up in a golden custom doing dances by myself on the side walk; hustling men and leading them into Satyr's House of Horrors."

"I got it." Peter said. "Tell me again what you do on the streets. Isn't it dangerous doing that in Muslin country?" Steve said; "Not really. It's about sex and that supersedes political and religious beliefs. The Turkish police are paid handsomely for their tolerance."

Peter didn't trust Steve to assess a situation correctly and, at times, be truthful under stress. He asked again; "Isn't the sale of sex illegal? I thought that the Muslins regulate everything including sex." Steve just shook his head and said, "Yes, marriage, divorce, slavery and adultery are regulated by the Ottoman laws, by the Muslim laws, and by the sharia law, but sex is above the law provided the price is paid regularly."

Steve needed to express his thoughts or he would explode again; "I was better off cleaning the bar and kitchen. I'm doing something far worse. I'm now a minion of Eros; except he's a wonderful myth and I'm a God-damn clown. – I've become an Istanbul "pimp. He makes me prance around in brightly colored golden clothing on the sidewalk in front of his 'dump of a place'. My job is to attract and hustle customers. He says my words are like golden arrows piercing the hearts of these men and making them lust for time with a pretty girl.

After I put someone together with one of the girls and

the sexual experience has been consummated, he is trapped. The girls have set their hearts on fire with torches of sex and sweet remembrances. Once they are hooked, they fall in love and become repeat business."

Steve was so upset that he was shouting his indignation. Peter said, "Speak softly. My ears are inches away from your mouth. When you are loud and excited, people hear what you are saying. You might attract the wrong people."

He calmed down a bit and said, "The Meyhanes (taverns) are now open all over Istanbul, from Yenikapı to Hasköy tp Galata to Kadıköy. There are young boys like us and young 'gals' dancing and singing in all these places.

The gangs are bringing in more beautiful women and boys from the Balkans to work as prostitutes and these gangs are recruiting and circulating women and boys throughout Izmir and Trieste. Because they are foreigners, they can work in these places if they are located in certain areas of the city. Muslim women are technically forbidden from engaging in 'sex for money'. But truth is, I hear that many poor muslin women are secretly selling sex."

Peter just listened.

"Satyr told me about the myth of Eros and his numerous golden arrows and he revealed the secrets and the many pathways to love and sex. Satyr told me about the golden arrows of beauty, desire, lust, passion, loneliness and need. He told me that that there are many holes in the heart and other parts of the body that people needed to fill. Passions need to be quelled. He said that we do it all for them at a fair price."

Peter didn't know whether to laugh or cry with Steve. But as he thought about Steve prancing around in a golden custom, he couldn't hold back any more. He just started laughing and couldn't stop. Steve was surprised at his seemingly non-caring response and was irritated by it. Then he couldn't hold back either. Both of them were laughing at the absurdity of the situation. Steve finally stopped and said, "There is nothing like a good laugh to chase all the bad spirits away."

After they finished laughing, Steve said, "In a way, I deserve what I'm getting. It's a lesson. I thought that sex was so special and even spiritual and now I'm seeing that sex is commonplace on the streets. I ruined my life and a poor innocent girl's life. For what? The gods are punishing me for my hubris. They made me a trickster and a clown to pimp for sex."

Ever the philosopher, Peter tried to calm him down with some logos. He said; "Forget reality and have some fun with it. Be a clown for a short time while we are waiting to leave. Wear any custom he wants you to wear and adopt any title you want. You can call yourself an 'Apostle', a 'Prophet', even a 'General', a 'Warrior' is impressive or a famous 'Entertainer'. People put titles next to their name all the time; yet, most of them are just poverty pimps strutting their foolishness making money off foolish believers.

Steve, strut your stuff on the sidewalk and call yourself a famous entertainer or something else that sounds important. Remember, even priests used to have two costumes – a black gowns and a colorful jester attire. They played different roles in royal courts. All these titled people were clowns before they made themselves look important."

It wasn't working. Steve knew that it was all bull shit. He was smiling. Peter had worked his magic and gave him a new perspective; "Peter, you are the calmest man I've ever met. I'm mad as hell and you find a way to bring me back to a quiet place within myself. Your crazy stories make me laugh at myself and at the absurdity of life. What difference does this momentary madness make? Everything will change soon. Nothing last forever and we can't change a damn thing."

They were both enjoying the madness of the moment. They were both laughing about the crazy illusions of their lives, all lives.

Steve change his face. He became thoughtful. Should he tell Peter or not? He knew that Peter was the leader and had helped him escape; "Peter, I have a confession to make. I'm in love with a beautiful Russian girl. She is a Hetaerae. Captured in a raid by Turkish bandits and sold into sexual slavery. She and I are leaving Istanbul and making a new start together in Russia."

Peter just stared at him. He was shocked. He said, "You're in love again? In love with another girl. You just told me that they are tricksters trying to trap an unsuspecting man by any means possible to get away from their horrible business. Their horrible fate.

You used to say that what you had with Cleis was beyond special. Your mother said that love is two hearts singing together. You sang to her and she sang back."

Steve remained quiet while Peter gave his 'I don't believe it speech'. Peter reminded him; "Your first love and reality was Cleis. She is the dream and now she is also your fantasy. One day, you will return to her. During the meantime, you will do what you always do. When you are unhappy with your life, you look homeward to Cleis.

Steve, after you are married to this Russian lady and someday you two see Cleis coming up the street, what will you do?" He said sadly; "I'll cry."

He thanked Peter for his helpful words. He was relieved that Peter didn't make fun of him. Steve told Peter; "When my thoughts turn to Cleis, it is a 'mystical' moment. But, she is gone. I am lost to her. She will move on and make a life for herself. I'm in love with an illusion.

I believe Inga, the Russian girl, is in loves with me and it is not just a 'Hetaerae' hustle. She is real. She is beautiful. She is now. She is beside me. I can be happy with her."

Peter remembered the words 'when you don't have anything to say that makes sense, silence is golden.' He ended the conversation by saying; "Only you can decide what's right for you."

He 'man-hugged' Peter 'goodbye'. As they parted, Peter said, "We're young. Let's enjoy our fantasies and try to understand what life is all about and why we are going through the ecstasy of life's madness."

Beneath his 'let's live life' talk, Peter felt sorry for Steve. He believed that Steve should be with Cleis again. They had a moment of exquisite joy, deeply felt passion and love immersed in a great confusion of the senses. It was Steve's first bitter taste of unattainable love.

Peter felt Steve's deep sadness. It was a love that was not meant to be, could never be fulfilled and would forever be unrequited. She would become his fantasy and also a joyful, but tragic memory. But then, Peter had another thought. Was he putting his own 'stuff' on Steve? Was he finally realizing his own truth? Was he projecting his fears about Antigone? Was he projecting a premonition? Was he feeling the pain of never being able to possess Antigone? Were they both going through the same thing? Fear about losing a loved one?

LOVE'S ENCHANTED KEY

"In his writings, Homer described a woman's beauty best: "I look at you and a sense of wonder takes me." Homer

Peter was an early riser. He couldn't wait to get up. Early mornings were magic for him. The solitude of the night cleared the prior day's madness and made him whole again. Mornings offered a quiet time and a chance to consider where he was in life and where he was going. It was his prayer time and he always felt like there was magic in these moments. He made his plans in the quiet of the morning rise. It was the time of day when the gods were listening to him and were breathing life into his plans.

When he emerged from the back door of the grocery store, he saw Antigone waving at him to come over and sit with her. It was their favorite place in the green grass under the majesty of the trees.

She hugged Peter right away and held him tight. She apologized for greeting him with bad news, but it was so series that she had to let him know what was happening. Through her tears, she told Peter that the Father of her Church told the congregation that they had to close the church. He told us that everyone should leave Turkey as soon as possible. The Muslin forces are killing Greeks, Jews and Armenians. They are killing Christians and other faiths. Nothing is sacred to them.

Peter said; "I'm not surprised. I knew this time would come, but it was still a shock to hear the message. Istanbul had become a 'killing field'. He tried to reassure Antigone, by telling her; "We have plans to get away. I'll talk to Costas about the escape plan. We'll sail away and go to Northern Greece where it will be safe."

She could only nod her head 'yes'.

When she told Peter the bad news, it took her breath away. She swallowed her fears to avoid making their last moments 'tearful and tragic'. Antigone said; "My mind is playing tricks with me. Today was a reaction to my time in Church and what happened. It was more than a strange day. I suddenly felt like life was just an illusion. And, if that is true, then death is an illusion. My head tells me one thing and my heart tells me something different. Sometimes I think that we are playing roles in a divine stage play?"

At some level of consciousness, I know that every thing is real. I am alive. I am a woman - free in mind, body and spirit. But, my 'gut' is tormenting me with the feeling that life is just a rehearsal for death. I also have the feeling that death hovers over us all the time waiting to snatch us away. It is a sickening feeling. The specter of death stacks us. It seems to be stalking all of Istanbul. I'm scared Peter; is our time over?"

They both wanted to change the subject and release the tension of the bad news about the pending disasters. Antigone told him that she took notes during his sermon. Peter asked; "Do you want to read your notes to me?"

She smiled and said; "Okay, but I tried to put his sermon in a poetic format. It is easier to read and understand. Poetry take the some of the edge off of the bad news. My poem is short and, probably, not very good. His sermon was titled: "They are coming for us." Here goes:

"They are coming, why God why?
We are scared, we hide, we cry

We tremble in the pitch of night
No place to go, choked by fright
The Spector of Death stacks us.

Hope is beyond hope, it never was
Our live are only rehearsal for death
Our Fate, the Holy Fires of creation
We leave only our tears of goodbye
Into the abyss, we end with a cry."

Peter stood up and gave her a tribute' clap; "The poem has drama and truth about the Spector of Death. I like it and respect your wisdom."

She relaxed. His approval meant a lot to her. She asked; "Peter, do you think that there is life after death?" Peter answered; "I don't know. If I die and never wake up again that will be okay with me. If I am given another life, that's okay with me too." She said; "I asked the wrong question. Do you think that we are spiritual beings?"

He answered; "Yes, it is an ancient Greek belief. Everything is spiritual. The universe is too big and complicated. Something powerful had to create and maintain a universe of such beauty. "

"Peter, I need to tell you something. I've lived with a gaping wound in my heart. I suffered a great loss early in my life. It almost destroyed me. I didn't tell you about it and kept my story close to my heart. I wanted us to have our own moment and not have my tragedy influence our story.

This almost sounds and feels like I'm making a confession. I wouldn't even put you through this; except that we are all in great danger. I need to be honest with you in case we die and still exist."

Peter interrupted her. "Does it make any difference if we are dead? We can't do anything about what happened to us when we were alive."

"Yes. It does make a difference to me. If there is life after death, I know what I must do and I don't want you to be hurt by my decisions and actions. There is pain everywhere and, it must be so, on the other side."

Peter felt her agony. She suffered the death of her brother; but there must be more 'life changing' tragedies that are tormenting her. She never talked about them and must have relived them constantly. Her pain must have ravaged her. "How brave of her. She bore her tragedies with dignity. Held her head high, stood tall and was unafraid." The more she told him about her life, the closer he felt to her.

"Peter, "I am a widow. I lost my husband and son in a horrible boating accident. My husband's father was a very powerful politician who didn't want him to marry me. It was all about my family not having wealth and political connections. "

He was a typical wealthy Greek man. They forced their children to marry for advantage. It's all about power and wealth. But my husband was defiant and would not bow down to his pressure and threats. He was all about love and not about his father's demands. We fell madly in love with each other and were secretly married against his father's demands.

It is a lesson that these men had to learn. Many young Greek boys from powerful and wealthy families had the same problem with their fathers. Most times, their son's defied their fathers proving that the essence of love and embracing love is the meaning and purpose of life. The power of love is the wisdom at the heart of all Greek mythology. The ancient poets and philosophers knew that Greek mythology is the words of God."

Antigone continued her life story; "We left his father's island and moved to Istanbul. In our first year, we had a beautiful son who filled our lives with parent's pride and happiness. When he was five years old my husband decided to take his son to see his father. My inner sense was one of fear.

I was terrified. The night before he left, I had a premonition of death. He didn't believe in divine warnings. He left with our son and steered his boat to his father's island. When I heard the news of their deaths, it broke my heart. Our son was playing on the deck when he fell off the boat into the strong currents of the Aegean. He was underwater and drowning before my husband realized what had happened.

Without even a moment's hesitation, he jumped overboard in a vain attempt to save our son. There are times when I think that, perhaps, he took his own life because he couldn't face me. I know he loved me dearly and that he couldn't bear to tell me that our son had died."

Peter came to her and held her. This was a time when words have no meaning. Only hearts can express the sadness of the moment. Peter said "I know that you live by divine law and that the laws of Heaven overrules the actions of man. We are not in control. We are all ruled and doomed by the forcing power of preordained destiny. That is the story of your life."

Through a forced smile she told him; "I was well-named: 'the eternal, sufferer.'

It was a delicate moment, but Peter mustered the courage

to ask her what she is trying to tell him about the other side. She collected her thoughts and said; "If we exist again as spiritual beings, I belong to my husband and son and I must be with them. But I want you to know that we are still connected by our memories and that if you ever need me I will be there in the moment. It will be as if we never said goodbye."

Peter didn't know how best to respond to her. The emotions between them were intense. He expressed what was in his heart; "My feelings for you will never change. You filled my days with endless wonder. You are still the dream that teases my heart".

"One thing more, Peter. The Church is having a farewell 'dinner dance' event tonight. They will have a Greek band. Let's go. Peter was 'all in' for a party. He smiled, almost giggled; 'How typical of Greeks to drink, dance and celebrate in good times and bad'.

DIVINE PLEASURES

Sappho the perfumed poetess wrote: "When you were living, never did you smell the roses by Olympus, where the Muses dwell. Now that you're dead, your faded ghost in hell is unremembered here on earth. You rang no bell. She felt that life should be lived and examined in the context of one's Kleos. That just getting by was a waste of this precious thing called life."

Peter, the early riser, slept a little longer that morning, Greek parties take their toll which is paid the next day. He wasn't sure he see Antigone in the morning and was ecstatic to see her waving at him e over and be with her under the trees in the back yard. He could see the coffee pot steaming on the table in front of her. Even the next day after an exciting Church party, she was a vision delight.

She gave him a 'long full body' hug instead of her usual morning polite one. Looked him in his eyes and whispered; "When I am with you, I feel young again. These thoughts make me feel foolish at times; but I enjoy the excitement of young love. It makes my heart sing. When we danced, our souls danced too.

Peter was overwhelmed. She was so articulate that he knew he would be foolish if he tried to say pretty things back to her. He remembered a song from the night before and quietly sang it; "I looked in your eyes and saw my first love." That's all he needed to say. She kissed him and they were good.

They had a quiet breakfast. Both of them lost in what they had to do that day. Antigone told Peter she had to go to Church and make arrangements to transfer the ownership of the grocery store to the Church. Peter described his day plans as having to meet Costas and Yianni to make arrangements for both of them to leave Istanbul.

Antigone put her arms around Peter and they told each other how much in love they were. She cried and held him tight as if she was saying goodbye. It was intense for both of them.

He needed a good laugh or two to overcome the sadness of the moment. And that where Steve came to mind. He was always good for laugh. His life was always haphazard. Peter realized that Satyr was clever enough to put Steve in a jester's costume.

Time mends. There were times when Peter got irritated with Steve's habit of feigned helplessness. But time restores good feelings and heals relationships. He was happy to hear from Steve, who sent word that Costas and Yianni were in town and that they wanted to get together.

Peter thought that Steve was good for him. The gods compensate fools for their condition. For now, at least, Peter, still had Steve who could make him laugh and feel good. Peter thought it ironic and humorous that Steve was forced to act like a "dandy of sorts" pimping for the Hetaerae.

Yet, Steve seemed to have settled with his lot in life. He made some peace and a degree of contentment with his job. It offered him one benefit. He had access to several Hetaerae which made him feel like he was a big man. He had become Eros reincarnate, the god of lust, desire and sexual passion.

But then reality struck. Peter realized that they were both doomed if they didn't make changes and find their way out of Turkey before the war started. Peter was silently calling on the gods, fates, guiding angels and anyone and anything to help them.

After they caught up with each other, they made their way over to the Kafenio looking for Costas and Yianni. They found them playing cards. After greetings were done and the hand played, they all sat down. To Peter's surprise, Steve told Costas about the goodbye party Satyr was holding and all of them were invited. Steve made a point of offering to set Peter up with the most beautiful Hetaerae of all – Calypso.

Costas said; "You should have a good time with one of the Hetaerae. She can be young or old, experienced or inexperienced, beautiful or ugly, married or single, purchased or not. Antigone is a dream that you can never possess. No one can. She will never get over losing her husband and son to Poseidon."

After listening intently to what Costas said, Peter thanked him for his advice. Costas took the edge off his remarks by saying; "Somehow, I think that being madly in love with an older woman is a normal condition at your age. Enjoy the madness."

They could hear the Greek band playing as they approached what Steve called the 'Palace of the Hetaerae'. They went in and everyone's mood changed. Steve had reserved a large table stacked with food and drink.

The Hetaerae joined them at an adjoining table. Steve nudged Peter to get his attention and then whispered in his ear that Calypso was sitting at the head of their table. Peter whispered back; "You can talk about beauty, but when you see it for the first time it takes your breath away." Steve said; "Wait. You haven't seen anything yet."

Steve had an announcement to make. He told everyone that there was a contest being held between Costas and Yianni. They both prepared poems describing 'who the Greeks are?' The winner will be honored with the first choice of our volunteered Hetaerae. Peter remembered Steve saying they were dreamers and poets and they were excited about the contest.

Nikos introduced Costas as the intellectual poet. Costas stood up and said; "My poem speaks to our roots: 'angelic spirits melded with savage horsemen from the North'. These horsemen fell in love with the beauty of Greece and the Aegean. Their achievements as a people changed Western Civilization." He cleared his throat and started his recitation:

We are the Greeks

Angelic Spirits came to Greece
Melded with the savage tribes
Who tamed by Greece's beauty
Remained, a new race became

The Spirits divine, lovers of truth
Inspired the intellect to create
Mythology, poetry and spiritualty
Religion, science and philosophy
Greek wisdom

The Spirits of truth and reason,
Seekers of justice, fairness, hope
The foundations of society created
Morality, ritual, precedent stated
Greek traditions

The Spirits of common cause,
Teachers, education, scholarship
Devoted to the war on ignorance
Inspired the use of common sense
Greece's legacy."

There was polite applause from everyone. Nikos stood up and introduced Yianni as a pseudo-intellectual. Yianni stood up. He had a big smile on his face. He said; " This is something new to me. My poem is about 'who I think we are now':

We Are Who We Are

"Steeped in tradition, ruled by our passions
We are wise, and at times we are the fool
We laugh, we sing, we hate and love life
We are who we are and don't give a damn

We dance to remember the loves we lost
We dance to forget what we cannot forget
We search to find ourselves, to find a God
We dance with our soul to know death
We are who we are: the Greeks."

Based on the applause, Yianni was the clear winner. Costas held Yianni's arm up in triumph. Suddenly, the band added to the applause for Yianni and played a loud 'line dance' song. Everyone jumped up and rushed to the dance floor to get in line. Four steps forward, two steps back, stop, kick step and off they went.

Peter stayed at the table. He was intrigued by the thought and excited to see the underworld of sex and willing women. Costas came over and sat with him. He too was excited just to watch all the beautiful women dancing and singing. He called them the 'Sirens', a reference to those dangerous yet beautiful creatures from Greek mythology who lured sailors with their enchanting music and voices and become the shipwrecks of life.

He spoke of another Greek version of the Sirens, not as sea deities; but as "Winged maidens, daughters of the Earth" in their meadows starred with flowers. Peter could feel the excitement rising with the anticipation of sexual delights sure to be followed after drinks and entertainment by the dancing maidens. The theme of the night was 'no drinks untasted, no songs unsung.'

Steve brought some of his girls to the table to meet and mingle with the gang. Costas was the first to go with a pretty young girl from Bulgaria. She knew a little Greek and just enough to negotiate a price for her services. Yianni was occupied with another girl from the Balkans.

Peter was by himself watching all these transactions take place. Steve's golden arrows were now directed at Peter and his love of beauty. He told Peter that he learned something Peter already knew: 'that beauty is more than a prelude to sexual pleasure. It is pleasure itself.'

He went over to the other table and escorted Calypso to their table. He introduced her to Peter as the beautiful cultured goddess of Istanbul. Steve told her, "This is my friend Peter. We talked about him."

Calypso put her hand on his shoulder, bent over and put her cheek on his. She was almost kissing him, but not quite. Her skin was soft and was a hint of what could be in store for him. He was intoxicated by the smell of her perfume. She whispered in his ear; "Stay the night and we'll enjoy the last night in Istanbul together." She tossed his wavy black hair and just said; "Cute." Peter stood up to face her, but she was gone.

Steve came and whispered; "Watch out. She will steel your heart." More advice. Nikos came over and said; "You will eventually tire of 'reaching for the unreachable and untouchable object in your dreams. Remember what the old Greeks say, if you must suffer for the love of a woman, do so in the arms of another beautiful woman."

Peter wondered if Calypso was a dream come true. He couldn't believe that one of his childhood fantasies was coming true. He recalled the name 'Calypso' from Homer's story of the Odyssey. There was one story event that always intrigued him. He was enthralled by the part of the story when Odysseus was held captive by the beautiful nymph Calypso.

He wondered, "Was he to be so lucky in life to 'have' an affair with a beautiful nymph named Calypso. Or were the gods just tricksters teasing him with lust for a fantasy that could never be? He remembered the part of the story where Odysseus was tempted by Calypso to stay with her on her Island and she would give him immortality. But love prevailed. Odysseus' love for his wife was so powerful that he had to go back to Ithaca and be with her.

Peter suddenly felt an overwhelming need to go to Antigone. For some reason, he heard Yaya's words about premonitions. There is a 'knowing' and a surge of anxiety that takes possession of your heart and mind. When that happens, it is a warning and information from the other side. He told Costas, "I have to go."

As he went out the door, he realized that Antigone, and not Calypso, was his fantasy come true.

A FRAGILE WORLD

"Hidden....in the light of thought, singing hymns unbidden till the world is wrought to sympathy with hopes and fears it heeded not." Shelley

When he arrived at the grocery store, Peter noticed that the front door was locked and that the store was closed. He went in the back door to look for her, he found her moving "stuff" around. It looked like more than "busy" work and the thought occurred to him that, perhaps, she was preparing to leave. "But where would she go and to what?" There wasn't any real choices for her and, likely, no real long-term hope for either of them together. .

She turned to look at him and smiled lovingly. Peter was overcome with a sense of relief that she was safe. Then he felt a wave of love and great compassion for her. He felt her sweetness and her 'inner beauty'. He had a moment of 'sadness'. Everything was coming to an end. He was feeling the loss of his life with Antigone.

"Peter, I heard that the Turkish army was sweeping the City killing many people. The Father of our Church was caught in the whirling currents of people rioting in the streets. He was in a large crowd of people who were marching to the square before the Chamber of Deputies. They were calling for the restoration of the Sacred Law.

Their numbers were overwhelmed by still other converging crowds of religious groups shouting their demands and cries of "Down with the Constitution!" "Down with the Committee!" Here then was the rallying cry of still another revolution in Turkey. The Chamber was stripped of any power and was disbanded after all the Committee Members walked out."

Peter said; "I heard that a skirmish between Armenians and Turks on April 13 set off a riot that resulted in the pillaging of the bazaars and attacks upon the Armenian quarters." Two days later, more than 2,000 Armenians had been killed as a result."

Antigone showed some concern; but didn't exhibit any fearfulness. She said; "Peter you must be very careful on your trips to the City proper to meet your friends."

He was calm when he replied; "I have to meet with Costas and Yianni to make arrangements for us. I don't have any details on our escape plan. I have to leave later in the day. I'm supposed to meet them at the Kafenio and get the details and timing of our boat trip out of here. I'll be careful and take the 'back' streets."

Antigone changed the subject. "We had our last sermon yesterday." He went with the change and away from the bad news. He always wondered what the teachings of the Church were. So he asked her about it.

She said; "We believe that Greek mythology comes from God. It is the word of God. Our Church is founded on this principle. Our angelic spirits, our goddesses, are many – from Gaia to Aphrodite to Athena to Demeter –and in the complex and many layered symbolism and ritual that we find the Eleusinian mysteries — we are graced with a vision of the sacred feminine."

Peter asked; "What does all that mean?" She answered, "Think of it as finding the sacred feminine in the myths and mystical writings of the ancient Greek poets and philosophers. If you wish you can say that we find the encoded wisdoms in the myths and mystic writings of the ancient wise men and women."

He asked; "Does your religious or mystical beliefs say anything about how the world came to be and how it operates?"

She said; "It is a little complex." He said; "Try me."

"We believe that the world was formed by a higher consciousness. That we are one in the all and the all is in the one. Everything is spiritual. We are spiritual beings. We are in the all and the all is in us. At death, we will take a true measure of our life and all will be revealed to us."

Peter said; "Doesn't seem like there is anything to fear from death. We probably get reincarnated and live another life or more."

Antigone said; "Let's leave it at that. I have to go to the Church later this afternoon and sign some documents regarding the transfer of the grocery store to the Church.

The myth that was Antigone was alive in her. He suddenly felt a longing to always be with her. His young life was filled with a spiritual yearning for her. His feelings for Antigone were sacred, and he would have no other goddess, but her. He would not leave her no matter what the cost was to stay.

Their time together was cut short. She had to go to the Church to conduct what she described as 'late business". He had to go back to the City and make arrangements to leave. Peter knew that this was a 'forever' time and that all their decisions were irrevocable.

Before she left, they held each other as if it was forever goodbye. She kissed him and broke their embrace in tears. Peter reluctantly left for the City. He remembered his conversation with Costas yesterday. He realized that the world is really fragile. It can change in an instant. He didn't know that the Ottoman Empire had collapsed and was replaced by the very aggressive Young Turks. And he didn't know that he was in a very dangerous place about to explode into chaos and deaths.

PASSAGE VII

THE SPECTER OF DEATH

Choral Forward: The Bloodless Revolution

The world spun and the power structure in Turkey changed. The Young Turks came to power in a bloodless revolution in 1908. Within a year, Turkey's Armenian population, empowered by the dismissal of Abdul Hamid II, began organizing politically in support of the new government, which promised to place them on equal legal footing with their Muslim counterparts.

The Countercoup of March 1909 wrested control of the government out of the hands of the secularist Young Turks, and Abdul Hamid II briefly recovered his dictatorial powers. Appealing to the reactionary Muslim population with populist rhetoric calling for the re-institution of Islamic law under the banner of a pan-Islamic caliphate, the Sultan mobilized popular support against the Young Turks by identifying himself with the historically Islamic character of the state.

"Tortured soul, tell me what we are seeing this night
The sound of troops and equipment rumbling in the streets,
Foreboding terror, a night filled with fear, a grasping stillness
Men marked for death on the run.

The land is haunted, many things hidden, death roams unbound

No lights to be seen, kitchens black, everything closed into doubt,

The air suffocates, no movement, only a quiet dread prevails

Fate remains hidden in the dark.

A sense of horrible happenings, man facing God, truth, judgment

Everything moving against us, tears held back, ears to the ground,

An agony to this moment, a cruel reality and death burn in our eyes

The world will never be the same."

The tragic Adana massacre occurred in the Adana VilaYet of the Ottoman Empire in April 1909. A massacre of Armenian Christians in the city of Adana amidst the Ottoman countercoup of 1909 resulted in a series of anti-Armenian pogroms throughout the district.

Reports estimated that the massacres in Adana Province resulted in the deaths of as many as 20,000–30,000 Armenians. About 1,300 Assyrians are reported to have been killed during the massacre.

When news of a mutiny in Constantinople arrived in Adana, speculation circulated among the Muslim population of an imminent Armenian insurrection. By April 14 the Armenian quarter was attacked by a mob, and many thousands of Armenians were killed in the ensuing weeks.

NIGHT OF THE LONG KNIVES

"Nothing lasts. Everything dies. All things are swept away. My soul and I are being destroyed. This realization gave rise to an old Greek proverb: "Don't waste fresh tears over old griefs."

The Young Turk's decision to solve the Armenian Question through genocide was adopted in the beginning of 1910's. There were several secret sessions and conferences of the Union and Progress Party's Central Committee and the decision was made. In this regard, the 1911 Salonika conference stood out. At this meeting, the leadership explicitly decided to 'Turkify' all the non-Turkish areas of the Empire. This most acutely impacted the Armenians throughout the Empire's territories.

The decisions made at the conference became the official strategy of the policy adopted by Young Turks. Secret orders were then signed by Talaat and sent to the Empire's local authorities for them to take prior necessary measures for exterminating the Armenians and other minority groups. It was May 1911, a month that would see the end of the Ottoman Empire and the rise of the Turkish nation under control of the young Turks.

Peter, found himself in a strange, hostile and dangerous City racing through its back streets. He was trying to find his friends so that they could escape from this 'hell-hole' called Istanbul.

There were police and troops everywhere, who were trying to bring order to the chaotic frenzy of panicking and rioting people. There were screams and shouts and wild rumors sweeping the streets of Istanbul. Once again, this part of the world was about to be 'torched' by men prepared for war, one that would be even bloodier with more deaths and losses than anyone could imagine.

There were more countries that would be involved; the stakes would be higher, and the weapons would be more advanced. The future looked bleak for ordinary people trying to survive and live out their lives in peace with some hope of safety and prosperity.

Peter was running through the 'back' streets of Istanbul. He could hear the shooting and screams of people in pain. He stopped every once in a while to get his bearings. He watched the chaos from a safe vantage place. People were running in the streets with the look of fear and apprehension in their faces and were confused. They wondered what was happening; but they knew that it was bad and that ordinary people were the targets.

He came to a street where there was fighting between the Turkish militia and resistance groups. Bodies were everywhere. Fresh blood ran down the sidewalks and in the streets. He stayed close to the buildings so as not to be a wide open target. He turned a corner and was stopped by a Greek resistance group of ordinary civilians turned warriors.

The leader of the group came up to Peter and questioned him. Once they knew Peter was a Greek there was some friendly advice given to Peter. He was told to pick up a weapon and ammo from one of the dead fighters to engage in the resistance. Peter was led by one of the fighters to the body Costas was there.

Peter immediately went to the Kafenio to get off the streets. He was surprised that it was quiet, not like the usual steaming boiling pot of Greeks and other crazies yelling at each other. People were either running or shooting at Turkish militia setting up posts to hold major traffic areas.

Peter fired off a couple of rounds at the Turkish militia and then ran like hell to get out of there. It was nightfall when he arrived at the building that housed the Kafenio. He was getting ready to make a run for the doorway, but there were Turkish police in front of the building. He was confused. 'What is that all about?'

He watched for a while. There were ordinary people going into and out the building and the police were not stopping them. It was time to take a chance. He kept his rifle when he went to the doorway of the Kafenio. A couple of policemen came up to him and questioned him. Peter told them that he had the rifle for protection and they seemed to accept his explanation. They told him to lose the rifle. It was dangerous to carry it around. They let him go into the Kafenio with the rifle.

Upstairs in the Kafenio, everything was quiet. They didn't want to draw any attention. There was no arguing, no shouting; no one was playing cards or any of the other games. Instead, they were huddled in small groups talking in quiet and hushed tones.

Peter saw Costas sitting at a corner table by himself and went over to him. He sat down next to Costas. They were both silent for a few moments. Costas broke the silence by saying, "You probably think it strange that I am just sitting here. I'm not paying too much attention to Yianni and the others talking about the atrocities and what is taking place.

Quiet time helps me deal with the chaos. I went down to the Port early this morning to lose myself and all the sadness of what is happening. When I stare at the water, the sounds of the sea and the Port activity; I go to another place in time.

My quiet thoughts were about my own death. I was hearing whispers that I don't have much longer to live. I believe that we all know when it is time for us to go."

Costas stopped and looked at Peter who seemed shocked and upset by Costas' comments about his death. Costas quickly changed the subject and rhapsodized about how supernatural his time at the Poet was and the calming energy that came from the waters.

Peter didn't know what to say. But then he remembered his own strange experiences when he went to the Port and gazed at the water, the waves, the seagulls, the jumping fishes, the ships and all the many songs of nature. He told Costas; "I understood what you are feeling and saying. When I go to the water, I feel like I can touch and dip into other worlds."

Costas was surprised that Peter had the same thoughts when he went to the Port. He said; "I also had strangest feelings when I was at the Port. I imagined that there was no such thing as 'time'. That the eternities of past, present and future all exist at the same time. My imagination was running away with me. I fell asleep and dreamed that these eternities were passing each other, touching each other at their extremes, coming together and moving apart. The Port and the sea waters creates many strange thoughts for me and takes me to other realities."

Costas added a concluding thought, "I don't know what kind of messages we are getting from our time at the Port. There is more to life than we can know."

They were both relieved when Yianni came to their table and interrupted their conversation about multiple worlds and dimensions. Yianni told them, "The arrangements have been made. We have one day to get ready and then we leave at 4pm on the second day."

Peter asked about Antigone. Yianni said, "Tell Antigone that she is more than welcome to go with us; but it will be very dangerous trying to get out of the Port. We should have no trouble getting through the Italian navy's blockade of the Port. But, we will make it. We are going back to Greece."

There was a short pause, Peter revealed his truth. He told them, "I'm scared for Antigone." Costas lowered his head and said, "Yes. We all have reason to be scared." There was a moment of silence and all they could do was stare at each other. Costas broke the silence, "Our world here in Turkey is coming to an end. We are already suffering the atrocities and the madness caused by the Turkish militia."

WAS IT ALL A DREAM

"Under the influence of love and the prospect of death, lovers sink into the realm of need and feelings for each other without reservation, no longer under the influence of fear or calculating their losses."

He came out the backdoor at the same time she did.. He said; "Have you heard the news about the riots and the killings?" Peter suddenly realized that he made a mistake by starting their morning with bad news.

She nodded her head 'yes'. A million thoughts suddenly raced through his head. The circumstances of their lives had changed, but the personal emotions between them were stronger than ever.

She held his arm as they walked to the table under the trees. Peter noticed that she didn't seem scared. They both were enveloped in a sense of foreboding. They talked and exchange information about what they were told by various sources. Their information was somewhat sketchy, maybe not even accurate; but they knew that their world was changing quickly and collapsing.

Peter noticed that her gaze had softened. She seemed lost in her thoughts. He wondered, "What was this, her look about? Was it a look of a woman suppressing her fears? Was it a comforting look to relax me? What was it?" He went over to her and she fell naturally into his arms. It was time for fears and tears. They hugged each other for what seemed like an eternity. After the moment, she pulled away slowly, gently.

She told Peter, "I need some time to think about you and me and where we might go. I've spent most of my time organizing my business affairs and destroying my personal papers. This was painful. While I did this, I rummaged through my private thoughts and I realized that there were few if any options for me and for us as a couple."

Peter was getting nervous about her conversation and their personal situation. He told her that he was at the Kafenio last night and that he met with Costas and Yianni. He told her about the escape plan.

She said, "Our time here will go quickly." She smiled and told Peter she needed some time to be alone with her thoughts. Then she went back into the grocery store and went straight into her bedroom. She closed the door behind her.

Peter was a little confused. He didn't know what she was thinking or what was happening with her. He assumed that leaving her life behind and starting over was like the end of the world for her.

He stayed outside and searched the sky. He could see the smoke of war rising in different parts of the City. He remembered the foul smell of death coming from the 'rotting' bodies in the streets. The riots, the arrests and the killings were disturbing.

His thoughts turned to their escape from Istanbul. No doubt large groups of people were preparing to leave Istanbul. He thought to himself, "Who knows anything." Everything was moving too fast. He was worried about their own frightening circumstances. What was in front of them was 'earth shattering'.

Peter had to clear his mind and walked a couple of blocks to get some perspective again. He was surprised to see empty streets and he had a hollow feeling in his stomach. Maybe it was clear because an attack by the Turkish militia was imminent. He quickly made his way back into the grocery store.

When he went up the stairs, he could see her at her writing desk in a 'dimly lit' room. He went in and tried to give her hope by telling her about the timing of their escape plan. She had to get ready to leave tomorrow at 2pm to make the 4pm launch time. She was quiet.

Then her mood seemed to change. She said; "I feel the weight of all the tragedies taking place and it makes me think about what could happen to us. The thought of death made me think of how I lived my life. I have nothing to be ashamed of and I am prepared to face my God."

It also made me think of your young life. It made me think about your spiritual journey and what is ahead of you. I can't get rid of the thought that you will end up in the Greek army. They will make you do terrible things all in the banner of freedom. I worry about your soul and your need to protect it by always doing the right thing.

Please remember that the right way is God's way. The military way is death and carnage and they will try and make you do terrible things. It is all justified by saying it is the military way and that you are serving your country. Promise me, that you will only do the right thing and make your decisions based upon divine law".

Peter didn't completely understand her message, but said; "I will."

She then said; "Peter I will give you my jewelry to bribe the Port Authorities. Be careful. I've heard from other parishioners that they are holding people hostage and taking all their assets. The cruelty was their deception. They took their assets and didn't give them safe passage."

Antigone had prepared a candle-light meal in her sitting room. She had set up a small table and chairs for them. After they finished her delicately prepared meal, her mood seemed to change.

He stared at her and tried to understand what she was really thinking. But she revealed nothing. Just a kind expression on her face was all he could get. They had a long look at each other. Their eyes were locked together. And then they went into her bedroom for the night.

FOR FREEDOM

"At death, we take the full measure of our lives."

The next day they met at breakfast under the trees and in the midst of nature. She had prepared breakfast and dark coffee the way Peter liked it. He heard her singing when he came into the back yard and he felt some relief when he saw her and heard her sweet voice. His first thought was that she got through her dark period.

She greeted Peter with a hug and a kiss. And after that sweetness, they sat down to eat breakfast. There was an excitement emanating from her. There was no doubt; she wanted to share some news with him. She was almost shouting when she said; "Peter, I', free! I'm free!"

Peter had a smile on his face, but wasn't sure why except that he always felt good when she was happy. He asked; "What are you excited about?"

Sje told him that she had some early morning dreams that she wanted to share with him. "The dreams made everything clear to her. I dreamed that when I was in our Church I was in a dark hall, but when I left it and went outside into the fresh clear air and the bright light of the sun shining on me I was nearer to God. I'm sure that means that the Church is interpreting the Greek mythology which is the basis of our dogma in a negative way and not how it was meant by the ancient Greeks."

Peter looked at her in a quizzical way. "Does that mean you are going back to the ancient wisdoms encoded in the Greek myths and are free of the dark interpretations of the Church?" She said; "Yes. In my dreams, I was told that the ancients wanted their myths to be viewed in a positive way, in a 'harmonious way'.

For example, the ancient myths make the point that opposites meet at their extreme and derive their harmony when they meet. Life is death and death is life. Life is a dying process and death is rebirth. The ancient myths say that 'Up is down and down is up'. Life and everything about it is different than I thought it was. We are opposites and yet we derive our harmony, our love, from each other."

Peter observed; "I think what you are saying is that you are free of the Church's negative interpretation of the Greek myths and can now see the encoded wisdoms of the ancient's view of them. The Church focus is on death and the myths are meant to be a celebration of life and death. You are free to believe in both Mythologies. As for me, I believe that life and death should be celebrated; although many Greeks cry at birth about all the pain and hardships of life for the new born and celebrate the freedom from this pain at death."

Antigone said; "By God, you got it. One day you will be a great story teller and philosopher. I always enjoy our little talks, but now It's time for us to go about our business. I have to complete the transfer of the Grocery store to the Church and do other important personal business. Before I go I want you to know that I love you and that I enjoyed our time together last night."

For some reason, Peter felt a wave of sadness come over him. He said; "You are my myth come true. And in my myth you are my goddess. He went up to her and looked deep into her eyes. He learned on this journey and believed that a person's eyes were openings to the soul. What he saw in her eyes scared him. He was overwhelmed by the feeling that she was disappearing. And there was nothing he could do about it.

Peter had to get away from this feeling. He told her that he was going to the Kafenio in the City to confirm that arrangements to leave were made. He told her that he wanted to make sure the plan was still a go before he exposed her to any danger.

One last goodbye and they were both off and headed in

different directions.

He carefully made his way through the alleys and back streets. He was relieved to see the Kafenio. He was almost joyous to see Costas there.

Costas told Peter that their plans were still 'a go' and that they had to leave Istanbul before things got much worse. He told Peter to get ready to leave. "And Peter just a reminder. If Antigone comes with us and brings her jewelry, we can buy our way out. It will be a safe escape. If she doesn't come, then we must make a run through the blockade. It will be dangerous." Peter responded, "We'll be there ready to go."

Costas confirmed that they were making room for Antigone in their boat and that they would take her to Lesbos. He told Peter, "Everything is set to go." Peter thanked Costas and left. He told them that he would return tomorrow in time for the escape.

Peter was curious about a huddle in the middle of the room. Most of the men were huddled around Yianni, who was very animated, but at the same time, he seemed careful. He didn't want the wrong people to hear him. It was typical Kafenio Theater. Yianni had created a scene and was playing a role; a bit part in the great unfolding Istanbul drama. He talked in hush tones; perhaps, for greater effect.

The other Greeks in the kafenio gathered round him to hear his quiet and guarded words – he talked of the rumors circulating around the Port, rumors probably both true and false, no doubt exaggerated for effect, misleading, informative, interesting and profound. His message: "Their world had changed. They were all facing death." Typical Greek street drama!

Peter passed close to Yianni but didn't make contact with him. He could hear him tell the old Greeks huddled around him that he heard Greece and the Christian Orthodox Balkan nations had combined forces and that the armies were taking up positions across Northern Greece and in the Balkan countries.

He learned that the combined Eastern Christian forces were moving against the forces of the Ottoman Empire and their Muslim allies to drive them from Europe. The objective was to free territories and areas that contained large populations of Greek and Balkan nationals.

All this was expected. The Greeks knew – in fact, everyone knew - that for years the Greeks were preparing for the savage battles to free northern Greece and the large Islands of the eastern Aegean, including Lesbos and Crete.

The Ottoman Empire had crumbled from within and that it was just a matter of time before the Greeks combined with their Balkan cousins (their new allies) would be strong enough to seriously contest the Ottoman Empire's great armies.

Yianni pulled out a copy of a Greek newspaper that he smuggled into Istanbul which he kept hidden. The newspaper was, of course, filled with the speeches by Greek leaders. It also had reports that skirmishes were taking place in northern Greece and the Eastern Islands. These areas of Greece had a long history of successfully defying and fighting off the Ottoman Turks.

There was also news about Electrinos Venizelos. He was emerging as the most dynamic and distinguished Greek statesman of his time; perhaps, of the century. Having led a civilian campaign for Crete's redemption to Greece, he was elected prime minister of Greece in 1910. It took him two years to organize an alliance with Serbia, Romania and Bulgaria to fight the Ottoman Turks.

After Yianni was done, an excited old Greek who was relating the news from the Aegean. They all started laughing when they heard what had happened in the Island of Ikaria. The crazy Greeks on that Island were the first to revolt in the east Aegean, and, in typically idiosyncratic fashion, they quickly declared their Island's independence flying their own flag.

This new Island nation lasted a mere five months. What happened was the Greek fleet showed up in November after being rerouted from landings on Hios, Lesbos and Limnos, and brought these wild Greeks gently under control. They were now part of the Greek nation.

The war for independence had started. For freedom Greece.

EYES EMPTY OF LIGHT

"Life is a narrow vale between the cold and barren peaks of two eternities. We strive in vain to look beyond the heights, we cry aloud, the only answer is the echo of our wailing cry."

Peter made his way through the 'back streets'. He felt safe thinking that there were no lights to reveal his movements. There were a few stars to light his way; but the outskirts of the city were deathly quiet. He remembered what his mother said. "The tigers come at night. It occurred to him that the Turkish secret police were 'waiting in ambush' for all who ventured into the streets.

He was in a 'devil's nightmare'. The 'night air' was filled with the sickening smells of death and despair. He was close to the center of the city and he could hear tanks and marching death. The horrid sounds of screams and crying filled the night air. Feelings of panic were taking control of him. Istanbul had become 'hell on earth'.

Peter was fortunate that night. He managed to avoid the chaos that smelled of death. Innocent people and their loved ones being slaughtered in front of each other. No one could help them.

He had no sense of time, but he found himself standing in front of the Kafenio. The building was dark. It seemed deserted. He went to the door and gave it a slight push. It opened. When he looked in the door, he could see Costas and Yianni waving at him to come over to him.

There were hushed discussions about the carnage taking place. Vianni was there and told him that to leave tomorrow night. They had word that the Western Allies were going to allow traffic to come and go for a 'twenty=four period to allow humanitarian shipments into and out of the Port.

The 'devil's nightmare' engulfed again. He made his way through the deserted streets going into and out of the small alleyways until he found his way back to the grocery store. It was closed. It was dark, except for a small light in the back of the store. He raced up the stairs. He had good news; they had a plan and they were going to leave Istanbul. They were going to their homeland – Greece.

He raced up the stairs. The double doors to the sitting room were partially open. He took a deep breath and went in quickly to keep the light from shining down the stairs.

He mustered the courage and went to her bedroom door and gently knocked on it. There was no answer from inside. Peter was scared for her. He felt empty inside. He feared that she may have done something drastic and took her life. He panicked. "He was too late to save her."

He pushed on the door and opened it - cautiously, almost fearfully. He looked in the dim-lit room and could see her lying in the bed, more beautiful and radiant and serene than even he could have imagined she would be. He spoke her name in low tones, quietly. There was no answer.

He knelt by the side of her bed. She was gone. He laid his head on her heart and cried. Her body was still warm, and he still felt connected to her even in death. He lost track of time and when he felt her body, it was cold. He looked deeply into her eyes. They were dark, empty of light. She was gone.

Peter believed that she would always be with him. But now that she was gone, he felt that she was never there, never real, a spirit walking through his life. He wondered, "Was it all a dream?" She left this world. He gently put her hands on her chest in a holy cross position. He was devastated. Antigone was no more. And Peter never felt more alone in the world. It was a sad ending of a dream.

He had to make a decision. She needed to be buried and he had to make the arrangements. Proper burials were a Greek tradition. The Greeks believed that the soul cannot transition to heaven without the sanctity of the burial. But there was no time. Costas and Yianni were leaving at 4pm that day and he would be left behind if he missed that launch time.

His love for her wouldn't let him abandon her. He remembered her life story. She risked her life to make sure her brother's body didn't rot in the streets. He decided to miss the launch of the boat and escape from Istanbul. He wasn't sure if it was a divine obligation, but he wanted to do it as a last gesture of his love for her.

He felt good doing the right thing. He would risk his life

to make sure she got a proper burial. He was living his own Antigone tale. Peter was able to fall asleep knowing that he did the right thing. He had a wild thought that somehow she was able to know that he risked his life for her spiritual salvation.

He woke up to loud knocking on the door. He was surprised to hear them enter the door and come to the bedroom. Peter watched as five men and women came into the bedroom. A tall, stately woman came up to Peter and introduced herself as Angela. She told Peter that Antigone told her about him and that she had a leather bag filled with her valuable jewelry and a farewell letter of goodbye she wrote to him. To Angela

The other people were around her bed. Angela told Peter Antigone made the arrangements for her burial through the Church and she would be buried at the Church graveyard in the hills. She told him that they were going to say a short prayer for her before they took her away.

Peter watched and listened as they gathered around her body and Angela with tears in her eyes, recited a poem of remembrance before they took her away:

Antigone's Prayer

"She dreamed a dream of life\
One of purpose and meaning
She lived the life she dreamed
A life of love, trust, achieving

She lived by God's divine law
Justice, morality and equality
Defying man's unjust laws

Risking all for loyalty causes

Her time all too soon ended
Still young and still unafraid
Her angels took her soul away
One in the all, the Divine is all."

Angela came over to Peter and gave him a leather bag filled with Antigone's precious jewelry and a farewell letter from Antigone. Peter thanked and went to his room. He opened the letter slowly and carefully so that he would not damage the contents. The letter was written on beautiful parchment paper. Antigone's touch was always perfection. Peter was dreading her words of goodbye and when he read her letter he was shaking with sadness.

"Peter my dear
I don't know how to start this letter, how to end it and what to say. It is my letter of goodbye. There are no good options for me, and I will only be a burden for you and your friends. Please forgive and please don't be sad for I will go to my husband and my son. They are my soulmates.

I remember my father saying that the Greeks celebrated death for it liberated us from the pain and sorrows of life. I've always thought of death as a new dream waiting to happen.

I wish you happiness and a God speed. As you go through life, welcome the sweetness of love, but remember that love is linked with pain. I've always thought that the gods made it that way to help us understand that the pain and suffering makes us wiser and helps us to make our decisions about love based upon its sweetness and not anthing else.

Peter, I enjoyed our time together. It was a blessing to have our sweet moments together. My feeling for you were confusing. At times you were like a son to me; a brother to me and at times something sweet. But your journey is just beginning and mine is ending.

Sail on, Peter, Sail on. Love Antigone"

Peter packed his duffle bag with his traveling clothes, put her letter in it along with the leather bag with her jewelry. He took his rifle and his ammo strap and headed to the Kafenio hoping that Costas and gang didn't leave yesterday. He didn't know what he would do if they did.

THE GUIDING HAND OF FATE

"Your face was hidden in the leaves. I cut the leaves one by one to get near you. When I cut the last leaf, you were gone." Yianni Ritsos – A Wreath

Peter raced to the Kafenio in hopes that Yianni and Costas did not leave.

The gods were with him. He made it to the Kafenio without incident. The Turkish police were still guarding the entry to the Kafenio. He had no choice. He had to go forward and get into the Kafenio and see if Costas and the gang were there or had already left.

The Turkish police were surprisingly friendly. They told him to lose the rifle and ammo belt as he would be killed immediately by the Turkish militia group patrolling the streets. Peter thanked them and went up.

After he opened the door to the Kafenio, he was greeted by the proprietor who recognized him. Peter asked why the

Turkish police were guarding the entry to his place. He told Peter that he had bribe them for protection which would run out at 5 pm that day.

Peter went in and to his surprise Costas and the gang were sitting at a table if front of the windows. He was elated. They were also surprised as they thought that Peter and Antigone were killed or captured by a Turkish militia group. 'Hand shakes' all around.

Costas asked him, "Where is Antigone?" Peter answered, "I can't talk without crying. She is no more. She is dead. There are dreams that cannot be and that dream is over for me.

My mother used to say, "The angels came, and closed her eyes." Everyone understood. They assumed (rightly) that Antigone took her own life. By the way, how come you are still here?" Yianni answered; "We are waiting the blockade by the Italian navy. Did Antigone give you her jewelry? That would be enough for those greedy bastards at the Port Authority."

Peter said' "Yes." He opened the Leather bag that Antigone left him. It contained her gold necklaces, jewels and other precious items that she gave him to use in his escape from Istanbul. Costas noticed that among her gifts was her Christian gold cross necklace, which he took out and gave back to Peter. The cross will spook them and who knows what they will do." Yianni said; "The jewelry will work aNd get us safe passage out of this 'shit hole."

Costas said, "We'll honor her memory at sea. We'll have a ceremony after we leave the Port area and are on the open sea."

Yianni was monitoring the events of the war to get news on the blockade. He learned and told everyone that the primary theater of war was North Africa. Everybody was surprised to hear that the Ottoman territory of Tunisia had fallen to French forces and was now a protectorate of the French. Seeing that, the Italians coveting a share of the imperial spoils for themselves. They claimed as "compensation" the territory of Libya. Their claim was based upon the historical record, which indicated that the two historic Roman provinces of Tripolitania and Cyrenaica were formerly integral subjects of the Roman Empire. They were the last African lands to remain in Ottoman possession

The news of what was happening came loud and clear. On September 28, 1911, Italy sent Turkey an abrupt ultimatum declaring Italy's intention to occupy Tripoli and the province, whose "state of disorder and neglect" under the Turkish authorities endangered its own Italian subjects. Nationalist aspirations in Italy were roused, and with the all-important financial interests motivating them; the very next day, the Italian government declared war against the Ottoman Empire.

Yianni was told by Port officials that the Turks would not be able to defend the province because they would not be able to get munitions to the Turkish soldiers in the war zone because of the inadequacy of the Turkish naval forces.

The world had changed for the Turks. In earlier times, they could have prevented an Italian landing; but now, because of the decline of the Turkish navy, the Italian navy had control of the Adriatic.

Italy now landed an army of some fifty thousand men at Tripoli and they soon occupied the coast line with its all the ports. Turkey was stretched thin trying to preserve the remnants of the Ottoman Empire and they were learning too late a lesson of modern warfare. 'Apply overwhelming force at point of contact'.

It was an old tactic; one that Alexander the Great employed successfully long ago. Italy with the tacit support of Britain taught the Turks another lesson in power politics: deny the field to your enemy. The Turks were unable to dispatch troops overland through Egypt to defend and retake Tripoli from the Italians.

Egypt proclaimed its neutrality through Britain and forbade the dispatch of Turkish forces overland. But all the news that Yianni heard was not favorable to Italy. Turkey taught the Italians some bitter lessons. The Turks were great fighters and over the centuries had learned and perfected their own strategies and tactics, which would never be obsolete. They had an answer to the use of overwhelming force. Modern weaponry and tactics may have enabled Italy to take Tripoli, but the Turks showed that "taking was different than holding."

The Turks went to their old allies – the fierce desert tribesmen and gained their support. The Turks organized them into military units and instructed them in guerrilla tactics. These desert fighters would ultimately harass the Italians with raids and deny them control over the country. The result was a stalemate.

Yianni was heartened by the stalemate; perhaps, it would result in a truce and they could finally escape. As they made their plans, they had to call them off again. Port officials told Yianni that the situation had changed for the worse. The Italians were not finished. They showed that modern warfare was not completely helpless against guerilla tactics. The Italians had changed theaters and their emphasis shifted to naval engagements with the Italians bombarding other Turkish ports and coastal cities. Their new lesson: "If it is not possible to hold and control key areas, then destroy them."

He was told that the Italian navy had bombarded Beirut and Smyrna. He also heard that they had occupied Rhodes, Kos and other Islands. There were rumors that the Italians had bombarded the two Turkish forts that guarded the Dardanelles. The war was coming closer to Istanbul.

Yianni was discouraged as it appeared that they would not be able to escape and that they and all other non-Turkish residents were in serious trouble and danger. The Turks usual reaction to bad news was to kill all foreigners. He felt that their time was running out. They had to make a move.

Finally, a chance came for their escape. On October 18, 1912, Turkey gave up its territories and signed a peace treaty ceding Tripoli, evacuating from Libya and leaving the Dodecanese Islands to Italy. The world was quiet again. With the cessation of hostilities and fighting, there was an opportunity for an escape. Yianni went to arrange passage through his Port contacts.

Before meeting with the Port Authorities, Yianni looked over the Antigone's gold jewelry. He told Peter, "You put the gold cross back in the bag. Did you take some crazy oath of poverty?. Take the gold crosses out of the bag and hide it under your shirt. I'm sure she wanted you to have it. Keep them away from those greedy bastards at the Port. You may need it later. The rest we'll give them for the release of our boat and our escape."

All of them, the gang, went over to negotiate their release. After much haggling, in the dead of night, with the cooperation of the bribed Turkish Port officials, they were able to board Yianni's boat. He immediately fired up his engines and sped out of the Port onto the high seas and freedom.

It wasn't long before they were in a position to have Antigone's ceremony. Costas agreed to make the dedication. "I am not a priest so I will not make this a Cristian burial. It will be an entreaty to God to protect this dear soul and our farewell song to Antigone:"

Antigone Sea Prayer

"We lost a dear soul
Who graced our lives with her presence?
A life dedicated to God's divine essence

We ask God to bless
A life that was committed to divine law
And let the light of her sweet love soar

We speak of purity
Embrace this soul to protect from harm
Bring her lonely heart to its family arms

We commit this soul
To the deep sea and rapture of its roar
There to rest in eternity forever more"

They were all relieved when the ceremony was over. Antigone's spirit was symbolically remanded to Poseidon to be with her son and husband who drowned many years ago. Costas awkwardly ended the ceremony with the words 'goodbye Antigone'. After a short pause, each of them in turn uttered the word 'amen'. It was over.

Costas had one last thing to say: "The poets, priests, song writers, teachers all tell us that life is a rehearsal for death;

but they also held out the hope and promise of eternity." Peter thought that they may be life after death and that she would live through eternity.

Their thoughts turned to freedom. They were free to think of their escape from bloody Istanbul. Steve and Peter were yelling for joy and the old men were smiling and laughing. They had escaped from Turkish control and the gruesome fate that awaited many of the minority groups that would be destroyed. The Turkish militias were continuing to 'Turkify' all the areas of their country.

On the world stage, the war raged on between the forces of the Great Powers, supported by Greece and the Balkan Countries, and Turkey and their Muslim allies. Spurred on by the Turkey's entanglement with Italy, Serbia and Bulgaria accelerated their negotiations for an alliance; however, their differences proved difficult to overcome. Only pressure from the Russian government, which was eager to regain ground in the Balkans, led to the signing of a Treaty of Alliance on 7 March 1912.

The Treaty was ostensibly applied to Austria-Hungary, but it also provided for a partition of European Turkey: Albania and Kosovo to Serbia, Thrace to Bulgaria; southern Macedonia would be received by Bulgaria, while its northern areas would be partitioned between the two under the arbitration of the Russian Tsar.[1]

Feelers about a rapprochement and an alliance had been put forward to Bulgaria by Venizelos in early 1911, but not until after the conclusion of the Serbian-Bulgarian pact did negotiations commence in earnest. Bulgaria, the "Prussia of the Balkans", had the region's strongest army and in light of the 1897 debacle, the Greek army was held in low esteem. Given these and other unresolved issues, the war against the

Turks continued with the remaining fighting left for Greece and their Balkan allies to resolve.

Once they were on the high seas heading for somewhere, anywhere but Turkey; Peter reveled in the beauty of the Aegean. He was immersed in the life of this vibrant sea world. The blue of the water and the taste of wet salt from it was invigorating and at the same time relaxing. Peter escaped from the cares of his world and found a temporary sanctuary lost in his thoughts.

The water stayed calm, even on the high sea. There was a sense of peace and tranquility. Peter's experience was far different than Odysseus' battle with Poseidon. Peter and the gang did not battle Poseidon and have dangerously high sea currents as the ones described in Homer's epic sea battle. Peter and gang were given safe passage to their next adventure.

In his reverie, Peter remembered the last line from Antigone's letter: "Sail on Peter, sail on."

PASSAGE VIII

ELEFTHERIA I THANATOS – FREEDOM OR DEATH

Choral Foreword: The War Hymn

Greece of 1833 consisted of the Peloponnese, an area of the mainland between and south of the Greek cities of Arta and Volos, and the Islands immediately adjacent in the Aegean. The Greeks wanted more of their territory freed and the territories that was historically part of the Greek nation and which were still occupied by large Greek populations. But the Powers decided – to avoid a continuing struggle they choose a small Greece without the major islands and other territories. The smaller footprint of Greece would be fully independent and the other territories would remain in the Ottoman Empire.

The 'deals' and decisions by the so-called Great Powers caused and created havoc for many people around the world. They carved up conquered territories in ways that separated tribes and peoples and attempted to protect and maintain their power bases by their 'divide and conquer' strategies. The decision to keep the large Greek Islands under the control of the Ottoman Empire was just another unresolved human disaster and it would take the Greeks another series of bloody wars and economic dislocations and struggles and more European intervention before the Greek Islands would be freed and for Greece to achieve its present boundaries.

It was not long before the war for independence started. As the Greek soldiers marched to the front, the singing of war hymns started. Many of the young men sang an old hymn by Rhigas Pheraios. It was written in the 1700's and it became a rallying cry:

"How long my heroes, shall we live in bondage, alone like lions on ridges, on peaks?

Living in caves, seeing our children turned from the world to bitter enslavement?

Losing our land, brothers, and parents, our friends, our children and all our relations?

Better an hour of life that is free than forty years in slavery.

In the east, west, south and north, let us all have one heart for one land.

Let each worship God in the fashion he pleases, let us hasten together to the glory of war, Let each whom tyranny has exiled now return to his own.

Bulgarians, Albanians, Armenians, Greeks, black and white, let us belt the sword

All together in a surge for freedom, so the world will know that we are brave!"

Let the Cross shine on land and sea, let justice make the enemy kneel,

Let the world be healed of this grievous wound, let us live on earth as brothers – free."

These hymns inspired the young warriors and helped take their minds off the tedium of the march and the prospect of their death. Their lives were no longer their own. This war hymn and others songs made these Greek soldiers of one mind and heart. As they marched to the front these words echoed down the long line of soldiers.

The Turkish armies were considered militarily formidable, almost unbeatable; but they would face the combined armies of Greece and its Balkan allies and it would prove to be a bloody encounter between determined armies and arch enemies. Greece would sustain many losses and pay a heavy price in human life, but it was a price that Greece's young men now turned warriors were willing to pay for freedom.

FOR FREEDOM, SONS OF GREECE

"Never acknowledge the limitations of man. Smash all boundaries! Deny whatever your eyes see. Die every moment, but say: Death does not exist." Kazantzakis

Although the Greek army was held in low esteem at the start of the war, it could offer its navy, which alone could prevent Turkish reinforcements from being transported from Asia directly to the European fronts. As the Greek ambassador to Sofia noted, "Greece can provide 600,000 men for the war effort, 200,000 men in the field, and the fleet will be able to stop 400,000 men being moved by Turkey to Salonica and Gallipoli."

An Alliance Treaty of Defensive was thus signed at Sofia on 29 May 1912. The Balkan Alliance was formed and the nations were posed for a fight for independence from the Young Turks.

After making it to Greece, this small crew of Yianni, Costas, Peter and Steve docked at a port they discovered that the peace only lasted one day. Had the war not stopped for that one day or had they waited one day more to escape; they would not have been able to leave Istanbul. For the very next day after peace was declared with Italy, Turkey was in a new war in the Balkans with Greece, Serbia and Bulgaria.

They wondered and discussed, "How strange life seems to be. It was filled with coincidences? They wondered If there was a grand plan for humanity - all of us?"

These were holy days. There were festivals and celebrations going on all over Greece and in Volos, the city where they landed. Peter, Steve, Costas and Yianni were excited about this. They wanted to play for a while, listen to Greek music, and dance with beautiful girls and women. It was time to drink, to enjoy Greek cooking and revel in the pleasures of life.

As they walked to the festival grounds, Costas and Yianni told them what the celebrations were all about. Yianni told them, "There are many different kinds of celebrations and festivals in Greece. Even many of the ancient rituals have been turned into celebrations by the 'fun-loving' Greeks. There is the ancient Olympian and Chthonic Ritual which are associated with "chilly gloom" and which deal with magical curses, exorcisms and the like. It puts people in the mood to celebrate after these demons are driven away?"

Costas added, "There are a number of rituals involving ghosts and spirits. In ancient times a victim is sacrificed and devoted to the gods. It is sad to think that the ancients entertained such demanding gods and thought that sacrifices were a way to satisfy them."

Yianni said, "Not all the ceremonies and rituals were about doom and gloom. There were the harvest festivals and the women's festivals. Of course, the women's festivals involved magical spells, curses and then a long silence for contemplation." He and Steve were also intrigued by the festival that was dedicated to "the making of the goddess."

Steve really liked the myth of Aphrodite and the story of her sea-birth. He commented, "How wonderfully erotic a thought that is." The myth of the "mother and maid" sounded familiar to Peter. He became aware that there are different stories and forms of women-goddesses.

Peter and Steve were surprised to hear that the ancients believed that ghosts could become gods. Yianni said, "I really don't know what the hero-feasts are all about. These festivals have something to do with heroes and their antagonism with gods. Somehow, the Olympian system is involved."

As they explored the fair grounds they met a priest at the food bar who told them, "There are many mystery feasts." The discussion about the celebration of Orpheus was interesting, but his introduction of "Divine Possession" into Greek religion was confusing to Peter and Steve.

They found the feasts of "raw flesh" a little barbaric. The priest told them, "It relates to the sacramental union with god by eating his flesh." He told them, "You can think of these festivals as purification and rebirth." Peter and Steve didn't understand what the attainment of divinity through purification was all about, but it seemed as good a reason as any to have a celebration.

They had a little fun with all these Greek stories as they walked around the festival. They could hear the music just a short way away. When they arrived there were lines and lines within lines of people dancing in unison. It was a joyous time and a wondrous time to be back in Greece.

They walked by a make-shift stage where a amateur poet was reciting a war poem. He told everyone who were grouped there that there is a poem of war, which talks of a God who remained hidden while the passion and delirium for war were taking place. He told them that Lynda Bengalis describe these moments as the rehearsals for the deaths to come:

"Memory has no end here and no beginning ......
And there, from my beings' depths, from the depths
where a god lay hidden in my mind's shadow,
the holy delirium was now set free,
and from the obscurity of my silence
powerful verses suddenly engulfed
my brain, quick versus, and they spoke these words:

You seem all hidden in Your passion's sun
and from there You aim Your arrows where
creation's stubbornness has not yet dawned.
For You this passion is a rehearsal for death:
rehearse it as is worthy of the holy fire deep inside You,"

They left and found a bar and were surprised to hear that drinks were free. Costas said, "Let's be careful. Free things are never really free. There is always an expensive price to pay."

It soon became apparant why the drinks were free. After a lot of drinking and wonderful heroic Greek songs, the price was made clear. They had to listen to Greek politicians

PASSAGE VIII   255

and army recruiters. Their messages were clear and to the point. It started with the story of Greek heroes and poetry of bravery and honor.

They recited lyric poet Simonides words. Etched in stone on the walls of Thermopylae were the words: "Tell them in Lacedaemon, passer-by, that here obedient to their words we lie." When all the drinking and the speeches were over, many of the young men were ready, no they were eager, to join the Greek army and fight for "liberty". They were young and unafraid and were willing to make the ultimate sacrifice. They embraced "death" to free Greece from the torturous 'choke-hold' of the Turks.

Even though Costas was approaching old age, he was eager to volunteer and join the fight against the Turk'. The rallying words that were spoken that day: "Even more honor was due" could apply to Costas for he must have known that if he joined, he would never survive the war and, yet, he was willing to go. Yianni pulled Costas away from the recruiters and they went back to the bar for free drinks.

More drinks and they all lost control of their emotions which led to 'silly talk' and stupid laughing. Peter and Steve were mocking the idea of becoming soldiers by marching in unison to the booths, getting free drinks and marching back to their grassy knoll. They looked ridiculous; particularly Steve who was still in his fancy 'pimp' clothes. He had to leave so quickly he didn't have a chance to change. Peter had on his work clothes and looked like a grocery clerk or a waiter.

Yianni was concerned about the thought of Peter and Steve in the Greek army and 'facing up' to the toughest killers in the world - the Turkish soldiers and their murderous muslin allies. He thought that what a disaster for them and for Greece if all the young men being recruited were like these two young men.

There were some protestors who were against recruiting young boys into the Greek army. One was a beautiful lady dressed in black. She was shouting, "I lost my husband and my two sons." She then quoted some words from a Greek poem:

"And death never came to me, so now I can only waste away in tears."

There were more words but muted as they move farther away: They heard her words: *"There was a world…..or was it all a dream?"*

The woman was not done yelling her beliefs. She said:

The world hasn't learned anything nor is there any memory of the beginnings and the endings. The passion for war is a rehearsal for death and war is the descent into the holy fires deep inside the devil's belly"

Peter and Steve were now unwilling recruits, new bodies for the hastily assembled Greek army and the chances were good that they would die in combat. They had to get away. If they stayed they would be forced into the army and, no doubt, they were not being thought of as 'nameless heroes-to-be'; but more like 'cannon fodder' to be used and wasted in runs across the battle fields.

The burly Greek soldier with the epilates on his shoulders, indicated rank, and seemed to be in charge. Maybe he was a sergeant. He was talking to Yianni who was pleading with him, "Take it easy on the boys. Leave them alone. They are too young."

Clearly, there was no chance of that happening. It was a time-tested concept that a recruit must be broken mentally, even spiritually, before he can be made into an obedient soldier ready to lay down his life upon an order given.

The sergeant told Yianni, "The boys are no longer free. They belong to Greece and its army." He pointed out that: "Throughout the ages, soldiers have to be ready to sacrifice their lives without hesitation, question or explanation and the goal of training was to inculcate this belief and willingness in new recruits so that they will serve their country and its people and pay any price, including laying down their lives. They will be broken, trained and sent into battle fully prepared to fight to the death."

They were also discussing whether Yianni and Costas would be impressed into the Greek army. Yianni said, "I'm a little too old, my legs are no good and I have to bring back our boat to Lesbos."

Costas took a different tact. He said, "Only old men should go to battle and not young boys. They need a chance to live." He was especially vocal and critical about the old men who started and caused the wars and sent the youth of the country to die or be manned the rest of their lives. It was clear that Costas wanted to go with the boys and perhaps serve his country. Perhaps, he knew what the boys were facing and he wanted to help them get through what would be a hazardous one-way journey.

The sergeant listened politely to Costas and responded in a very serious way. "You can join the army along with the boys; but you will not interfere with me and the treatment of them. This is about 'love and glory'. Love of country and the glory of being a soldier fighting for the independence of Greek Islands."

Peter and Steve were no longer in Costas' charge; they were now under the control and at the mercy of the sergeant. He represented the army and ultimately Greece and its people. The sergeant did not comment on the larger philosophical question of the 'old men' fighting the wars started by other 'old men'. There is no value in a soldier questioning why life is the way it is. He is to do as he is told by his superiors.

Yianni asked the sergeant for a moment to pray with Costas and the youngsters. He called them to him and they went under a small tree away from the other soldiers, although a few other soldiers joined them. They prayed for forgiveness of their sins.

Peter went up to Yianni and asked him for a favor. Yianni said, "Anything." Peter took one of the gold crosses around his neck off and asked, "Please give this to my mother. It's the gold cross I tried to get for her in the church. She will understand. Tell her to use it to get Dad back to Greece. It will be a dream come true if he gets back."

Nothing else was said. Nothing asked of the gods. They would do their duty as men responsible for their own survival. After the prayers were done, the sergeant then turned to the boys and asked them their age. They told him they were fifteen years old. He responded with his first order: 'You are now both eighteen years old and if asked, that is the answer you will give.'

Costas asked, "What age do I give?" The sergeant answered, "Only God knows why an old man wants to join the army; but if they ask you tell them that you are eighteen years old." Everyone just smiled.

SIR, YES SIR

"The great tragedy: the violent fields of death are littered with the corpses of brave, young men who are no more.

Peter, Steve and Costas were sent to a boot camp for training and preparation for the horrors of war. Their T.I. or training instructor was the Sergeant who forced them into the Greek army. Peter asked; "What is your name?" The Sergeant screamed; "My name is 'Sir or Sergeant' to all of you and when I give an order you don't question me. You salute and answer "Sir Yes Sir."

The three of them walked away and under his breath Peter said; "What an asshole." Steve wondered out loud; "Doesn't anyone use their real name?"

The first step in their training was to shave heads and start the process of destroying everyone's ego. They were going to become the 'lowest form of animal life'. They were all dressed in the same green fatigues. They were forced to march in unison. No individuality allowed.

The Sergeant looked for any excuse to 'dressed a soldier down' by screaming and yelling at him. He made them run together, crawl on their stomachs in the mud, hope on one foot at a time, skip together, traverse over water obstacles by shimming on a rope high above the water. All the while the Sergeant yelled at them to go faster. Stop and then more obstacles to crawl over, under, around, and through. The recruits forgot who they were and followed his orders blindly. It was all about being willing to give up their lives on a bloody battlefield.

The only training they liked was on the shooting range.

Ammunition was limited to ten rounds per soldier. The Sergeant told them they'll get plenty of practice on the battlefield.

They also liked the indoctrination sessions. Not that anyone really listened. The first orientation session was given by the Sergeant. The theme of the speech was about the impact of the violence of war on the senses:

"War plays strange tricks with the senses and the mind. Soldiers learn that they are not individuals. They are part of a larger picture – a machine. They are forced to disappear – their identities all hidden. Everybody is expendable."

Costas whispered; "Our memories of our past lives has ended. They are being replaced by new memories: 'what they went through not to be shocked by the horrors of the battlefield. If we survive, the horrors will be in our psyches forever."

Training seemed endless. Day after day. They had constant drills and are always rehearsals and preparation to die. They didn't have much time to get ready so everything was concentrated. Training was brutal and intense to get them ready for the battlefield. All soldiers are trained to be stoic. Feelings and passions are forbidden. The military mind believes that the passion for life generates fear of death.

Peter heard the constant calls to duty and obedience. Nothing else mattered. Any thoughts of God's words for peace and love must 'lay hidden in the mind's shadow.' The thoughts of love and peace must be replaced by a belief that a good soldier must be willing to sacrifice everything and fight to the death for freedom. The purpose of training to make every recruit a good soldier.

The Sergeant surprised everyone by introducing them to their Field Commander. He started his address by telling them who the Greeks were and how they can be again:

"It was Alexander the Great with his brutal innovations of iron discipline, technological superiority in methods and tactics and his brilliance in management of battles that changed the face of war. Alexander's techniques of warfare made it so that individual soldiers are no longer an exemplar of valor and instead are part of a massed field force so lethal as to raise abject terror and horror in their opponents.

This who we were and who we must be again if we are to defeat the Turkish Empire and their muslim allies.

It was a typical 'rah, rah' speech with one exception. He included a quote by Homer in his speech:

"Shed down a kindly ray from above upon my life, and strength of war, that I may be able to drive away bitter cowardice from my head and crush down the deceitful impulses of my soul. Restrain also the keen fury of my heart which provokes me to tread the ways of blood-curdling strife. Rather, 'O blessed one, give me boldness to abide within the harmless laws of peace, avoiding strife and hatred and the violent fiends of death."

We chose the way of peace to obtain our independence from the yoke of tranny; but we are forced to take up arms to attain freedom for all our people."

He closed his talk by telling them that this was the last sessions before they went to the front. He apologized for the shortness of their training period. The Field commander made the point that foot soldiers are the "heart of the Greek army." It was typical military jargon and motivation psychology.

The Field Commander introduced the assembled group to a young lieutenant. He said; "He will lead the charge and the Sergeant will remain at the rear. His job will be to shoot anyone who gets scared and runs."

Training and speeches were over and the gang of Peter, Steve and Costas would soon be heading to the front lines and were about to participate in the 'trench and charge' ground war. They form their ranks and began their march to the front lines along with hundreds of other Greek soldiers.

It seemed to Peter that that there were a lot of young men in their ranks. Peter and Steve were forced to say that they were eighteen years old instead of fifteen. When asked, Costas told the lieutenant that he was in his fifties, instead of his sixties, so that he could join the army and shepherd the young men. Ages didn't seem important to anyone. Greece needed bodies to throw into the battles with the Turkish armies. What difference did it make if they were young or old men?

The march to the front was grueling, almost torturous, but almost had an air of excitement about it. There were jokes about their uniforms which didn't fit and made them look foolish. They couldn't wash themselves for days and they all had an order about them. They suffered in close quarters with each other. They were crusted with sweat and dirt and plagued with little pests oo fast to kill. Food and rations were short. Sometimes they were fed by Greek families on their march, or they wouldn't eat for days on end.

Peter thought back to the speeches at the festival. What was all that noise that the Greek politicians were making? He remembered clearly the words:

"War may be hell, but it is a glorious hell, the height of human suffering combining the ultimate tragedy of death with the lasting grace of the great deeds – the greatest of great deeds, courage in battle and devotion to country.

Serving in the army of Greece was an honor and a tribute to the ideals of liberty and freedom and protecting the homeland?"

What these politicians didn't say, perhaps didn't know, that although modern warfare had eliminated new myths and concept of heroes and personal glory; the horrors of armies engaged in combat didn't change over time. Homer described the sounds of struggle and the horrors of war as follows:

"At last the armies clashed at one strategic point, they slammed their shields together. Pike scraped pike with the grapping strength of fighters armed in bronze and their round shields pounded, boss on boss, and the sounds of the struggle roared and rocked the earth. Screams of men and cries of triumph breaking in one breath, Fighters killing, fighters killed, and the ground streamed blood."

It is hard to imagine that anyone could find glory in such horrors and the massive waste of young lives. The usual culprits for war are the bankers, businessmen, politicians; but the poets must also assume blame for such carnage because of their glorification of the heroics of war. They needed to participate in a bloody battle and their poems would be far different.

Peter thought: "Let all of them come here. What was glorious about this hell?" For the first time, Peter understood Antigone's words and warnings: "Don't listen to the military mind. They send young men to die in war to die for a cause. The women are left and must bury them and morn over their remains."

Yes, it is hell, but he looked around and saw young Greek men in the prime of their lives. He was proud to be with them and maybe even a little enthused about the struggle.

These young men were intense, ready to fight and die for their country. Even Steve looked a little more heroic. They were bound together in common cause – one heart, one spirit, one purpose. The training in boot camp was over, they were marching to the battlefields and many of them would never return. Yet, forward they marched as one in song, determined and in good cheer.

Peter stayed with Steve and Costas. They were teamed up with an old grizzled fighter – a Klephts, a veteran from the hills who spent most of his life fighting the Turks in 'never-ending' guerilla battles with them. Peter didn't know his name, so he called him Mikos, after the first guerilla fighter that he met at the Lesbos' Kafenio.

He didn't understand Mikos who wanted to spend his last years in the thrill of battle. Only a crazy man and, not surprisingly an old veteran at that: "could be steeled at the heart and mind and enjoy the thrill of battle and deaths and never feel the terror. He was here to fight for freedom — his life crusade."

As they marched to the front, the singing of war hymns by everyone started to inspire and take their minds off the tedium of the march. Many of the young men knew the hymn and were singing. More singing, the young soldiers came to the lines that thrilled all of them and made them of one mind, one heart and one spirit.

After what seemed like an eternity, they arrived at the front. They were greeted by the first sounds of war. Many were surprised and scared by the loud booms of artillery and smaller staccato sounds of small arms, rifles and pistols. Yet, to the man, they gathered themselves and moved forward under the lead of the young officers. These young men were given gold bars on their shoulders, some authority, special uniforms and a little extra pay and for that they had to lead the charge against the enemy lines. The Turkish soldiers would line up their sights on the shiny gold bars on their helmets and fire at them. They were fed up as cannon fodder.

To the rear were older men, many were sergeants, whose orders were to shoot anyone who ran away. These men, hastily drawn together as a specialized unit, fortified with the very brave fighters from the mountains. They were assigned a special mission and that was to take the hills that flanked the Turkish lines and hold them. They were to serve as a checkmate against the highly trained and equipped Turkish army. If the Turks were able to stop the charging Greek attacks, they would not be able to advance for fear of an attack on their flank by this unit.

Peter was proud to be a soldier and a comrade. He wanted to serve his country. His inner demons had to be quenched. He could not let himself get in touch with his gut-wrenching fear – the hysteria of a young teenager facing combat for the first time. He made up his mind to accept his fate no matter what it was. He needed to mentally stay outside himself and to accept, more likely ignore and overcome the reality of the bloody scene about to take place.

Costas, now his philosophical guru, told him about Plato's interview with a Greek soldier who died on the battlefield and came back to life after he was ministered to and restored. The Greek soldier told Plato that after he died he went to a spiritual world which was filled with love and acceptance. He felt like he had come home. He had a soul which survived death.

Peter asked; "What do you think this all means?"

Costas answered; "It could mean that our ancestors were

right and that everything in the universe is spiritual and that there is such a thing as reincarnation. We have a soul that has many physical lives. In fact, I think that life is a journey of our soul and that we are just one journey along the way. True existence is a journey of soul living many lives in physical bodies. It must mean that there is purpose and meaning to life. The ancient Greek philosophers may have been right when they said that it is pain and suffering which makes us wiser in his life and for all the other ones."

"Thanks Costas. Not sure that's the way it is; but it is interesting. We could find out real soon." My mother used to say; "What's up is down and what is down is up. She always practiced an economy of words. Peter said with a smile.

Their attention turned to Steve. He never had any coping skills and he was in touch with his core feelings and the terrors that always lurked in his mind and soul. He was talking gibberish. His fears had surfaced. He was frightened to death about what was going to take place; but he was trapped and couldn't run for fear of being shot.

Costas and the other old man tried to calm him down, but they were also preoccupied by their own preordained fates were – what Homer described as:

"Why so much grief for me? No man will hurl me down to Death, against my fate. No one alive has ever escaped it, neither brave man nor coward, I tell you —- it's born with us the day that we are born."

The philosophical session was over and Steve was on his own for now.

They started jogging to the front again and could see the battle scene in front of them. The ground was blood-red and fresh blood was streaming from the littered bodies. The armies were in close contact and the sound of the struggle roared and rocked the earth.

There were men screaming and charging forward toward the Turkish lines. Many were falling, breathing their last. The screams and cries of pain by dying men were frightening. Fighters killing fighters and the ground drenched and streamed blood. There were dead bodies everywhere; some had been there so long that they had stopped bleeding and their stench mixed with gunfire was like a poison cloud that blanketed and covered the hell and inferno of the battlefield.

Steve stopped running forward. He tried to look around, but was scared to see what was happening. His fears took over him. He was bewildered, scared, crying and unable to know or sense what was happening. His body was shaking from fright. He wondered if everyone or anyone was feeling what he was feeling. Was he a coward? He didn't care what anyone thought. Panic had infected every bone is his body and, yet, he moved forward. There was no other place for him to go but forward toward the enemy. His training had prevailed over his fears.

Peter was resigned to his fate and unafraid. His will power had overcome his fear. He kept jogging forward without the choking halt of panic to stop him. He made his peace with God and was willing to die if that was to be his fate. Everything was now tolerable fortified by his determination to serve his country.

The fear of death had subsided, peace was restored in his being and the chaos of war was now only background noise. The orders to push forward were accepted without fear or doubt. He had become a soldier. He still harbored a need to survive and still had some fear; but his fear was now manageable and buried somewhere deep in his subconscious mind.

Their trot to and on the battlefield was now a full run. Costas was yelling; "Stay close to me Peter. Stay close Steve." He told them to follow him and not go ahead of him. They were at the front line and were now behind the first charging line of Greek soldiers. They were battling the heavily entrenched Turks. The charging line was met with a blistering hail of gunfire and men were slowly dropping and silently rolling over to their sides into the blood and stench that covered the battle ground.

Costas continued to move forward, but at a cautious trot. The order was given to hold their positions behind the charging line. They were then ordered to start digging a trench at their position. They would have to work most of the night. Greek snipers were positioned to return fire against any Turkish soldier who fired at them as they dug the trench. It was an effective tactic.

Peter went from a happy, carefree teenager to a soldier trapped and hoping to survive a vicious war. He wondered: 'what purpose does all this tragic waste of treasure and lives serve'. He would never forget its savagery, cruelty and waste of human life. He felt that if God was near, why all this hell – why did so many brave and innocent souls have to be wasted? Why doesn't God show his "hand and stop this viciousness? Where is God's love of humanity? Why doesn't he save us from ourselves?

THE HEART OF THE WARRIOR

"Let the Cross shine on land and sea, let justice make the enemy kneel, Let the world be healed of this grievous wound, let us live on earth as brothers –free."

They were back in their tranches again and everything was peaceful with only sporadic shots being fired. Before they went to sleep, Peter asked Costas; "Why is so much blood and treasure being spent on this small entrance to the valley?"

Costas said; "The entrance to the valley is an opening to Turkish soil. If we are able to overcome the Turkish position, we will be able to charge up the valley and team up with the Balkan forces. Together, we will take the land bridge into Turkey and attack their bases guarding Istanbul. The war would be fought on Turkish soil."

Early morning came and they woke up to chaos, blinding smoke, the sounds of rapid and ceaseless gun and cannon fire, screams of fallen men dead and wounded. Costas. Peter and Steve rushed to their positions. Orders were given to advance and then orders given to retreat and more orders contradicting the orders given. They were unclear what to do, but the Sergeant ordered them to move forward to support the charging line.

It wasn't long before Peter was mired in this insane hell. He was knee deep in mud and the blood of falling over and dead men. Men who had given their all. He loved them, who had become his brothers. Peter felt his anger and was ready to fight for them, for his country and for all the Greek people. It made no difference what happened to him anymore. He became a Greek soldier baptized in the blood, sweat and tears of his fallen comrades.

They were at the rear of a newly assembled platoon of Greek soldiers and they were charging forward with suicidal courage at the enemy's trenches. After horrific fighting and loss of life, the order was given to retreat. The Turkish line held and the Greeks retreated slowly back to their trench line that they dug for a possible retreat and holding point for them.

Looking at the dead bodies across the killing fields, Peter felt that God was not there on the battlefield. He knew that there would be another bloody battle tomorrow and he felt that it could be the last day of his life and maybe for Steve and Costas too. There was always going to be another battle; another deadly run and blind charge across the violent bloody killing fields. All he could do was utter the words, 'Why, God why?'

They moved back to their lines feeling that day's disappointment. The Turks were formidable enemies and crazy-brave soldiers. When they got back to their lines, they were greeted by their comrades. It was time to find something to eat and find someplace to rest. Tomorrow was looming large in his mind.

Peter, Costas and Steve found a small lone tree to sit under. Peter called the tree, 'The lone survivor.' Across from them was a small group of soldiers who were talking about a Greek officer with the name Kazantzakis. Costas asked them, "Are you talking about the writer from Crete?" The group answered in unison, "Yes. He is with another division. We think that they are marching to the right flank of the Turkish lines to turn them into themselves. When we go at them tomorrow, they may be in a state of confusion if their flank doesn't hold."

Costas asked, "Are you guys' poets and writers?" One of them answered, we are 'Poets, philosophers, writers, teachers.' Steve asked, "Why are you here? Couldn't you get deferments as some kind of 'wise men'? They laughed. "We wanted to be with all the other artists who joined. We hoped to be in their unit, but that was not to be."

Costas, who had the heart and intellect of a poet asked them, "What do poets and philosophers know about war? This is serious business. You could get killed or maimed for life."

One of the more serious young men rose and said, "Let me tell you a true story about how a poet saved the city-state of Athens from destruction. After a number of years of battle between Sparta and Athens, the Spartan Army was camped outside Athens ready to sack and destroy the city the next day. As was the habit of Greek armies, they had a banquet, played music and listen to poetry and other readings of literature.

When the poetry of Euripides was read to them, it deeply affected the sensitivities of the Spartan soldiers. And to a man; they agreed that they would not destroy Athens. It was reported that the Spartans said; "Any city that could produce such a great poet should not be destroyed and deny the world the great art and poetry that the Athens's poets will inspire."

Another young man took his place and made the point, "That to be a Greek writer, the tradition is to be a warrior. You must fight for Greece to have any credibility. Aeschylus set the rule when he fought at Marathon. He was the father of Greek tragedy, but he wanted his epitaph to be about his wartime service at Marathon."

It was clear that Costas had opened his heart to these beautiful young men who were willing to sacrifice everything; including their lives for an ideal. He didn't warn them about the dangers they would face. Peter remembered Costas saying to him that the bullets will tear a hole in your stomach so large you could put a fist through it. But Costas had clearly soften and was moved to tears thinking about the fate of these idealistic young men who were about to be sacrificed as cannon fodder. He changed the subject and asked, "What does this man Kazantzakis tell us about war?"

Another young man stood up and recited: "It is our duty to set ourselves an end beyond our individual concerns, beyond our convenient agreeable habits, higher than ourselves, disdaining laughter, hunger, even death, to toil night and day to attain that end." Another writer added, "Try to make your life glorious. Never surrender to mediocrity. Remember his words that, "Only thus does life acquire nobility and oneness."

Costas asked, "And what does this man from Crete say about death?" The group was totally charged and animated. One of them answered, "He tries to give people who agonize over this great tragedy an answer; but all he could only say: "Where are we going? Do not ask! Ascend, descend. There is no beginning and no end." Still another added; "The moment is spiritual: Leave the heart and mind behind. We must obey orders and go forward. Otherwise, Greece is doomed if we fail. "

Then there was a brief silence which was quickly broken by a short quotation from one of these poet soldiers, "Conquer the last great temptation of all – Hope. It is an illusion on the battlefield."

Peter lamented; "I knew that the scenes of battle will be glorified and become new legends by the poets. They will one day say; "Greece, as we know it today, eventually emerged successfully from the fire of hell – the House of Death". Costas added; "They will glorify the price that was paid: 'so many young, sturdy souls, so brave fighters' who gave their lives and souls for their country." Pavlos, one of the young 'poet soldiers' said, "I remember an old Greek philosopher who made a statement that "Good is bad and bad is good."

I forget his name and I'm not sure what he meant. But, I think he meant that the fight for independence is good, but having to kill for it is bad. When a Greek poet writes a war poem with all its gory, he is celebrating the struggle and warning the price in human life paid." Peter asked him; "What was in the bag slug over your shoulder?" Pavlos was getting ready to sleep, but he uttered it is my bouzouki. I'm a poet, a singer and I play in Greek bands. I love music and poetry."

This was the last statement before they all went silent and dozed off.

Night time brought the thought that there is no rest on the battlefield. Nights are for one charge after another against enemy lines. Everything is a torment and mornings couldn't come quick enough. They were so uncomfortable and miserable that they were almost to the point that they didn't seem to care what happened to them. Death had become the only freedom from this hell on earth.

Peter never forgot his first sight of a bloody battle field. It was far different from any poet's rendition of it. His attitude about life had changed forever by the horrors and the wholesale butchering of lives. And yet, he and his comrades would step out on the battlefield again and again and be willing to give their lives side by side with their comrades and for their country.

THE SMELL OF DEATH

"Those thoughts that wander through the universe." Kazantzakis

One of these thoughts was recounted many centuries before Aeschylus' play: 'Agamemnon' when the chorus sang:

"But dark fear now; shows me dim, dreadful forms hid in the night.
Men who shed the blood of men, their ways are not unseen of God,
Black the spirits that avenge."

Costas wanted to talk to Peter before the next major assault against enemy lines. These two early risers grab a cup of coffee at the service trailer and found a secluded spot to talk about a thought and feeling that wandered into Costas' mind.

He told Peter; "I'll get straight to the point. My time is up. I dreamed that my father came to me and told me that the end was near. My gut is telling me that I won't survive this next assault."

Peter was visibly moved by the thought that Costas would die that night on the battlefield. "I'm sick to hear you say that. My heart aches at the thought. Steve and I have come to care for you."

There was a pause to absorb the pain that they both feeling about Costas' premonition. Peter tried to take the edge off the sadness of what Costas was saying; "This thought of end times, death, is wandering all over the camp. Maybe you picked up that thought."

Costas said; "I think that we know when it's time."

"Costas why did you volunteered to join the army. It was too dangerous and you didn't have to do it. I assumed that it was your concern for Steve and me. Why did you put your life on the line for us?"

"It's about a lot of things; but one of them is how I wanted to live and how I wanted to die – my Kleos. There is a Greek tradition that we must live a worthwhile life and that includes a 'good death'. My life was spent selfishly, perhaps foolishly. After my wife died, I lived only for myself. It was about: 'no song unsung, no wine untasted, no line dance not joined and no woman met that I didn't love. It was intoxicating.

Trying to guide and protect you and Steve was my atonement. I had to do it. I don't want to die; but if I do it will be a good death. " They hugged each other. It was an unconscious and spiritual goodbye; perhaps forever. They went silent and joined the ranks that were lining up for an assault.

The Greek army was moving into position for a major assault against the Turkish lines. They were anxious to get it over and were ready to sacrifice their lives for Greece's freedom. Legions of man were forming ranks in the field of combat. They were determined to bring the fight to 'hand to hand' combat with the Turkish soldiers in their trenches.

The Turks were entrenched, but were exposed to 'overhead fire' from the Greeks on the hill side. They were not in a position to retreat; all their men were on the front line holding off the major assaults by the Greeks. Their reserves were withdrawn and moved to the front against the Bulgarian forces, the Prussians of Southern Europe. It was 'do or die' for them and it was shaping up to be a major battle that could turn the 'tide' of the war in Greece and their Balkan cousin's favor.

The Greek army moved a gunnery unit forward where it could provide cover fire. Costas, Peter and Steve's unit were on the charging line. They were charge and fire at the Turkish army units that were entranced in a long continuous trench. Everyone was waiting for the Greek bugle call to charge and then the firing would begin from both sides.

The Sergeant told Peter to be the one to stand and fire. Steve was told to drop on the ground and load rifles for Peter to fire. They were to advance and hold ten feet on the killing fields. Peter was to stand and fire and then advance a few feet against withering fire. He would fall to the ground next to Steve, grab the reloaded rifle, stand and fire at the Turkish lines again. Costas and Mikos were next to them doing the same thing.

Everyone to the man obeyed orders. During the first charge, all of them bent over with their heads down and were slowly making their way across the killing fields trying to gain and keep footage. They did as they were told: fire their rifles as they moved forward and dropped to the ground /for reloaded rifles. They did this against withering fire.

They made some progress and then the Sergeant made his way to the front line and told them to retreat and establish a new holding position. The young lieutenants leading the charge had been killed and the Greek army forced to retreat and reorganize themselves.

Peter never forgot this moment. He told Steve; "I couldn't see anything. There was smoke everywhere. I just jumped up and fired off a round and quickly dropped to the ground. When you handed me a new rifle, I would stand up and shoot. I never had a chance to aim. It was just rise, shoot and fall down and then rise again to charge and fire."

Before they could catch their breath, orders were given again to advance. A new surge forward was ordered. The men on the field rose and pushed forward with renewed intensity. There was no time to think of survival. Retreat was not an option. They were where they were. They were ordered forward, abandoning all hope of survival.

Costas signaled Peter with a wave of his hand to follow him in the charge against the Turkish lines. Peter had a bad feeling about this charge forward: "I saw men rising and running forward; and I went forward with them. It was as in a dream where I was running in a dazed state of delirium shooting, falling, jumping up and firing and doing it again and again."

Greek soldiers were lurching backwards and downwards after they were shot. Others shot paused, their heads bowed and then sank slowly to their knees, rolled over and were still forever. Costas, Peter and Steve were trapped in a mass of running men shooting and trying to kill the enemy.

Then their world changed. As they surged forward behind Costas, there was an explosion and they were knocked to the ground. After a confusing moment, Peter soon realized that he was still alive. Up ahead, he could see Costas slowly falling to his knees, and then rolling slowly over to his side.

The two young men searched the battlefield, all the while hoping to find Costas wounded but alive; hoping that it was all a nightmare and they would wake to find alive the old man that they had come to love. They searched the field looking at one body after another looking at the "grim remains" of the battle.

Peter saw Costas' body and could only point at him. When Steve saw him he howled in grief like a wounded animal. They ran over to his body. Damn the fighting. Damn the risks. They hoped that he was only wounded, but in their hearts they knew that it was over. Their souls and hearts were ripped open. He had become a 'father-figure' to them.

They crawled on the ground to Costas. He was dead; lying face down in the dirt, still clutching his rifle. There was grief, deep, deep within his empty eyes. Steve wondered out loud; "Is that is how God sees him. Would he hold his rifle for all time, throughout eternity? Steve was worried that the rifle had become an extension of his soldier's arm and his arms an extension of his soul. He started crying. What if God doesn't take him?

Under heavy fire, Peter and then Steve made their way to him; they clutched his head in their hands and began to cry. He was dead. His eyes were wide open and the light never seemed to leave him. They had lost a father, a comrade, a brother, and a friend who had tendered and protected them. Costas' mission and his time were over. He had taken leave of the seas, the sun and the fields that he loved so well.

They both felt grief—deep, deep, within. Steve started hallucinating. He was shouting; "That's how God will receive him – a man holding a gun rushing to kill other men. What a price to pay. Would his soul be taken from him?"

Peter was concerned. Steve was beside himself and was no help at all. Pavlos, the tall, thin poet-soldier, saw what was happening and came to help Peter remove Costas' body. Peter told Steve to go ahead of Pavlos and him. As they lifted his body, Peter realized he was still warm. He knew that Costas would never get up again, but maybe his spirit could still be around. Peter's heart hurt, tears filled his eyes and he was gasping for breath as he carried Costas' body. He suddenly realized how final Death is.

Peter and Pavlos carried and at times dragged Costas body off the battlefield. They looked around and saw that there was no escape from the chaos. Pavlos said; "The fighters on both sides have fallen into a hell for lost souls."

They participated and witnessed the true horrors of a battle of attrition and the savagery that comes from extreme violence. They saw fighters killing other fighters, historic enemies righting past atrocities and injustices, the oppressed against their oppressors, Muslims against Christians – there were so many justifications, reasons and excuses for this war and no mention of the barbarism of unbridles warfare that had to be endured to gain Greece's freedom. 'For freedom our sons'.

THE BURIALS

Aeschylus' expressed God's role in the death and despair of war: *"Black smoke, I would be nearing the clouds of God."*

The Sergeant watched Peter and Pavlos carry Costas' body off the battlefield. He couldn't make out what Steve was doing. They were easy targets for the Turkish soldiers who held t as intrigued by the Turkish soldiers who held their fire until they could make it off the battlefield. At great risks to themselves, Peter and Pavlos removed Costas body before it was mangled by the vultures.

Peter also noticed that the Turkish soldiers held their fire and he assumed that they were holding their fire because ey were honoring the dead. He remembered what Panos at the Church grounds told them that the Turkish soldiers and people were very superstitious. No doubt, they were being respectful of the dead and soldiers protecting them. They probably did not want to anger the gods.

Peter and Pavlos were standing over the dead body and

not sure what they should do with it. Pavlos, the young poet, was equally confused. The Sergeant came over and told them 'good work' and that he was promoting the three of them to the rank of 'grave diggers'. He told them to take Costas' body to one of the 'mule-driven' carts to the road behind the battlefield.

The Sergeant also told them that the field commanders from both sides were on the battlefield negotiating a '24 hour' truce. Both sides had suffered heavy losses and everybody needed a break in the action.. The blood bath was over for a short, sweet moment of peace. The battlefield was littered with the dead and with gruesome vultures flying around getting ready to feast on the dead.

After the Sergeant left, Peter said; "He must think he is funny or he is still a shithead. Steve said; "He is so full of shit. Pavlos asked; "Should I write a poem about Sargent-shit?" There was a resounding 'no' from Peter and Steve.

Peter said; "Let me change my mind about his tactics. I feel a different 'vibe' about him. I think he really likes us, but he acts like a tough guy. All of the Sergeants act that way to make us know they mean business and they can't have us questioning him." Peter realized that the Sergeant and the officer core had played them. The Sergeants are the so-called tough guys giving out tough orders and the officers' job was to calm the soldiers down when he was too rough. It is a 'good guy/bad guy' act.

Pavlos saw the Sergeant returning and he 'hushed' them. The Sergeant said; "The terms of the truce are soldier-simple. The Turkish soldiers would shoot and remove all the vultures. The Turkish finished the job of shooting the vultures and removing them. They were enjoying themselves and made quick work of killing and removing them. They probably are going to fry and eat them. It would be ironic if that were the case"

Peter, Steve and Pavlos and the other so-called 'grave diggers' entered the battlefield and remove their dead for burial. Priority was given to teams that were moving the wounded to the tents at remote locations at the rear for medical help and treatment.

As they worked, they talked about how they participated in a heroic battle. They looked around and saw that it was a mighty clash resulting in the death of many brave young fighters on both sides. They were saddened about the carnage that took place on the bloody battlefield, and were horrified and repulsed by the torn and the mangled bodies that littered the battlefield.

Miraculously, Peter, Pavlos and Steve survived the carnage; and they would never forget their bewildering descent into the 'battle' and darkness of that descent into hell. Many souls were lost and left behind in the battlefield inferno. Upset, Peter looked up at the sky hoping to find some sign that God had come to bless the dead and to honor the sacrifices that these brave young souls had made. What he saw horrified him. Hawks and vultures were circling the battlefield; they had come to feast on the dead.

Peter was depressed and preoccupied with thoughts of life and death. He wondered if there was a God and, if so, He must see the carnage taking place. He wondered why He didn't stop it. All the soldiers were 'shell shocked' over the many deaths. Peter had used up all his tears. He learned how to bear pain and the unbearable agony of loss and despair. He had become a soldier and was taught how to bear the pain that never ceases; but, deep inside, he still retained his boyish personality and humility. The carnage did not take away his essence.

When they arrived at the burial site, they threw the dead bodies one-by-one unceremoniously into a ravine. Steve wanted to 'lay hands' one last time on Costas' body and took Pavlos place. Peter and Steve carefully placed Costas' body on the top of the pile of human remains and began to toss dirt over the dead bodies. The grave-diggers felt the sadness and the finality of death.

Peter got into position to say a prayer. He told everyone Costas had a premonition that he was going to die and he wrote a short prayer and celebration of their heroic deaths, their Kleos deaths. He told everyone that Costas wanted his last words to be light-hearted and positive in tone. Through tears that he was holding back, he read Costas' last words:

> "Say a little prayer for us
> For all of us who gave our lives in battle
> For freedom, for country, love of family
> We died a good death for a Kleos ascent
> Hold us in your memory, till we meet again
>
> Sing a little song for us
> To celebrate our lives, purpose achieved
> To dance for joy, to sing, to shout ascend
> Up is down, down is up; we are spiritual
> Life is death, death is life; there is no end
>
> See you all on the other side, blessings"

Everyone was silent. It was over and everyone put the mules away and made their way back to their positions at the front lines.

That night was different. Under a flag of truce with the Turks, the Greek soldiers felt safe enough to celebrate. The sounds of Greek music and men yelling and dancing reverberated over the battlefield and Peter could swear that he could see Turkish soldiers on the other side of the killing fields, dancing 'shoulder to shoulder' in a circle. They were singing Turkish lyrics to the Greek music. There was a short moment of brotherhood between the opposing warriors allowing their souls to touch each other.

This moment was planned well in advance. Leaders on both sides wanted a short respite and a celebration of the heroic efforts and sacrifices made by fallen. It was planned in advance and was made more complete when bottles of wine and ouzo were released to the men. They were possessed by a touch of exhilarating madness. Some of Greek soldiers didn't participate in the celebration because they felt that it was disrespectful of their brothers who had died on the battlefield and that everyone was dancing on the graves of their 'comrade-brothers'.

Peter had a different attitude about everything that night. It was crying time again and he was dancing alone, but celebrating with everyone. He understood the meaning of the celebration. He knew that everyone was just trying to free themselves of their pain. Music, songs and weeping filled the air and for a few short moments, the world was bearable.

He had witnessed again the insanity of warfare. He witnessed how killing takes control of the senses as life and time disappear. The past, present and future merge. All thoughts of death and loss became one cry. But that night was different.

Peter was by himself and away from the other soldiers; but he still heard the echoes of the lyrics and the music being played by the small Greek band entertaining everyone. The song went:

> "We say our prayers of loss and remorse
> For all the young men who gave their lives
> For freedom, for country, for love of family
> Their sacrifice heroic, called by God to leave
> We will miss their love, we are left to grieve
> We sing our sad song of celebration and joy
> They are free, purpose achieved, souls mend
> Good lives, good death, Kleos heroes ascend."

Peter smiled. Pavlos took Costas last words and made a song of it. For now, Peter was dancing his sorrows away: Greek style-by himself with his soul.

THE INTELLIGENCE REPORT

The Greek poet Ritsos captured the intensity of the fighting:

"They gasp. No water. All are thirsty. For years now,
All chew a mouthful of sky to choke down their bitterness.
Their eyes are red from the vigil
a deep line wedged between their eyebrows
When they are killed, life marches up high with banners and with drums."

Despite the sadness of the day, Peter found some solace in the celebration that night. He rose early that morning feeling the joys of life and went for his morning coffee before it was all distributed in the rush of mid-morning madness and the struggle of the late risers for a cup of java. While he was relaxing and enjoying the morning calm before the fighting began again, Pavlos came up to him and inquired about Steve's 'where-abouts'.

Peter had a chuckle in his voice when he said; "He is probably in the fields chasing the butterflies, the squirrels, rabbits and the other field creatures. Pavlos said there is some poetry in that vision. Those little creatures are young souls and Steve is dancing with them. You could be right, The Greeks think that butterflies are visiting souls. Their light chatter was interrupted by the Sergeant who asked where Steve was. Peter answered; "He chasing butterflies in the fields above.

The Sergeant was not amused. He told them to tell Steve to stay put that there is an Intelligence Report to be read to our section at late morning about 11am. He told them that after that reading Pavlos and Steve are assigned to the charging line and Peter you are assigned to the trench line on the small hill overlooking the battlefield. Peter asked; "What am I supposed to do back there?" The Sergeant answered; "Shoot any Greek who deserts the battlefield and shoot any Turk that breaks through our ranks."

The Field Commander Mehalikis arrived at 11 am to read the Intelligence Report to Peter's unit. He started by saying; "We are taking the unusual step of sharing our 'intel' with you, our front line troops. The Report indicates that Greece and its Balkan allies are winning the war against the Turkish forces. The end is near and we will be on the winning end of it. I've been authorized to read the following Report to our fighting forces in this theater of the war:

"The war plan by Venizelos and the General Staff called

for a rapid advance with overwhelming force. The objective was to take Thessaloniki with its vitally important harbor. A minute force of little more than a division proper, just enough to forestall a possible Turkish redeployment eastwards, was to be sent west as the "Army of Epirus", while the bulk of the army and artillery would embark on what would later be called "blitzkrieg" tactics against the Turks in the east.

The Greek plan worked brilliantly: advancing on foot, the Greeks defeated the Turks soundly twice, and were in Thessaloniki within 4 weeks. The Greek plan for overwhelming attack and speedy advance hinged upon another factor: could the Greek Navy succeed in blockading the Turkish fleet within the Straits, any Turkish reinforcements from Asia would have no way of reaching Europe quickly. As matters turned out, Turkey would be slow to mobilize, and even when the masses of loyal troops raised in Asia were ready, they could go no further than the outskirts of Istanbul because they were fighting the Bulgarians in brutal trench warfare.

With the Bulgarians directing the bulk of their forces towards Constantinople, capture of Thessaloniki ensured that the railway axis between these two main cities was lost to the Turks, who then suffered total loss of logistics and supplies and severe impairment of command and control capability. The Turks were hard placed to recruit locals, as their loyalties would be liable to lie with the Balkan Allies. Ottoman armies in Europe were quickly cut off and their loss of morale and operational capability was forcing them to a quick surrender. The fighting was intense.

The Greek army has advanced from the south and overcame a strong force of Turkish soldiers. Defeating them was not enough; the Greeks then spent additional troops trapping them in a ravine. The goal was to capture all the modern armament, artillery and transport that the Germans had given to the Turks. After many brutal assaults, the remaining Turks surrender and the Greeks took possession of their 'much needed' armaments.

They reinforced their positions waiting for a counter-attack by the Turks. When the Turkish forces reinforced their positions for a counter charge, the Greeks guns mowed them down, putting them to flight like a disorderly rabble. Following up this victory and a series of other smaller but just as bloody clashes, the Greeks pursued the rest of the Ottoman army across the border to liberate Salonika."

The Field Commander closed with the following comments followed by command; "The sacrifices that we shed on this battlefield were not made in vain. We have tied up Turkish precious reserves that they need on other fronts. We are going to rattle their cages with another blistering attack and force them to deploy their reserves to protect their positions in this major choke point. If we force them to do that it will be a major victory for us. For freedom, sons of Greece."

He announced that he was deploying additional Greek reserves to this battlefield and they were moving forward to join the ranks of our other Greeks soldiers who have been conducting the battles against the Turkish forces lined against us. They will join us in the battle we will wage now. Brother-to- brother – we will fight them and relieve the pressure on the other Greek divisions – fighting the now retreating Turkish armies in the other war zones.

The charge began. The newly formed Greek army of brave young reservists and veterans was an elite fighting unit. Through the fiery pain, the screams of deaths, massive destruction, tears for their brothers, endless suffering, the agony of battle, the taking and giving of life, the rag-tag army of Greece had become an elite killing machine. Almost unexpectedly, the Turkish lines broke. The vaulted Turkish fighters were retreating and running for their lives.

Peter was on the battlefield with Pavlos. Steve was missing and Peter took his place. He and Pavlos were in the middle of the mass chaos and the carnage of deaths that was being shed. The Greek soldiers were exacting huge losses on the Turkish soldiers. Wounded Turkish soldiers in and out of the tranches were killed on the spot; most were bayoneted and others had their throats slashed. The Turks that ran from the field were chased down and shot. Very few prisoners were taken. They paid a dear price for running and wanting to live. They paid a price for all the atrocities that had been committed against the Greek people by the Turkish and Muslim armies.

Meanwhile from the north, down the valley of the Vardar, came the Serbs to defeat a large Turkish army group at Kumanovo, then another Turkish army group at Monastir, whose remnants after a loss of ten thousand soldiers, fled across the frontier into Albania. In the east the Bulgarians invaded Thrace in strength, to defeat a Turkish divisions in a bloody two-day battle at Kirk-Kilissa, then moved to confront the main Turkish army at Lule Burgas and drove this army back to the Chatalja Lines, between the Black Sea and the Marmara. The Ottoman army, forever tenacious under siege, was able to halt the advance of the Bulgarian army.

The Turkish strategists determined that the Greeks were planning another two-prong attack east and west of the impassable Pindus mountain range, and they accordingly allotted their precious reserves and heavy armaments resources, again divided, on a defensive posture in order to fortify the approaches to Ioannina, capital of Epirus, and the mountain passes leading from Thessaly to Macedonia.

Word came that with great pride, Greek soldiers on another front had marched into the city on the feast date of its patron saint, Demetrius. The army was pelted with roses by delirious Greek crowds in the streets there to meet them. After almost five hundred years of Turkish domination, the blue-and-white Greek national flag flew from the windows and roof-tops of the city while the Star and Crescent vanished forever.

The Greek soldiers were proving to be the equal of the Turkish soldiers in terms of skill, discipline and bravery. They were physically strong and were able to endure the hardships of long marches into battle. Both sides knew that these wars would be long and arduous and it would be a battle to death. No quarter was given by either side. No quarter was asked for.

They had accomplished their goal of forcing the Turkish reserves to be deployed to the battle and hold their lines. Both sides reinforced their positions and were getting ready for the ensuing battles to come. The Turkish reserves were assigned the task of sealing the pass out of the ravine.

A large number of the Greek soldiers had scaled the walls on the back of the ravine and, once they were to the top, they looked down on this very strong reinforced Turkish force.

The battle started and because of their superior field position, the Greek guns began to mow down the forces trapped in the ravine. The Turkish soldiers were holding the narrow pass, but the Greek soldiers were holding their position against intense fire and wave after wave of attacking Turkish soldiers trying to dislodge the Greek positions on the hills which were proving to be a strangle hold on the Turkish reserves.

Both armies were sacrificing men in these attacks and counter-attacks and impairing the effectiveness of their armies. At first, the Turkish strategists were confident that the massing of their divisions and their superior firepower would carry the day; but as the battle wore on they realized that they too were taking on massive losses.

There were waves of men who took heavy fire and losses. The fallen dead just seemed to melt into the earth. Then a second wave of Greek soldiers charged forward and under heavy fire they too seemed to whither and disappear into the earth, and then a third wave of men merged into the remnants of the first and second, and after a while the fourth blundered into the remains of the others.

Greek officers and the Sergeant came running forward to 'head off' the charging Greek soldiers. They were shouting: "Stop and retreat to our forward tranches. The charging Greek soldiers followed their orders reluctantly.

The Turkish soldiers and their reserves stopped firing and were reorganizing their positions. They were replacing their dead and wounded.

The fighting stopped. It was time for burials. The burial squads went to work. Peter and Pavlos were handed masks to offset the stench of bodies rotting in the heat, gloves to protect them from diseases and butcher aprons to keep their uniforms from soiling from the profusions of blood from the dead men being thrown on the carts.

Peter was fascinated by a Greek priest who seemed to come out of the night; out of 'no-where'. He was dressed in a long, black robe which accentuated his long white beard. Peter watched as he moved from cart to cart giving the men their last rites and forgiving them for their sins. He was captivated by the sight of the priest kissing the bloody mangled bodies and thanking them for their sacrifice for the Greek people.

The thought of kissing all the bodies of these crushed heroes made Peter a little ill, but a 'heart-felt' jolt and a reassuring thought suddenly overwhelmed him. Everything he had been told about humanity being spirit and flesh was true. The pieces of body before him were nothing without the departed spirits. There was a refreshing revelation of hope and a next life in the darkness of death for everyone.

Peter and Pavlos and some of the other soldiers from the burial squads were getting 'spooked' by this old priest and what he was doing with the dead bodies. The old priest seemed to be a spirit from another world and time.

Peter whispered; "He seems to be an illusion. Where are all these poor souls going?" Pavlos whispered back; "There is a strangeness to this moment and this scene. The priest seems to be caught in a time warp. Time doesn't seem to exist. There is no beginning or end and the present, the past and the future exist at the same time and he seems to be able to move through all of them."

"Ah, you poets with your wild imaginings. I don't know about all that, but one thing is clear to me. This present moment exists and it is full of heartbreak, full of pain, full of sorrow and madness."

They heard chatter and were surprised to see the Sergeant talking to the good father. After they were done, he came over and told them that the Father Pious and some villagers came to help us with the burials. He ordered them to keep taking the bodies off the battlefield and bring them over to Father Pious and the villagers for burial.

The only words he had for them was; "Where is Steve?"

Both Peter and Pavlos shrugged their shoulders and said' "We don't know." They quickly left the Sergeant to be by himself.

PASSAGE IX

WHY GOD, WHY?
WHY ALL THE MADNESS?

Chorus Foreword

The poem below is a tearful look at the great tragedy of war. Ibn Arabi, the great Sufi poet, wrote following poem. It is one of his poems of tragic themes: "At the End of the war where are those we love?"

"Of all the army that set out, how few
Survived the Way; of the great retinue
A handful lived until the voyage was done –
of every thousand there remained but one.

Of many who set out no trace was found
Some deep within the ocean's depths were drowned;
Some died on mountaintops; some died of heat;
Some flew too close to the sun in their conceit,
Their hearts on fire with love – too late they learned
Their folly when their wings and feathers burned;

Some met their death between the lion's claws,
And some were ripped to death by monster's jaws;
Some died of thirst; some hunger sent insane,
Till suicide released them from their pain;
Some became weak and could no longer fly

(They faltered, fainted, and were left to die);

Some paused bewildered and then turned aside
To gaze at marvels as if stupefied,
Some looked for pleasure's path and soon confessed
They saw no purpose in the pilgrim's quest;
Not one in a thousand souls arrived –
In every hundred thousand one survived."

This poem describes the plight of warriors who suffer the trauma of war and all its horrors. Many of them are brought so far down by their grief that they become like dead men. In the Greek tradition, defiling one's head with dust is a sign that the anguish of war is unbearable and that death on the battlefield is horrifying. It is a pain so excruciating that it needs voicing, so gruesome that it must find expression, so primitive that it must throw itself back to an original source.

These warriors are immersed in the horrors of war where life or death decisions have to be made. The ancient Greek writers justified the carnage of war in poetic terms. The warriors who experience the horrors and tragedies of the battlefield know they cannot be justified through poetry. While poetry may elevate, it cannot make the pain bearable and those that suffer war are never the same.

The Intelligence Report II: Psychological Warfare

Homer's painful description of warfare:

"There — head falls forward, fatigued at evening,
and dreams of home,

PASSAGE IX 295

Spread of welcome, waving from windows,
Kissing of wife under single sheet:
But waking sees bird flocks nameless to him"

"Tears are not enough praise." A Greek proverb praising the bravery of their men in battle.

Peter and Pavlos were drinking their early morning coffee when the Sergeant came over to them and asked; "Where is Steve?" They gave the same answer; "We don't know." Peter added the thought; "Maybe he was on one of those carts?" That possibility seemed to satisfy him.

The Sergeant said; "Peter, I have news for you. The Greek navy and their marines had taking action to free Lesbos of Turkish rule. I was in the Field Office when I heard that while the ground battles were raging, the Greek navy was controlling the seas. On 8 November 1912, the Greek navy led by Admiral Koundouriotis occupied Mytilene harbor and political and administration was assumed by naval officer Koklos Melas. On December 6th the Battle of Klapados liberated Lesbos and it united with Greece.

He went on to say we will have another Intelligence Report today. Make sure that you are both there. This Report is the start of our new 'psychological warfare.' We are going to play with the minds of the Turkish soldiers. The goal is to depress the Turkish soldiers and ruin their morale. We are going to make sure that the Turks hear this report. It is a report that is truthful. The next reports will be full of half-truths. The goal is to mislead, discourage and get control of their belief systems so that they make mistakes and be less willing to risk their lives for a losing cause.

Peter and Pavlos were interested in seeing this new form

of warfare in action. They enjoyed the thought of Turkish mind control and were hoping that it worked.

The Field Commander broadcast his Report to the Greek soldiers in a way that the Turkish soldiers could hear it. He began:

"The strategies conceived and employed by King Constantine of Greece, who had studied at the Berlin Military Academy, were brilliant and had the Turkish soldiers on the run. Under his able leadership, the Greek army had faced overwhelming odds and overcame the invincible Ottoman force with courage, valor and great sacrifices of life.

There is a strangeness of destiny at work. Constantine married Sophia, the sister of Kaiser Wilhelm of Prussia and was identified with Germany. The oddness is that Germany supported the Ottoman Empire and Greece was being led by a member of the German royal family.

Life is so full of unknowns and contradictions. The Greek people hated the appointment of a King to rule them and they hated the Great European Powers for putting a king, one of their own, to rule them. Yet, that King was able to provide military leadership and emerged as a hero of the war against the Turks. Another contradiction: He was married to the sister of Kaiser Wilhelm of Prussia. Germany was supporting the Ottoman Turks. Was there a larger scheme to life? Was he sent by some higher power to lead?

The capture of Thessaloniki proved to be a crucial achievement. The pacts of the Balkan League had provided that in the forthcoming war against the Ottoman Empire, the four Balkan allies would provisionally hold any ground they took from the Turks, without contest from the other allies. Once an armistice was declared, then the facts on the ground would be the starting point of negotiations for the final drawing of the new borders in a forthcoming peace treaty. With the vital port firmly in Greek hands, all the other allies could hope for was a customs-free dock in the harbor.

In the meantime, operations in the Epirus front had stalled. Against the rough terrain and Ottoman fortifications at Bizani, the small Greek force could not make any headway. With operations in Macedonia complete, Constantine transferred the bulk of his forces to Epirus, and assumed command. After lengthy preparations, the Greeks broke through the Turkish defenses in the Battle of Bizani and captured Ioannina and most of Epirus up into what is today southern Albania (Northern Epirus). These victories dispelled the tarnish of the 1897 defeat, and raised Constantine to great popularity with the Greek people."

The Field Commander, inspired by the Greek victories in other sectors of the war, ordered his troops to attack the Turkish positions. He told his Field Officers that the objective was still the same. Put enough pressure on their [position to hold their precious reserves in place.

Wave after wave of Greek men attacked the Turkish positions, but they were driven back time and time again. Pavlos was in a reserve unit that was ordered to move forward and be the next wave of men to launch a suicide charge against the Turkish lines. During their attack, the Turkish soldiers made a surprise counter charge and the two armies met in the middle of a frenzied battlefield in hand to hand combat. The Greeks army took the onslaught and started to retreat slowly.

Peter was with the rear-guard troops who were ordered to shoot anyone leaving the battlefield. They were told to shoot to kill and spare no one. The discipline of the force had to be maintained at all costs for the safety of all and the victory that was at hand if they resisted this last gasp onslaught. Peter raised his rifle as ordered, but he could not bring himself to shoot his own men. He was shooting over the heads of the fleeing men, appearing to comply with orders; but not able to be an executioner of his countrymen.

The attacks against the Turkish lines were faltering. As a last resort, the battle-tested Klephts were called up from the rear and rushed to the center of the battle. After a ferocious battle, the Turkish onslaught was stopped and they retreated back to their positions with heads bloodied and bowed. They would not be able to launch another counter attack that day without new reinforcements. Both sides could not give anything more that day and they retreated to their safety zones for a rest before tomorrow battles.

And then the key refrain for all these unknown soldiers: "save me from hostile capture, from the sudden tiger's leap at the corner." The soldiers rested that evening and the lucky ones dreamed of home and their loved ones. Tomorrow, the fighting between the two great armies would begin anew and more brave men would die for family, country, cause and freedom. There are fragments of a poem written by Pablo Neruda entitled: *'Nothing but Death'* that describes the moment. It tells how Death desperately throws itself at human loss and cries silently in the presence of the losses:

"There are cemeteries that are lonely, graves full of bones that do not make a sound,
The heart moving through a tunnel, in it darkness, darkness, darkness,
Like a shipwreck we die going into ourselves, as though we were drowning inside our hearts, as though we lived falling out of

the skin into the soul.

And there are corpses, feet made of cold and sticky clay, death is inside the bones,
Like a barking where there are no dogs, coming out from bells somewhere,
from graves somewhere, growing in the damp air like tears or rain.

Death is inside the folding cots, its spends its life sleeping on the slow mattresses,
In the black blankets, and suddenly breathes out: it blows out a mournful sound that swells the sheets."

Somewhere deep inside, all soldiers cry silently about the deaths of their comrades and, surprisingly, even the losses suffered by their enemies. They know that Death waits for them and will come in the red-soaked dawn of morning's light.

In wartime, after the great battle, killings and slaughters, the spirit of Death comes like a thief in the night felt, but unseen and unknown and then is gone with the light of the day leaving only a corpse behind as proof that there was once a man who lived, but who lives no more. There are cemeteries and graves overflowing with all the lonely souls that fell in battle and were no more.

THE HISTORIC RECORD

The Historic Record shows that war had changed from ancient times when great words were written about the exploits and bravery of soldiers.

"The world wept at the bravery of Homer's soldiers and hailed the decision of Hector who loved honor more than love and life."

War was now a mass confrontation between large armies and suicidal charges of armored infantry. They moved forward slowly, row upon row of men, attired in faded green uniforms with tiny insignias and the clunking noise of tanks moving forward as monstrous killing machines.

Peter and his new companion Pavlos were going through their early morning ritual of drinking coffee and talking about whatever. The Sergeant knowing where to find them came up to them and joyously tormented them with the same question; "Where is your friend Steve?"

After their usual 'eye –rolls' they gave him; "We don't know."

He said, "I'll tell you where he is. The little shit deserted. He's gone."

Peter asked; "How do you know that?"

With a pretend scowl on his face, the Sergeant explained; "There were three of them who deserted. We caught one of them last night and he squealed on them. Seems they split up and they headed in different directions. Steve is still out there on the loose."

Pavlos asked; "What did you do to the one you caught?" The Sergeant mumbled; "He is no more. The Field Commander ordered the firing squad. It is an honorable form of death. Peter you are assigned to the search team and Pavlos you take his position on the back line."

Peter asked; "Why me? He's my friend."

"You'll be in a squad, so you will have no decision-making power. No responsibility for what happens. The Field Commander will decide what we do with him."

The Sergeant sensed some animosity, He changed the subject. He was smiling when he told Peter and Pavlos about the soldiers from Crete who defeated a major force of Turkish soldiers. He said; "It was incredible. A small contingent of soldiers from Crete dressed in their traditional black fighting clothes and their high tied boots and headbands attacked the Turkish troops.

The Cretan soldiers prove themselves to be fierce fighters in their struggles to free Crete from Turkish control. The very superstitious Turkish soldiers saw all these men dressed in black from head-to-toe and they must have thought they were ghostly apparitions. The Turkish soldiers all fled from the battlefield."

The sergeant added' "Their loyalty is to Prime Minister Venizelos, who put together the Balkan alliance. His strategy is working and the Turkish Empire is slowly collapsing under the pressure of having to defend multiple fronts. The Greek navy also played a pivotal role in troop movement and the blockades of Turkish and muslin ports. That plus freezing Turkish reserves made the Turkish army immobile and susceptible to wide sweeps on their flanks.

He also let loose other cultural groups who wanted to take revenge on the muslins for their past atrocities. The Turkish army and their muslin allies are crumbling under the pressures."

Peter asked; "How do you know all this?"

The Sergeant said; "Yesterday, the Field Commander brief the officers and sergeants. He told us that it was payback time for the Turks and Muslins armies. For centuries they abused the Christians and the Jews. The Greek army let volunteer militias bring up the rear of the liberation army. They are fighters from different parts of Greece that immigrated to Greece over the centuries." The Sergeant left them after saying more than he should have.

——— Author's Footnote ———

The Historical Record shows that prominent among these militia groups were the Greek Jews. They first arrived in Greece in large numbers as far back as 600 B.C.E., after they were expelled from Babylon. It is said that the ancient Greeks were intrigued by the new settlers and quickly learned and, to some extent, adopted Jewish lore and writings."

A second wave of Jewish refugees, fleeing the Maccabean wars, found safe harbor in Greece. Other waves of Jewish refugees followed and large communities of Jews lived in Athens, Crete, Corinth and Thessaloniki and along the coast of Asia Minor, on Rhodes and in the Aegean Islands.

The Muslims defined Christians and Jews equally as "people of the book" and as the Ottoman Empire started to crumble and the Greeks pressed forward with their struggle for independence, the Jews of Greece joined the fight for independence.

In the early days of fighting, almost all the Jewish communities of the Peloponnesus were destroyed. A number of the Romaniote Jews of Ioannina, Greece, many of whom spoke Greek joined the Greek army during the Balkan Wars and fought side-by-side with their Greek country men. The Greek Jews proved their valor in Greece's wars against the Ottoman Empire and their Muslim allies and they too were greeted that day in Salonika with roses.

The Greek Jews were a formidable community in the melting pot of people called Greece. They fought 'side-by-side' with the Greeks in their struggles for independence from the oppressive rule by the Ottoman Turks.

The Greek armies pursued the rest of the Turkish army and their muslin allies across the border and liberated Salonika. Marching into the city on the feast day of its patron saint, Demetrious, they were pelted with roses by delirious Greek crowds in the streets. Leading the liberating Greek army were King Constantine's regular Greek army dressed in classic heavy green uniforms soiled with the blood and dirt of their battles. Greece had an army built up with Greek nationals and others that came from America to fight for Greece's freedom.

The relationship between the Greeks and Jews lasted for centuries. When Mussolini invaded Greece, the Jewish community supported the Greek defensive effort and sent six thousand young men to help defend the border and deter the Italians. It wasn't until the Germans invaded and took control of Greece that the Jewish community in Greece was decimated.

When Israel was formed, Greece was a staging area for the transport and migration of many Jews. The Greeks never turned on the Jews even under pressure from the German occupiers.

THE DARK PASSIONS OF FEAR

"The passions that move us are instances of divine possessions."
Greek Proverb

It was time for early morning coffee. Peter and Pavlos enjoyed each other's company and found a remote tree to sit under and talk about the usual things: Steve, the Sergeant, the war and where they were taking them.

Peter said; "Steve belongs to another age before Alexander the Great and his iron discipline, tactics and strategy. Steve belongs to age when men could form a small groups of bandits and could go out and kill, rape. Pillage, destroy and then leave the group anytime they want.

Pavlos was anxious to tell Peter something. He whispered; "Peter, I've been thinking about you and Steve and I believe that you should not turn him in for sure death by a firing squad. I also think that if you find him you should both take off in the opposite direction and live the lives you were meant to live. The war is almost over. You serve your country with honor, you were and are 'under-age' and you should have the opportunity to live your destiny and achieve your life purpose."

Peter was moved by his words. They both reached out and hugged each other. They realized that it could be a forever goodbye.

As part of his early morning routine, the Sergeant came by and took supreme pleasure in harassing them. He said' "What the hell is wrong with you guys? Hugging each other on the battlefield. It is weird." Both Peter and Pavlos said; "Sir, mind your own damn business, sir." It was their first

PASSAGE IX 305

show of courage to put him in his place.

The Sergeant just smiled. He let it go; but he reminded Peter that he was assigned to the search party and he should be armed and ready to find his 'good - buddy' Steve. He has to answer for his cowardly act of desertion. He left smiling.

Pavlos said; "Peter, he's still a jerk. Don't pay attention to his little game of harassment. He gets us so angry so that we take our aggression out on the battlefield." Peter said; "I know his little games of harassing us and the pleasures he gets by doing so. It doesn't work anymore."

Peter left and went to his position on the back line. He was watching the battle taking place from his rear-guard position and was anxious to join his comrades fighting the Turks on the open battlefield. He was anxious, visibly distressed and helplessly watching all the carnage that was taking place before his eyes and all around him.

He heard the officers shouting, "For God and country" as they charged across the killing fields; many falling and making the ultimate sacrifice. He thought, "God has abandoned us and our country and he has forced us to give our lives as the price for freedom and peace."

He knew there was a need to free the Greek people and blood had to be shed as the price of that freedom. And were the generals and officers just doing their duty and making the hard decisions that were required? It was clear that all heroes have blood on their hands? Maybe they too are victims of a dire Fate. He was confused and felt so insignificant and helpless to change the chaos and violence of the battles that were taking place.

From his position on the back line, Peter was able to see the horrors and grief of the battlefield. He felt the agony of it, which was like a 'kick to his stomach and a knee to his groin. His heart ache for his comrades. It was a pain that was debilitating.

They knew without even being told that their fate was death by a firing squad. Peter could hear the cries of the night; those uttered and those of silence:

"The tear-socked ground gave out a sigh of wind that spewed itself in flame on a red sky,

and all my shattered senses left me. Blind, like one whom sleep comes over in a swoon,

I stumbled into the darkness and went down."

He couldn't conceive of medals given and poetic platitudes glorifying the battles and making the hell of war bearable. His only thought was that soldiers who suffer it are never the same again. They are shocked by the horrors of war and become like the dead men themselves. This happens over and over again throughout time and the images of war are always haunting and never forgotten. Nothing changes. Mankind is cursed.

The rear guards were ordered to shoot any deserter running from the battlefield. There was nothing Peter could do to help the flawed, tragic and luckless souls who were overcome with fear and deserted the battlefield. It occurred to him that he was the wrong man for a rear-guard position. He could not shoot a Greek soldier running from the battlefield.

He shot over the heads of the frightened men who were running for 'dear life'. The rear guards held their line, but once the fighting had stopped the rear guards were released from their positions and were ordered to track down the deserters and shoot them on sight or bring them back for execution.

The charge by the Turks had been stayed and the Sergeant came by and ordered Peter to join the search party. He ordered the search party to move out. The search was underway in all the hidden places in the small deserted villages near the battlefield, the cellars of half-standing buildings, abandoned small sheds, and all possible hidden places, nooks and crannies that were behind the battlefield.

The search parties formed naturally into several groups. A few men went alone as single hunters. Peter elected to go alone. Being with other hunters didn't feel right to him. He really didn't want to search for deserters and didn't know what he would do if he found one. It was best for him to be alone and have some freedom of choice and action.

Peter went in the different direction. He successfully made separation and was finally on his own. Fatigue was taking control of his body and mind and he was looking for a place to meditate and take a short nap. He saw a green patch and row of trees and went to them.

One tall tree attracted his attention and caused him to remember an old dream. It reminded him of Antigone's prayer tree in her back yard and the many quiet moments he shared with her under her tree. It was perfect location, remote and secluded, and a holy place where he could think about his situation, maybe meditate and release his cares go and rest his aching body. He felt safe under his 'newly adopted' prayer tree; laid down and let himself go into a peaceful and quiet sleep.

Peter usually had disjointed images in his rim sleep and most times could not remember what he even dreamed. He thought that if he even remembered any of the images or dreams, he would dream of Antigone; but if was Costas who inserted himself in Peter's reveries and he came to him in a 'giant form' holding a small shed in his hands.

He woke up, startled by the vision; but he was keenly aware of the shed that Costas was holding in his hand. Peter now knew that he had to find the small shed where Steve was probably hiding. He remembered his Yaya saying that the spirits come to you in your dreams and guide you along your destined path.

It was clear to him. He jumped up and started walking with a sense of direction and of purpose. He felt guided and his instinct was to go near the encampment not away from it. Steve was a scared little rabbit who wouldn't be able to go miles away. He would find the nearest hiding place to 'hunker down'. He was 'counter intuitive in his thinking and confusing to people.

After a long return walk and search, he saw a large field and felt compelled to go in that direction. At the far edge of the field, he saw a small shed, parts of which were still standing. He peered into the door. It was dark and he could not see clearly what was inside. He moved in slowly thinking if someone was there, he should be careful. He could be shot.

He went into the shed and could sense that there was a male presence inside; but he couldn't tell who and where he was. He said; "Show yourself." To his surprise, he heard a quiet whisper; "Peter, is that you?" He was stunned. It was Steve talking to him, "Peter, don't shoot. It's me Steve. Don't shoot me; I'm your friend, your brother."

Peter saw Steve pitifully huddled in the dark corner of the barn; he knew that he could not kill him. Peter was trapped. How could he be responsible for the death of his friend, someone he cared for, someone that war had made into a pathetic fearful creature? Peter felt like he was always forced to become involved with Steve's problems. He knew that he was trapped by his loyalty to his friend.

He put his rifle down and slowly sat down next to Steve. They hugged each other and Steve started to cry. Peter couldn't hold back his tears. These two young souls were tormented by the chaos of their lives and their dire circumstances. They were trapped. Peter knew that there was no way that they could escape and there was no way that they could go back. It would be certain death for Steve. They had passed the 'point of no return'.

THE WAILING WALL

The military achieves discipline by a 'mind control' process known as 'mass transformation'. It is a way of controlling their beliefs, their thinking and their reactions in certain circumstances. It is a form of hypnosis where raw recruits are trained to think as one. Instilled in them is 'blind obedience' and a willingness to die for a cause.

"*Why do you tear me from myself? Ovid*

Mankind eventually finds out that we are born flawed and many lives are destined to be tragic. Life teaches us that the pains we inflict upon ourselves, hurt the most."

Peter was dealing with a number of 'heart-wrenching' issues and decisions that he needed to make. His issues were complex and his choices painful. The harsh realities were clear. Loyalty to the military code of conduct or loyalty to his friend Steve.

He was plagued by one ominous thought after another. He was being torn apart by these ominous thoughts. Everything had come down to a struggle to survive and to save his friend. He was tormented by the thought that he was helping a deserter. And yet, that deserter was his friend and a terrified and helpless soul.

The question of honor was 'gut-wrenching' for him. The respect and love he had for Costa and the other men who paid the ultimate price made his decision even more difficult. He loved Costas the old man who guided them, protected them and fought by their side. He cared for Pavlos, the young poet, and even cared for the Sergeant. He cried for the young men who gave their lives to their country. Deserting was disrespect for their sacrifices and their memories. And what of the ancient Greeks and his much-loved ancestors? Peter's heart hurt trying to determine what was the right thing to do. He didn't want to betray their memory.

He understood what the military had to do. He even agreed with what they were doing. It went back to Alexander the Great and how he transformed a group of raw recruits into a disciplined fighting force. He perfected the technique of mass transformation and uniting a diverse group of men think as one. They were convinced that all their 'free floating troubles' had one solution – to destroy the enemy. Held together by the 'iron fist of discipline. He loved the brave young men who gave their lives for freedom.

Peter had the feeling that they were not really in control. What was in control was the unyielding and inextinguishable torment of man trying to survive by defying the terrifying power and darkness of the spiritual forces above, within and all around them. He wondered if destiny was just a form of spiritual control.

The problem of what to do was not complicated for Steve. It was simple. He ran to save his life. As to the matter of personal honor, he believed that: "Honor has no worth, if the trade for it was his life."

Peter knew that they were cornered. He couldn't reconcile what was irreconcilable. He couldn't bring himself to comply with military law and be an important cause in Steve's death. A fellow Greek— for what? It was all madness.

Steve was getting nervous with Peter's silent deliberations. He said, "Peter, this is all madness. Everyone has a rifle and is running around in circles shooting at each other and at everybody. Peter now they want you to stay at the back lines and kill Greek soldiers. They want you to track down us and bring me back to be killed. What is so glorious about that? You won't be killing Turks. Is that what you want to be – a killer of Greeks?"

Peter answered, "I know all that. It is painful to think about it." Then more silence.

Peter's silence was too much for Steve. He was panicky and only a positive answer would take his pain away; "Are you really serious about taking me back? They'll kill me on the spot. What the hell are we eve n doing here? Our uniforms are three sizes too big. We stink. I haven't had a shower since we left Istanbul. Where is the glory in war? I've got vermin crawling in my hair and all over my body. I can't tell you how many times I shit my pants."

Peter couldn't hold back a laugh over the thought of Steve shitting his pants from fear. Steve relaxed for a moment and he too was smiling. Then Steve got serious again and asked, "Don't tell me you are thinking about God and the after-life? Look up at the sky and tell me what you see."

He answered, "Vultures, birds and who knows what else." Steve said, "I'll tell you what happened to me. I saw myself lying dead and these vultures eating me. I ran. I got the hell out of there. Who cares what the military thinks about me." Peter was quiet again. He wondered; "What the hell is going on? What is life all about? Everything is mired in madness." Are we living in a hell on earth?"

He remembered an old Greek saying which served as a guide to making the right decision in complex situations. The Greeks say: "Look in the mirror and decide what you want to see." Peter was looking into the mirror of life and he had to decide what to do and what he wanted to see. His eyes only saw two simple helpless young men who were trapped by the circumstances of their lives.

Steve kept pestering him for an answer. Peter proposed a solution; "Why don't we split up and you escape and I go back." Steve was quick with an answer; "You will be feeding me to the vultures. I can't make it alone. I don't know what to do, where to go and how to get there. You've got to help me get out of this."

Peter told Steve; "Let's take a short nap and maybe we'll come up with a solution." Before he fell asleep, Peter recalled the short Greek prayer that he heard his mother say many times: "Kyrie Eleison" (Lord have mercy) and now he understood the meaning and beauty of that short, but powerful prayer.

THE POINT OF NO RETURN

Antigone's whispers: There is a quotation from a gospel that the 'word or thought must be aligned with one's emotion, passion and belief' and that can be a guide to what the right course of action should be.

Passage IX

Follow your heart: *"Be unafraid and adhere to divine law. Know that God will always be forgiving."*

Peter was tossing and turning in a 'rim sleep' state of confusion. He could hear whispers in his semi-sleep. It was Antigone's voice softly saying; "Obey divine law; not military law. Protect the goodness of your being – your soul." Her voice was like an echo from a distant past. A sweet soul.

Other broken images came to him and added to his rim sleep confusion. It was his Yaya. There was no stopping her. His grandmother was pushing her way into his vulnerable semi-awareness. It was a repeat of an old warning 'be careful' with him.

"Be careful. Steve is a trickster, a Hermes. Keep your guard up when you are with him. He cannot be trusted. The hymn of Hermes describes this type of person as one 'of many shifts', blandly cunning, a robber, a cattle driver, a bringer of dreams, a watcher by night and a thief at the gate. He is a creature of great appetites and must always satisfy his hunger at somebody else's expense."

Peter forced himself to get up. He had enough indecision, enough trauma and enough 'tossing and turning'. He just wanted to sleep peacefully. But deep inside, he knew what it was what was bothering him. He knew that a decision had to be made about Steve. He remembered that divine law starts with a basic premise which was 'to follow your heart' when making a decision. But, that's not he was. He was a 'follow your head and your heart' guy and he believed that kind of thinking will take you where you should go.

He knew that this was a 'life-defining' decision. A decision made in a Kairos moment, a decision made in spiritual time and made with Kleos overtones. There was no real choice for Peter. He knew he had one rule and that was he would not kill a Greek or, in Steve's situation, not be forced to be responsible for his death. It was clear. He was feeling like his humanity was at stake. His intuition was telling him that 'being a Greek' was more important than the great intangible, the lofty military code of honor and duty. Following military law blindly didn't make any sense to him.

Peter really wanted to stay and fight for his country. He was involved in the fight that stopped the Turkish advances and it was rumored that the Turkish government was getting ready to surrender. He wanted to be on the front lines when that happened. He wanted to be there for the final battles and celebrate Greece's victory with his comrades.

All of that joyously imagined, he made his decision. He chose to protect Steve. He would not be forced by military law to be responsible for the death of his friend, another Greek. Killing fellow Greeks was not what he was about. The love of his comrades and saving his friend's life was who he was and how he wanted to define himself. He would not betray his Greek spirit and he would not let himself be a pawn and a victim and turn his friend over to a military firing squad.

He would have to desert to help Steve. So, he let his temper take over. Peter became Peter; "What the hell am I thinking about? If the price is disobeying a military order; then so be it. If the price is to die by a firing squad, then so be it." That was Peter's truth. It will be what it's going to be. Who the hell cares? If the military kills us, we have a long sleep without any dreams or, if the ancient Greeks are right we will have a new life through reincarnation. I'm okay with either one."

Peter made a courageous decision. He would help Steve. It was the honorable thing to do and it was consistent with a loyalty to humanity and divine law. He had passed 'the point of no return' by sealing his fate with Steve's. He said to himself; "We started this damn journey together and we will complete it or end it together."

He was 'good' with his decision and now able to fall back to sleep. They both took a long nap waiting for nightfall to escape. Sleep lifted the weight of his concerns. Time quickly brought the nightfall and reality back. He looked across at Steve and both of them reluctantly rose and got ready to face a new world. They were leaving the shed when Peter was overwhelmed by the immensity of the moment. It was a dash against death.

He sensed 'the magnitude of his decision which the silence of his sleep concealed.' He would not see the world again as before.

At the peak of the night under its star lights, they made their move. There didn't seem to be any viable escape for them; but they had to try and escape. The options were slim or none:

"If they went east, they would be back to the front lines and would fall into the hands of the Turks – not a good choice. North would bring them to the fighting between the joint forces of the Serbs and Bulgarians fighting a large Turkish army across a wide front. West was into Albania which was still in Turkish hands and a very dangerous place with well protected borders. South was deeper into Greece which seemed to be their only hope. They had to merge into the countryside away from the fighting."

It was 'pitch-black' as they moved quietly from the shed into the field. They moved quickly across the open fields and tried to cover as much distance as they could. They had to make it to a safe area before daylight and discovery. The pathway was uncertain. Fear propelled them. They fought to overcome the fatigue of their bodies, their aching feet and heavy legs, the thirst of their parched throats and their sickened stomachs empty by hunger.

They saw a patrol at the edge of their field and they ducked and waited until they passed. Then they raced past the road into another field. They went from field to field; this seemed to work. It was their only hope. They successfully repeated it over and over again. Would their luck hold up? Could they last until daybreak? They were breathing easier and started to feel that God was going to spare them.

They crouched over and were making their way carefully across a large open field when, suddenly, they heard men yelling and shots being fired. They saw a big man – he looked like an officer or sergeant, some kind of commissioned officer - running up the road with several soldiers running behind and firing at him. He went down. Peter and Steve moved away quickly hoping not to be noticed. But such was not to be the case, they were spotted by one of the soldiers and a group of them took off in the direction of Peter and Steve.

They rolled down a small hill and ducked into a heavily wooded area. They were deathly still listening for the slightest movement and sounds. Then, there was the silent whispering of soldiers. Peter and Steve couldn't catch their breath; there wasn't enough oxygen and they shook and trembled with fear. Their breathing was heavy; it seemed loud and every movement that they made was blasting in their minds. They were trapped; their worst nightmare had come true.

It wasn't long before they were discovered by four soldiers. They surrounded Peter and Steve and pointed their guns at them. Peter and Steve had their guns raised and aimed at them. Peter just shook his head. Here he was pointing his gun at Greek soldiers again. He wondered why it was that he found himself in that horrible predicament again. It was a 'stand-off'.

One of soldiers asked, "Peter, what the hell are you doing here?" Peter responded, "I couldn't bring my friend back to a firing squad." Two of them saluted, nodded their heads slightly as a sign of respect, and said; "Yes, we understand." Peter put his hand on the barrel of Steve's gun and pushed it down slowly. They both placed their rifles down on the ground. No explanations, no excuses, no stories, no justification, no reasons could be given for being where they were. It was over.

They led Peter and Steve through the clearing to the road. A large man, a noncommissioned officer named Andros, was chained with his hands behind his back. Peter and Steve were chained to him. All three of them were marched down the road to meet their apparent fate. Steve was lost, confused, sobbing and Peter was resigned to his fate. Andros was quiet.

They were marched into a small "war torn" town and ended up in a bullet-battered jail located at the outskirts of town. The three of them ended up in the same cell, chained to a stone wall. It wasn't long before they were delirious with hunger and thirst and had descended into their own personal hell. All the while, they could hear shooting and the background noise of the battles taking place. It was over for them. They were 'chain-linked to their Fate, a wailing wall of no return.'

Peter put his arm on Steve's shoulder and looked into his eyes. He told Steve that before his father left for America to work on the railroad, his father told him that he should always be brave in life. He should not be scared of death. If you die, you sleep in eternity or be given another life.

Steve was holding back a tear when he said; "Thanks Peter, that helps."

A SPIRITUAL REVEAL

"Capture and execution by a firing squad, sometimes called fusillading (from the French fusil, rifle) is a method of capital punishment, particularly common in the military and in times of war."

Desertions are fueled by the sight of men 'butchering' men in the senseless carnage of war. It was terrifying what ordinary people could be trained to do. Those nameless men and boys would never see the light of day again or feel the tender heat of the sun's life-giving rays; nor would they ever feel the tender caress of their loved ones again. They had lost the most precious thing of all and there was nothing left. Their bodies were thrown on a mule wagon and buried in the cold, black earth — in the field of military honor.

They were trapped in the lonely cell of regrets and tears. It is the place where military sinners have to wait for death and begin to feel the black earth cover them. It is a place where 'disobedience turns to pain' for all eternity. They were sentenced to a cell that had the smell of countless prisoners. The jailer told them the cell is commonly known as the waiting room of Hell.

He remembered being told in training camp how deserters are treated. To instill discipline and to frighten them, they were told how fusillade works. The instructor told them that a firing squad is normally composed of several soldiers who are instructed to fire simultaneously, thus preventing both disruption of the process by a single member and identification of the member who fired the lethal shot. The prisoner is typically blindfolded or hooded, as well as restrained, although in some cases prisoners have asked to be allowed to face the firing squad without their eyes covered. Executions can be carried out with the condemned either standing or sitting.

The agony of men dying and the pathos of the moment is described in a fragment taken from a poem by the poetess Ioanna Tsatos:

"At the peak of the night under its lights
Man facing his God
Man facing his hangman.
The groans in that cell a nightmare.
The depth of this moment
I sense it the horrible happening
Which silence conceals.
I shall not see the world again as before."

Peter believed in the obvious. That death is final and beyond recall and that there are no meaningful words to describe it. He remembered the training instructor in boot camp saying that death by a firing squad is a soldier's death and not a criminal's death. Therefore, it is considered a honorable way of dying. None of that made any sense to Peter.

The TI or training instructor also told them that there is a tradition in some jurisdictions that such executions are carried out at first light or at sunrise. This gave rise to the phrase "shot at dawn". Once blindfolded and in front of the firing squad, prisoners have surrendered all hope. In Dante words: "And in their blind and un-attaining state their miserable lives have sunk so low that they must envy every other fate."

Some things never change. Steve was sobbing. His agony was that night time would soon be over and the early morning light will come and they will take him away.

Andros started screaming obscenities at everybody. Peter told him to maintain his dignity, "You cannot change your life and your fate. Try as much as you can not to degrade it." He told him, "No one wants to listen to your rantings before he most die. You are screaming for yourself. Your mouth is four inches from your ears; you don't have to scream so loud to hear yourself."

It was to no avail. Peter yelled, "Let us have our last moments. Must we listen only to you and go to our graves with only your pain and not our own?" Andros calm down. He asked: 'What crime did I commit that I must pay with my life? Before God, I ask is it not my first obligation to care and protect my family? Why was I forced to kill young men and other fathers? I only want to return to my family and my little children and care for them. For that, I must forfeit my life and their safety."

"Andros, we all have our pain to deal with and we are about to die with you. In your mind go to your love ones. Be with them. Don't spend your time screaming through the night in a jail cell. Be with them in thought and prayer during your last moments."

The tactic seemed to work. Andros quieted down. Once Andros was still, Steve stopped crying. He asked, "Do you think that there is life after death?" Andros answered, "The ancient Greeks said that the Elysian Fields was the final resting place for the souls of heroes and virtuous men; but I guess that leaves us out of there." Peter contributed the thought, "The priests at the Greek Orthodox Church preach the concept of heaven and hell." Steve added his thoughts to the dialogue, "I want to go to Heaven; but I don't want to die to go there. I'm scared to die; but life is too hard. It is unreal, unjust."

Andros was quiet for a moment and then said; "The ancient Greeks believed that everything is spiritual and that we are eternal. My wife and I believed that we are soul mates and that we will be together for all eternity. She used to recite a little poem she wrote about our connection through all eternity. It went something like this:

"If you came to me with a face that I have not seen and with a voice that I have never heard; I would still know you. Even if centuries separated us,, I would still remember and feel you. Somewhere between the sand and the sky, through every creation, there's a pulse that echoes and connects us. When we leave this world, love is the only thing we take with us from one life to the next. It is the memory of our hearts."

The thought that he would see his wife, his soul mate, again made him calm down. It was almost daybreak. Andros was quiet. He had made his peace with himself and with God. He was resigned to his fate. Two guards came and as he was led out of the cell.

Yet, he was still bitter; but he went without emotion, in dignity and faced his death as a man. Peter believed that Andros would die a hero's death bearing forever his tragic and unbearable pain over the safety of his wife and his children.

Peter had a different thought about what was in store for all of them. His view was that; "Our deaths will be a long sleep and a forgetting. There is nothing more - no judgment and there is no punishment. He was now at his 'tipping point' and was resigned to his fate, His attitude: "To hell with it all".

Two soldiers came and Andros was led to an adjoining cell for his final confession. Steve started to talk and Peter told him to be quiet and listen to what was being said. They heard Andros making his final confession and when it was over he asked the priest, "Do you think that there is life after death?" The answer he got was a surprising one. The priest quoted a passage from the Book of Ecclesiastes about the cycles of time:

"For everything its season, and for every activity under heaven its time: a time to be born and a time to die....whatever is has been already, and whatever is to come has been already—-and God summons each event back in its turn."

Peter heard Andros ask; "What does that mean? Do I have another life after they kill me?" The priest gave him a guarded answer, "Although it is not taught by our religion, it is my personal belief that there are spiritual cycles of death and rebirth. There is a discussion in the ancient texts that says 'The soul has neither a beginning nor an end'. I believe that you will be spiritually restored. Take heart, there is life after death."

He sounded relieved as he thanked the priest for his words. He told the soldiers that he was ready. Peter could hear him being led outside before a firing squad and after a few moments, shots were heard. Andros was no more.

While this was happening, Peter looked up into a round opening in the roof of the jail cell and saw some of those things of beauty that Heaven bears. He hoped that there was a God and that Andros witnessed the same rising golden dawn, the deep blue of the sky and the shinning glory of Heaven as he ascended. Peter hoped that life was not over for him. He hoped that he found his peace and his Maker and was safe in His arms.

He looked up again. In a silent prayer, he asked to be saved. Peter had finally reached out to God for salvation.

THE ETERNITY OF THE MOMENT

"There is a life that is higher than the measure of humanity: men will live that is higher than the measure of humanity: men will live it not by the measure of their humanity; but by something in them that is divine. We ought not to listen tp those who exhort who exhort a man tp keep to a man's thoughts, but to live according to the highest thing that is in him, but small though it be, in power and worth it is far above the rest." Aristotle

A Greek proverb. The Spark of Divinity: *"A divine spark connects our souls."*

After they took Andros out, Steve was fearful. He said, "Peter I'm scared of dying. Do you think that there is another life after this one?" Peter answered, "Look at this way. It is either a long sleep or we get to do this over again. Either way, it's good." Steve wouldn't be cut off. He persisted. His fears were driving his need to know. "Do you think that the shots will hurt a lot? How long will it be before we die?" Peter answered, "No one alive can answer your questions. I guess that it will only hurt for a split second. Then it's over."

Steve couldn't help himself and he continued to ask more questions; but there was no way Peter could help him. Steve asked again, "Do you think about what is going to happen to us?" Peter said, "I don't stay in the moment. I go the port area of Plomari and watch the waves, the seagulls diving to catch the small fish and the boats coming and going into the port. It makes me peaceful, 'kind-of' happy."

Everything went quiet. Sounding a little panic, Steve said, "We're like small fish, aren't we?" Peter didn't answer. Steve spoke again, "There really is no hope for us. Is there?" Peter thought about it and said, "Not really." Steve asked, "Are you going to pray?" Peter said, "Yes, I have been – a little." Peter was getting annoyed with Steve, but he knew that he was in pain and he let him rattle on with his 'trying to feel good about something' questions.

And then it was time for Peter to go. The security guards came to their cell and unlocked Peter's chains. Steve was yelling, "Peter I love you like a brother. I am so sorry that I caused all this. Goodbye. I'll see you on the other side." Peter waved goodbye. He was caught up in his own emotions and couldn't manage any words of goodbye.

The security guards took him to a cell they called the waiting room. Peter asked; "Waiting for what?" A security guard was laughing when he said; "For death to come." Before they left, the soldiers told him that he had his last moments for himself and that a priest would join him to hear his last confession.

Peter was having a difficult time getting his head around what was happening to him. It was hard for him to believe that he was at his 'end time' and so early in life. He did what always worked for him in times of stress or contemplation, he escaped to the Plomari port and visualized the 'wine dark' sea, the ships coming and going and the seagulls and other birds flying high and free.

Once he visualized the port and the activity at the port; his fear left him, his depression lifted, his 'food and thirst' dizziness eased and a magical wonderment took possession of him. He felt clean and free. He accepted his fate and let go of his fear, pain and anger. He was no longer heavy with remorse, he made his peace with the world and he was ready to leave it. He had cried. He had prayed. He was no longer afraid of death.

With that burden lifted, he started to reminisce about old times and sweet times. "I have lived a good life; short though it may be. I had a wonderful childhood and a loving family. I had many happy times, sad and even crazy moments, all at same time. I sang songs. I danced when I was sad. I danced when I was happy. I loved a beautiful woman who took me to her heart. Anything more is just going to be a repeat performance of what my life has already been."

Peter enjoyed reminiscing. It was like being at the port. But then, the dreaded knock on the door came and a priest came into the cell. Peter was shocked to see him. It was Father Paris. When Father Paris saw Peter, he was aghast. "Peter, what are you doing here?" Peter said, "We ran away from the army. They caught Steve and me and brought us here."

"You're too young to even be in the army. What happened?" Peter started to tell him, but Father Paris cut him short and said, "Never mind. The fact is that you're too young to be in the army and that's what we have to deal with, before it's too late."

Father Paris left. After a dizzying, short time, he returned with a little bread and grape wine. Although it was not a

Holy Eucharist and a sacrament, it gave Peter some much needed nourishment. Father Paris said; "The word "Eucharist" means a "Thanks giving" and this ritual serves both a practical purpose as well a symbolic purpose.

After Peter finished drinking the grape wine, he watched Father Paris rise and quickly walk out of the room. Suddenly, Peter felt a bolt of hope go through him. His head and his heart surged with new energy. He said, "Father Paris, I don't understand what wars and all the killing is about." Father Paris answered, "We are meant to love and help each other. Not destroy each other. We are all cursed with 'original sin'. It is a 'tragic flaw'. The madness of war are crimes inflicting on ourselves. We have only ourselves to blame."

Father Paris left the cell and in just a few moments he could hear him yelling at the Sergeant. He was shouting, "We do not kill children, young boys before their time; before they can know what, they are doing, before they learn what is right from what is wrong and how to find God's way in this world." He could feel Father Paris determination and his power surge through him. He was arguing with the sergeant who was the grim reaper in charge of the firing squad.

The Sergeant was taking the position that there are no extenuating circumstances that can or must be considered. He said, "Desertion is the gravest of all battlefield violations. The lesson must be taught to all that a military order must always be obeyed without question." He was a soldier who was handicapped with an 'unthinking' mind that was encased in a military 'strait-jacket' of archaic beliefs. He believed that orders were inviolate and must be obeyed; otherwise, the army would have no coherence or direction, no backbone or discipline, no power or strength, no loyalty or allegiance and could not be counted on to complete assigned missions.

After talking and arguing with the Sergeant, Father Paris gave up on him. He went away thinking that the joy of executions has possessed that man and that the spirit of God and mercy had left him, leaving him hollow to the core. The sergeant was inflexible and getting belligerent with his remarks and his stance.

He asked Father Paris if he knew what the word 'Fusillading' meant. – Father Paris was silent. The Sergeant said, "It means 'death by a firing squad'; but here it means soldiers facing God through the barrel of a gun." Father Paris told the sergeant, "Do not do anything until I talk to your Lieutenant." Peter's hopes were dashed by the Sergeant's attitude. Father Paris left the Sergeant.

His hopes were quickly revived when Father Paris walked into his cell with a young lieutenant who immediately asked Peter how old he was. He was hesitant, but told the lieutenant that he was fourteen but had been ordered to say he was eighteen. There was another moment of hesitation. Should he say more? Yes, why not. He told the young officer that he was forced into the army and that he was ordered to always lie about his age. Peter was feeling some relief and he experienced a glimmer of hope in his mind and heart.

After hearing Peter's age and his story of forced conscription into the army, the young officer seemed clearly agitated. He walked out the cell and the jail and stood in the night air. He could hear the Officer and the Sergeant arguing and then complete silence. When the lieutenant returned, he put his hand on Peter's shoulder and told him, "You are free." Peter couldn't believe what was happening.

Peter told the lieutenant about Steve in the next cell. The young officer went into the building again and Peter could hear him ordering the Sergeant to free Steve. When Steve walked out of the building, he had a big grin on his face. Peter noticed that the tears had left his eyes. It immediately got a little confusing as everyone was talking at once. Peter felt like he was born again. He could hardly believe that they were free.

Once outside the small stone prison, Peter and Steve hugged Father Paris. Peter was at a loss for words. But Father Paris understood. He told him that words were not necessary. He said, "What we do is sometimes more than what we can say. There are times when words cannot be uttered as when the glory of Him moves into us and into all things. It gives value to each life and gives meaning to each moment of life. You haven't lived long enough, you are not ready to accept Him and you cannot go to Him as you are." He blessed them both.

Peter wondered, "Why God why does everything seem like it is madness? And yet, is there a purpose for everything and did God hear his silent heartfelt prayer in the cell block? Peter chose to believe that the decisions he made to comply with Divine law may have been a silent prayer. He was willing to die before he took the lives of Steve and his comrades. His honor was restored by the appearance and actions of Father Paris and the young officer. He now understood what Father Paris told him about the Spark of Divinity that connects souls to each other. It instills mercy for one another and for all people.

Peter and Steve took a break and found a water spigot to wash up as best they could. The cold water gave them some relief from the heat. As he washed away the dirt, Peter's gave silent thanks. He was happy to be free, he felt like maybe the universe had blessed them and that maybe, just maybe; there was purpose and justice in this world.

After they finished cleaning up and were ready to get away from the jail house, the young officer emerged to see them off. He put his arm around Peter's shoulders and told him that he too was from Mytilene, Lesbos and that there had been enough deaths. He was glad that he was there to save them. Peter felt the exhilaration of freedom and reached out and hugged him. Both men had tears in their eyes. It was a moment when they connected at a deep soul level.

He told Peter that the peace would not last many more days as Greece and the Balkan Nations would reject the peace treaty in front of them. He told them that the Greek army was anticipating that the Turkish forces would make ridiculous demands at the surrender talks. The Greek army was preparing for a major attack and a push into Turkey; which, if successful, would end the war. The Greek nation couldn't believe their audacity. They lost. It was apparent that they still believed they were in control. A major lesson would be taught them by Greece and their allies.

The young officer feeling his own mortality said; "Peter, I must go to the front and I am sure that I will not return. You go and live your life for both of us." They looked into each eyes and connected again at a very deep soul level. There was another brief hug between them. It was another instance of just feeling without words. They both felt the spark of divinity that connected their souls. The Lieutenant left.

Steve seemed perplexed. He told Father Paris that Peter and the Lieutenant were acting strange. "Why are they hugging and why do they have tears in their eyes? What's going on? They don't even know each other."

Father Paris said; "Most men from Lesbos know how to cry and express their emotions. I think you just need a hug." And so, Steve hugged Father Paris and cried away the tension of his near death and during the war and the firing squad. Father Paris said; "We all need a hug and a cry once in a while."

Peter came over and was still feeling the exhilaration of freedom. He approached Father Paris and offered him the gold cross as a gesture of gratitude. With a bug smile on his face Father Paris said; "That's your gold cross Peter. I have my beautiful wooden cross and that's how it should be. You will need it for your journey." They both remembered the incident of the gold cross at the Church. It was clear that they had bonded during their short time together.

PASSAGE X

DISTANT SHORES

Choral Foreword: Scientic Mythology

The large body of Greek mythology and poetry contains still relevant theories regarding what turns out to be modern concepts about the spiritual and energetic nature of the universe. They contain encoded wisdoms regarding such topics as:

The meaning and purpose of life and its spiritual evolution.

Hardship, pain and suffering as a means tp attain wisdom.

The simulation of the universe, humankind and the illusions of reality.

The assisting role of higher powers in the fulfillment of life plans.

The reality of past lives, life after death and reincarnation.

The journey of souls in the ascension and fulfillment of purpose.

Old ideas are the foundation of modern science. The above subjects, and many more, are the underpinnings of the newly-emerging language of science, philosophy, religion and other theories and explanations of our very mysterious universe and its spiritual realities. The role of the scientific method serves as a discipline in the development of new scientific explanations of reality that are based upon ancient beliefs and that serve the higher purpose of understanding who we are.

The love of art, poetry and the enjoyment and pursuit of beauty are celebrated in the Greek culture and its mythology. There is a true story and now also a tale about the beauty of the human body. Being naked in public, even representations of nudity, was prohibited in ancient Greece. One very brave model named Pyre was tried in court and her defense was to disrobe in the court room and show the naked beauty of the human body. She was unanimously declared not guilty of any crime by the jury and the law was changed in Greece to permit nudity as an art form.

There is great diversity in Greek mythology and poetry and they contain wisdoms on all subjects from the creation of the universe to the nature of reality. The ancient Greeks even dared to speak of love, its sweetness, its madness and love's companion pain and heartache. There is the tale of Jason, which is about Greek heroics. It also has a sub plot about 'how NOT to treat a woman in love'.

Jason was a great Greek hero who retrieved the Golden Fleece. He did it with the help of a blind prophet who told him how to fool the jaws of the rocks. He told Jason to send a little bird ahead of him. The rocks would crash in on it and then reopen, at which point he could successfully sail through. Great though he may have been, he didn't know how to respect and handle a woman. It cost him dearly.

Fortunately, there are other voices in Greek mythology and poetry that dealt with the complex and mysterious subject of love and how to handle a woman. Their advice was very simple. 'How to handle a woman; just tell her 'you love her'. It is the connectivity of love that holds the cosmos, and everybody in it, together.

A SERMON ON A HILLSIDE

What is 'Kairos time'?" it is the right time or supreme moment. It is a spiritual term which it was thought applied to spiritual journeys and experiences. The ancient Greeks had two words for time: Chronos and Kairos. We all live through Chronos or chronological time. Kairos is a period of indeterminate time in which in something spiritual happens. While Chronos is quantitative, Kairos has a qualitative nature, permeant, divine nature."

It is a spiritual period during which lives are defined. It is filled with opportunities for teachable moments and spiritual growth. It is the right moment for change and experiences and achievements. When people are in a spiritual zone, living out their destiny, they do so under the watchful and protective eyes of the gods. They are blessed."

Father Paris told Peter and Steve that he would help them get started on their new journey. He knew that they would have difficulties getting started and finding the pathway. He told them that the first step would be to go to the Greek Orthodox Church in the mostly deserted town, clean up and find and eat whatever scraps of food we find and then look for and change into civilian clothes. "Then we head north."

Before they left the war zone, the Lieutenant gave Father Paris some good news. He told him that the Serbs and Bulgarians took Adrianople and we took Janina inflicting heavy losses on the Turks. Now there are escape routes and they can make it to freedom by going north. But they need to move quickly because the fighting will start up again. Wars have a life of their own and they suffer their own slow and agonizing deaths. The thoughts of vengeance remain and are lodged deep inside their consciousness. More hostilities will be necessary to make the paper declarations of peace take hold."

After hearing the news, the three of them carefully made their way into town. There were a number of empty houses that looked promising. After rummaging through a couple houses, they were thrilled when they found some civilian clothes that were left behind. Peter and Steve joyfully changed into them and they were immediately transformed. The young soldiers who were lost in 'ridiculously large' military fatigues were transformed back into young teenagers sporting a 'not so fashionable refugee' look.

Father Paris told them that they were headed for a church that was outside the war zone. "Estimate, about three miles." He also told them that they would leave right away and not take a chance on some accident happening and a recapture by the Greek army scouts who were roaming around looking for stragglers. He said; "The excitement of being free will give you the energy you need for the long trek north.

It was a long scary journey out of the war zone. As daybreak came, Peter saw the sun rise from the heavens and 'bath' them in the warm light of day. Father Paris was leading the way toward a small town that had an historic church in the middle of the square. He told them that he knew the priest there and he was sure that he would help them with transportation north.

Peter felt the warmth of the Holy Spirit go through him. For the first time, Peter felt connected to something beyond his own illusions of reality. He now had the feeling that there was something more to life than the madness of the human experience.

They walked about a mile or so when Father Paris saw a beautiful hill laced with stately trees and suggested that they go up there and rest a while. Once there, Father Paris said; "There is some thoughts that I want to share with both of you. It is about your journey."

I believe that we are all on spiritual journeys searching for the purpose and meaning of life. It can be perplexing. I remember what a wise old man who lived on a street corner once told me. He said and maybe thought that he was Socrates incarnate. I was young then and searching for my own life plan. He told me; "Live out your destiny with joy. It is the path of destiny that you must stay on to achieve your purpose and learn the meaning of your life."

Steve interrupted him and asked; "Are we all on a journey?" Father Paris answered; "Yes, everybody and, also, everything in the universe is on a journey of sorts. What I want to tell you about is his concept of destiny's joy. He told me that the dark passions of life such as anger, hate, jealousy and the other madness of life are caused by our fears and are dressing emotions. He said we open ourselves to the dark forces in life who lead us astray and we fail to achieve the purposes of our life plan. He warned me that every journey is meant to be hard so that we experience and learn the meaning of life and the joy that comes with wisdom and the understanding that life is about loving and helping one another."

Peter and Steve were smiling at each other. They felt the joy of Father Paris' convictions and shared it with him. He went on; "Accept your Fate without complaint or pity for yourself. Follow your heart. It is the highest source of wisdom that life offers us. Focus on how to deal with the dark moments of life and to reject the 'sad passions' of fear which cause the depressing feelings of hatred, selfishness, remorse and ultimately regret. Be joyful. There is purpose and meaning to life. Find it."

Father Paris was smiling at the end of his sermon on the small hillside where they resting. He started walking down the hill and beckon them to follow. They were all quiet with their own thoughts.

As they approached the church, Father Paris saw Father Alexander standing at the top of the stairs in front of the entrance to his church. When he saw Father Paris he smiled and waved at him to come forward. It was a wonderful reunion of two 'black robed' handsome men of God who couldn't wait to connect and bond with each other again. Introductions were made and they entered the church and went to the privacy of the church's backyard.

They were all seated on the benches of a large wooden table under a beautiful apple tree. Father Alexander invited them to sit on the benches under the tree and told them that he was having lunch prepared for them. It was time to get acquainted and to find out what brought them to this remote village in Macedonia. Father Paris told their story and their need to get transportation north toward Russia.

Father Alexander was understanding and sympathetic. The conversation then turned to lofty thoughts about the priest's favorite subject. Father Alexander asked, "Are you young men religious and members of the Greek Orthodox Church?" Although it was a slight exaggeration, Peter answered, "Yes, we went to church with our mothers and our family." Father Paris joined in and said, "The boys have been through a lot and that they had been nearer to their

God than ever before."

Peter had to be honest with these two wonderful men who gave their lives in service to the Greek people. He had to be truthful about his beliefs. He owed them that. He said, "After all he had been through, after all that had transpired, after he was faced with the reality of death and the workings of destiny and the intercession to save him; he still harbored some doubts. Steve confessed that he too had his doubts and wasn't sure what to believe.

Father Paris said, "Thank you being honest. What questions do you have? This would be a good time to talk about your doubts."

It was Peter's moment to talk seriously. He said. "I don't understand how Jesus could be the son of God. He was only a holy man." Father Paris agreed, "It was written in the early Greek bible that he was 'a' son of God and not 'the' only son of God. We are all God's children." That made sense to Peter and also Steve.

Steve had an observation and a question, "How can someone come back from death in bodily form?" Farther Alexander answered, "We That is a Roman belief. We believe that his spirit returned to earth." Peter and Steve had both lightened up and were accepting of the answers. They made sense to them. Father Paris said, "We have a little more time for one more question and then we have to get ready to leave."

Peter was anxious to ask that last question, He said, "I still believe that we have a free will and that we manifest our own destiny." Father Paris answered, "We do have free will, but we are guided on our destiny by our guiding angels." Peter thought. "There may be some truth to that. We had to have the help of a lot of angels to survive our ordeal."

Father Paris picked up Peter's vibe and said, "We are all heroes on wonderful but frightful journeys. We set out on a quest, meet great hardship and face our 'most feared' demons. Somehow, we overcome all this and we become more serious in outlook, deeper in our thoughts, more thankful, even more powerful and after all experienced, we are wiser. It is truly wonderful and much more than we could ever have imagined."

They all stood up. It was time to rest and get ready for the long journey ahead. Farther Paris went over to Steve and gave him a hug, blessed him and they said goodbye. He came over to Peter, he reached out and put his 'hands-on' Peter's shoulders. They stood there quietly and looked into each other's eyes. It was a 'father/son' moment. Father Paris blessed him and told him to go with God. They kissed goodbye and parted with the usual tears shed by Greek men in emotional moments and goodbyes.

Father Paris turned and walked over to Father Alex. They hugged each other, said goodbye and Father Alex reassured Father Paris that he would place them in good hands and get them started northward.

Peter watched Father Paris walk away. He wondered why his life was the way it was and why his goodbyes were always a parting of forever.

Father Alex walked with Father Paris down the road. After they were down the road to the front gate, Peter watched Father Alex waving goodbye to Father Paris.

FORESTALLING DEATH – HOMER'S ESSENCE

Greek proverbs

"Death is the great liberator. We lose our ego, our cares and our woes. But we also lose the beauty and essence of life."

"The gods envy us because we are mortal, because any moment may be our last. Everything is more beautiful because we're doomed. You will never be lovelier than you are now. We will never be here again." Homer's Iliad.

The next morning Peter and Steve were standing with Father Alex at the church front door waiting for Panos (aka: Homer) to come and take them on the next 'leg' of the journey. Eventually, they sat on the stairs waiting for him to come and get them. In an attempt to make conversation, Steve asked Father Alex whether there is 'life after death' as many of the soldiers discussed in their conversations before a big battle.

Father Alex said; "The Greek myths are replete with stories of the gods and a spiritual world and a waiting period before the next incarnation. Plato told of his experience with a Greek soldier who came back or had a near death experience who told him about another existence. It is well-documented that there is life after death, reincarnation and that we are all eternal beings.

Steve asked Father Alex; "Can you tell us a mythical story while we wait?"

"Yes. We'll call it a 'sermon on the doorsteps'. There is a mythical story about Orpheus or 'he who brings the music of love'. His name means the 'darkness of night'. Orpheus was a poet, a dreamer and a musician whose music had power, was mystical, enchanting and had a magical effect over everything. By the will and commandment of the gods,

Orpheus was made the music-maker to charm and inspire the world. As the world blossomed his song, Orpheus felt the pangs of Eros' arrow. The lovely Eurydice, his love-light was struck too. Quickly Orpheus sang his song capturing Eurydice's heart."

Steve interrupted Father Alex and said; "We may not time for the full story, please tell us about the 'other world stuff'.

Father Alex said; "You're right. The gods were envious and wanted Eurydice's beauty for themselves. They sent a poisonous snake to kill her and send her to the spiritual world of Hades. When Orpheus realized what happened he went into a state of depression and sang only sad songs driving the world and everything in it into a state of depression. Orpheus descended into the spiritual world of Hades and recused Eurydice."

Suddenly, they heard singing. Then they saw a brightly colored wagon pulled by two mules. It stopped in front of them. Sitting on the front seat of the wagon and obviously driving the wagon was a long white-haired man with a big smile on his face. His face was dominated by two gold, 'round rim' eye glasses which framed two sparkling bright blue eyes. Peter thought; "It was an interesting restart of their journey."

Father Alex waved at him and yelled "Welcome. Thank you for coming." They all walked down the stairs for introductions to this 'man sized' elf. He jumped off the driver's seat of the wagon and Father Alex came to him and hugged him. He brought him over to Peter and Steve and Father Alex made the introductions. He introduced him as Panos aka Homer and told them that he was a Greek gypsy and a traveling barb. He told Homer. "These are the young men

I told you about that need a ride as far north as you can get them. Homer seemed very receptive and apparently it was a go.

After the introductions, Peter asked, "Do you go by Panos or Homer?" He answered, "I go by my stage name Homer." So Homer is a stage name?" Homer answered' "Kind of. When I go to my favorite hill and trees and meditate, I zone out and get in touch with my inner truth and my alter ego Homer." Peter didn't know what to make of his answer and let the conversation go."

Steve asked; "What is a barb?"

The good Father Alex took the liberty of answering and said, "Homer is an entertainer, a poet, a musician, a singer and a song composer. It is an 'old-time' tradition on the order of ancient Homer and Hesiod, the great Greek barbs. He is a very talented man who makes a living going from 'town-to-town' along the Balkan shoreline stopping at the small towns and entertaining the populace with his bouzouki, Greek music, song and poetry. It is a wonderful tradition."

Father Alex couldn't resist one last sermon. He told them; "Our greatest triumphs often come out of meeting our greatest challenges. There are mysteries beyond man's immediate comprehension."

Peter said; "Father Alex, we've seen only death and despair. My mother used to say that everything dies." Father Alex softly answered; "There is another viewpoint. The ancient Greeks used to say that everything is spirit; even the planets and the entire universe. They and I happen to believe that; "Nothing really dies" and it is my view that "everything is eternal. We are all spiritually connected by a great consciousness. Don't let the dark, negative thoughts control your thinking. Go forward with the gift and joy of life. Go with and to God."

It was time to continue their journey. They thanked Father Alex and goodbyes were made. The three of them were off on their way to somewhere, anywhere. Peter rode up front on the wagon with Homer and adventurous Steve jumped on the extra mule that was attached to the back of the wagon. Homer told Peter that he was headed north along the shoreline toward Budapest, Hungary.

TRICKSTERS AND THE LITTLE BIRDS OF FATE

Jason realized that the Straits are extremely dangerous due to the rapid currents created by the flow of water from the Black Sea into the Straits. The ancient Greeks thought that the gods placed the large rocks there to guard the Straits. The powerful tides and the crashing currents careening through the rocks smashed ships trying to sail through."

They made their first stop on a knoll overlooking the sea. Steve jumped off his mule and was yelling that they were heroes on a journey like Jason and the Argonauts. Peter and Homer were watching him jump up and down, arms and head lifted toward the sky as if he was talking to the gods. It was 'play acting' and he was running in circles singing a song he made up that they were like Jason the first great hero.

Peter yelled back, "We are more like the little birds that sacrifice their lives to open the rocks." Steve was still laughing and strutting around like he was marching in a parade to the accolades of thousands. Peter didn't know what to make of Steve's absurdity. He shouted; "Steve quit acting the role of the fool. You are going nowhere, fast." Homer calmed Peter down and told him; "Let him go. Let him believe that he is Jason, the great Greek hero.

There was only one way to go. Peter and Steve had to make their way through Eastern Europe headed north toward Russia. They went past the Straits of Bosporus which is a narrow passageway of water between three waterways, the Sea of Marmara, the Aegean Sea and the Black Sea.

Homer told them mythical stories and recited poetry. One myth was based on exaggerated and some truth. It was an old Greek myth about Jason and his recovery of the Golden Fleece. To get it he had to go beyond the treacherous Straits which were thought to be at the edge of the known world. He told them, "It is not hard to believe that the ancients thought that large dangerous natural barriers were 'boundaries' drawn by the gods.

Jason met an old blind prophet who he believed was a 'heaven-sent' messenger who told him to release little birds into the straits to know the best time to sail through them. They would sacrifice their lives as the gods' price for showing a mortal when and how to sail through the dangerous straits. Jason was certain that the old ladies of Fate had opened the way for him as a reward for his faith and courage. Once through, Jason believed it to be a sign that he would achieve his goal.

Steve believed or let himself believe that he was a great, reincarnated hero like Jason. Peter had a different experience. Having survived a dangerous situation, he learned a great lesson and that is we cannot let ourselves be defeated, possessed, dominated and held back by the illusion of fear. Steve was now ready to embrace the challenges of his personal journey and embrace and enjoy all that it offered.

It wasn't clear to them where they were going, but they were going with a high degree of confidence and expectation. Peter wondered if life was such that we live for the moment or whether there was more to life than that. He wondered if there was any meaning to life. Having been saved by the intervention of Father Paris gave him hope that there was something more waiting for him and that we all may be guided by a divine plan. But he still couldn't reconcile their thoughts with the carnage and brutality of the war.

Peter just shook his head in disbelief. Steve was now ready to accept the challenges of their journey. He knew that Steve had serious shifts in mood, energy, thinking and behavior –from the highs of mania at one extreme to the lows of depression at the other. Peter gave him a bit of a pep talk. He asked, "Steve why are we heroes?" He answered, "Because we are still alive. We survived all the traps like Jason did. The little birds didn't. They were expendable." Peter caught Steve's enthusiasm, but he didn't feel like a hero. But it was true that they were survivors, which was a gallant achievement and close enough for them to believe that they were heroic.

They had many close calls and were about to face more danger, heartache and fatigue and, as they talked about the journey ahead, Steve's mood changed again. He was now gloomy and negative. His lament was, "Our walking will never end. I will never be happy again. My life will never be the same. I have almost been killed, have no money and I am walking from Greece to Russia. This is madness."

We never should have left Greece. I have lost my desire for adventure and quests. I can't believe that I have to walk to Russia. This is no quest. It is a disaster. Who knows what we will find when we get there? Sophia is right about one thing. I am coming out wiser and will never get myself involved with quests, heroics, wars and dangerous predicaments again. In the future, everything will be about women."

Peter expected a shift in Steve's mood, but he was losing his patience and was tired of Steve's negative remarks. He told him, "Quite whining and quit crying. Be a man! Stand up and look forward not back." He tried to get him to be a little more positive about everything and pointed out how fortunate they were and how good everything had turned out.

He told "Steve; "We did what we had to do. We escaped from Greece; we gained the help of two old mariners; we had an adventure in Istanbul; we enjoyed the love of beautiful women, we escaped from Istanbul during the only day possible; we live through the war, were saved from a firing squad and now we are heading to Russia and, hopefully, then to the United States. Father Paris saving us from certain death. He was our miracle. When I went to the Church and met him; little did I know that I was meant to go there and that he would save me one day. What an adventure, what an Odyssey it's been."

Steve said, "Peter you are just a dreamer. Worse still, you probably believe all those mythological fairy tales. There were real miracles. There were many beautiful women, but you let them go. You had a chance to be with Calypso and all the beautiful maidens in Istanbul and you passed on them because you were in love with a myth who ended up just being a dream of yours." Peter just smiled and said, "We both had our dreams and our moments. If it is meant to be, I will meet another Calypso and her willing maidens."

Homer interrupted their conversation with the comment;

"Beware of the sirens – they are Tricksters like the gods. They set the traps of sex to capture young men like you two and get you under their control."

Peter asked, "That's a little confusing. Sophia, our teacher, told us that Homer wrote many myths about Tricksters and many of them were humorous. I don't remember any of the myths, but she said that Tricksters set traps for people. She said these traps and schemes usually backfire on the Trickster, but they end up in a good way for the victims. She warned us to be careful of the Tricksters of the world;"

Homer picked up the conversation from there. He said, "Tricksters are interrupted anew by new generations and by different people. What drives a Trickster? He is a creature of appetite. He gets his creative intelligence from hiss deprivations and his actions by this need to be fed. He caters to the various kinds of hunger that we are born with and his tricks and actions to feed himself and others."

Steve blurted; "What's wrong with that?" Peter asked; "I'm confused too. Why is he important? Is there a myth you can tell us? Maybe one where he is a mythical hero". Homer replied; "Tricksters are agents of the gods who fool you and make you wiser about the risks of life."

Homer smiled. He had their attention. "He is a spiritual creature. He moves between heaven and earthier. "The road that Trickster travels is a spirit world as well as the road he travels. He is adept. Sometimes he travels as a messenger between heaven and earth, but if the road is closed he travels as a thief who steals from the gods the good things that humans need if they are to survive in this world. Prometheus fooling the gods and stealing fire to give to humanity is a famous mythical hero and Trickster."

Homer suddenly became serious. He found himself caring for them. He became concerned about them and how they would survive when they left him. He asked them; "The route to Russia will be dangerous. What are your thoughts about the danger and how you will handle a bad situation?"

Peter thought for a while and then said, "Death is no longer a stranger. Once I was forced to face this terror, I finally understood a great truth and that is there is nothing to lose and nothing to fear. I faced the deadly god Death and came away with the belief that he is the ultimate liberator. No more cares, no more worries. Just into the sleep of eternity forever. For the first time in my life, I knew that when my time is up and I have to go with Death; I would do so without a cry, tear or whimper."

He told them, "I'm free. I do not fear death anymore. I expect nothing when I die. I ask for nothing. We were saved time and time again and I know that everything is beyond our control. When my time comes, I will lay down forever and it will be an eternal sleep and forgetfulness. It is clear to me that we are all mortals. That's the way it is and it can't be changed. I accept this truth and, by doing so. I am free. Never will I tremble again at the threat of death.

Steve and I discussed the possibility of our deaths when we were going to face the firing squad. We were determined to be brave and accept our fate even if it meant our deaths. Our time on the killing fields had convinced us that everything is temporary. The gods couldn't be cruel enough to limit the lives of all these brave souls. We survived the fighting and were made stronger by it. And we have the will and confidence that will help us make it through the rough times ahead.

Peter looked at Steve. He smiled at Peter and said; "I agree……..sort of, sometimes." He paused for a moment……"I guess we grew up."

Homer raised his fist to the heavens. He felt better about letting them go on their own. He thought about what Peter just said and now he too was free. He could let them go on their own in good conscience. They had survived some serious situations and had the right attitude, the will and the luck to do what was needed to survive. They would be in the arms of destiny.

He said, "Okay. We're good. Let's go."

LET'S CELEBRATE, LET'S DANCE

"A Greek dance is about life; it starts with a small cry, a tear from the heart, and becomes defiance with a foot stomp on the ground and a loud shout."

Budapest, Hungry was in sight. Homer's slow moving wagon was entering the main square of that city. There were people everywhere celebrating, singing, dancing and just acting out whatever they felt. It was the news. They just heard of the victory of Greece and its Balkan allies over the Turkish and Muslin armies.

Everyone was gathered in the square celebrating. Peter and Steve raised their arms up to the sky and shouted cries of joy for the achievement and this historic moment. People were dancing in circle dances. Everyone was yelling for joy and Peter and Steve started jumping up and down. Strangers were embracing strangers who were suddenly kindred souls. The world was a wonderful place again. The war was over and Greece and the Balkan Nations were free of Turkish rule.

Peter thought of his fallen comrades and was holding back his tears. He was moved by the feelings of love, pity, gratitude and respect for his old comrades-in-arms. He felt a sense of reverence for those brave men who died to free Greece from the oppression of the Turks and their Muslim allies. He delighted in thinking about the courageous deeds of the young Greek soldiers. He reveled in the struggle that had been successfully waged against what was reputed to be the greatest army in the world.

His moment of personal remorse took possession of him as he sunk into his remembrances. He was thankful that he was there to participate in a number of battles and he would never forget charging across the killing fields with his comrades. He felt the pain again of Costas' death and he suffered again the untold personal agony when Costas, the grand old man and patriot, was killed. He bore witness to the bravery, the sacrifices, the hopelessness, the anguish, the miseries of the brave Greek warriors, and he was there to see the historic sight of the Greek soldiers holding their own against the vaulted Ottoman armies.

During the celebration, he heard that after the war there was a mysterious reveal. The people were talking about the role that the conscripted Christian youth may have played in the outcome of the war. At some deep mystical level, despite the indoctrination and attempted conversion of the Christian youth to the Muslim religion, there was an affinity, possibly a spiritual connection, between the fighters from Greece and the Balkan Nations and the Christian conscripts in the Turkish army.

Everyone was proud of these young fighters and, certainly,

the bravery and daring of the young fighters from Greece and their cousins from the Balkan nations were decisive in the war. Although it can never be proved that the mystical bond between them and the Christian conscripts had any real impact on the outcome of the war; there were indications that the Ottoman-formed army may have been weakened from within.

The old myth of the invincible Ottoman Turks was once and for all time destroyed, not by the hesitant Great Powers of Europe, but by Turkey's former subjects, who despised them and were willing to risk all they had including their lives in the frantic need to be free of Turkish and Muslin dominance.

There were various rumors circulating around the square. There was word that on December 3, 1912, an armistice was agreed between the Ottoman Empire and the Serbs and Bulgarians, but not yet with the Greeks who held out to obtain the release of the other Greek territories still under the dominance of the Turkish muslins. The European Powers intervened so that they could dictate the terms of the peace; but the fighting continued as the Balkan nations and Greece refused the terms of the peace that were being arranged.

Peter heard that the Greeks and their Balkan allies had prevailed in the war and that the Greek army had acquitted themselves in the final great assault. The Greek army made the Greek people proud again in the war for freedom and independence. The historic bravery of Greek warriors had been restored.

He also heard that the Greek people were in a state of joyous euphoria. Greece's territory and the captive Greek population had been recovered and, under the dual leadership of Constantine and Venizelos, her future seemed bright. Peter smiled thinking how happy his family and all the people of Lesbos were after they learn of Greece's victory. In all his joy he felt a slight tang of remorse and sadness thinking of home and family.

Peter said, "Okay. I don't feel blessed, but we were lucky. Honestly, I do feel blessed and it makes me want to celebrate and dance in the square with everyone." Homer tied up the mules and the wagon, took out his bouzouki and joined the festivities. He shouted, "Okay. Let's dance." And dance they did as others in the square joined their line. It was the right time for shouts of joy. A new age was starting with the historic victory over the Ottoman army. It was the freedom from their tyranny. It was a Kairos moment for the world and continuation of Peter's and Steve's spiritual journey. "Yashoo!"

PASSAGE XI

RIDING THE WAVES

Choral Forward: Nothing Changes

A Spector was hanging over the world:

"That Specter was communism. Marx and his associates wrote a fiery declaration of principles – a pamphlet entitled: The Communist Manifesto which describes in shocking terms that a specter is haunting Europe and that specter is the changes in the existing world order. The pamphlet sparked the fighting on the streets and in the alleys and it would inspire a revolution in Russia and other countries of the world."

Conditions on the ground were explosive. People were upset with the injustices of their world and their lives. They blamed the wealthy and the powerful international bankers and businessmen for brutalizing the workers and living off their labors as parasites."

It wasn't a complicated issue. Many of the European liberals say that capitalism is only a mask that covers the ugly reality of the most rapacious exploitation; the rape of the planet, the destruction of the environment without the slightest concern about the fate of future generations.

The sole concern of the international bankers and the-boards of the big companies who are the real rulers of the entire world are to enrich themselves through the plunder of the planet's assets, including the labour of the working class.

It was clear that the dialogue was irrational and dangerous. No one was listening. The people's complaint could be summarized as; "Just imagine all the money flowing upward into the hands of just a few selfish people. Nothing was flowing down to the great mass of people. What happened? Revolution.

Peter and Steve walked into the wailing cry for freedom and equity. It was the same cry that led to the war between the Ottoman Turks and Greece and their Balkan allies. Peter was starting to believe that 'nothing changes' and that mankind is plagued by one war after another. Life is precarious and one struggle after another.

BACK TO THE KAFENIO

"Dike, the goddess of justice, is responsible for the application of harmonious order to a chaotic world. Spiritual justice in the world is one of the great themes that is revealed by the Greek myths."

The myths are far different than the realities and truths of life for most people. There was much talk about justice; but, in actuality, divine justice was always ever-elusive in the final outcome. In life, the journeys and the escapes taken by adventurous souls are not joyful. New struggles and challenges are always going to change the romance of a journey to the drama of a death march.

Homer took them all the way to St. Petersburg, the largest shipping port in Russia. He couldn't leave them at

PASSAGE XI 355

the border and did all he could for them. He kept them safe and made them feel good about themselves. He entertained them, sang songs, recited poetry, told them stories to make them wiser about life and what was ahead for them. He tried to be witty and told Peter; "St. Petersburg must have been named after him and it was a good sign. The chances to leave Russia and continue their journey to somewhere were more feasible at this large shipping port."

Peter realized that they were helped by many different people, but didn't know why. They were not angels; but, perhaps, part of their journey was to be guiding spirits in their lifetimes. But now, they were now on their own and had to survive in turbulent Russia. It was a daunting part of their journey. Peter had the feeling that it would set the stage for the rest of their journey.

He remembered Sophia's lesson about the Odyssey and her discussion about the fun and romance of an Odyssey. At the time, he thought that if he was lucky he too would have such a mythical journey in his lifetime.

Then he remembered his Yaya's warning. She told him to be careful with what he wished. She said; "The gods will give you what you dreamed of as a kid; but they will extract a huge price."

She was right. Reality will be different than his dreams. Peter and Steve had suffered and labored through country after country and it seemed like nothing was going to change. Peter learned the lesson about wishes and the gods. He was coming to 'grips' with the reality of adventures and realized that it requires a lot of imagination to get hold of the 'ever elusive' joys of a journey.

As was his nature, Peter let go of his 'remorse and disappointment about the journey. He was 'nursing' the feeling that they were finely at an important stage of their journey. But, never-the-less, things looked bleak. They were at the outskirts of St, Petersburg and didn't really know where to go and what to do.

Suddenly, strangely, both Peter and Steve felt a rush of excitement and an energy. Their aches and pain and fatigue disappeared. Peter thought; could it be their birthdays that were subtly be that they were older and more experienced. Their birthdays had come and gone. They both began to celebrated with crazy antics and jumping up and down with joy. Why? They didn't know. So much for maturity and experience. They were still young and just 'tired' crazy.

They both had turned 19 years old and going on 100 in experiences. Looking back, how they survived and made it through this leg of their Odyssey was a mystery to them. They learned that when there is no alternative; it becomes a test of wills, persistence and endurance; but mostly luck.

Steve was bothered and blurted out loud; "I wonder if Cleis' dad survive the purge that most likely is taking place in Lesbos." Peter felt Steve's anger and was careful with his response. He told him; "Don't wish him harm. That shit will come back to haunt us."

They were in the center of the City and were witnessing the beginnings of a new war. They ran into a parade of protestors marching behind the leadership of communists who were calling on the people and workers to break their chains and unite in a great struggle to forcibly overthrow the existing royal social order and take their rightful control of the country's economic resources. Their message was that the workers produced the wealth and therefore the workers are entitled to a larger share of it as well as control of it. Only then they claimed could poverty vanish.

Peter and his sidekick Steve were now exposed to the passions of new ideas about egalitarianism and the communist movement and came to believe in the equal sharing of the world's resources. He joked to Steve that, "Costas once told me that Jesus was the first communist. He drove the money changers, the bankers, out of the temples."

They were in central St. Petersburg searching for a kafenio. They got lucky. They happened to hear a couple of old Greek protestors talking and they approached them for directions to the Kafenio. One of the old Greeks took pity on them and offered to take them there.

Eventually, they arrived at the kafenio and were looking and hoping for a source of help, a refuge and a shelter to protect them during the raging storms of the communist revolution. Peter thought, "Thank God for the kafenio. They served as temporary sanctuaries and staging areas for their next move; more likely more misadventures by these travelers, refugees and escapees in their 'not-so-joyous' romp through life.

It was a typical kafenio located on the second floor over a Greek deli and statuary shop. Peter and Steve walked up the creepy stairs and introduced themselves to the owner of Kafenio. Peter asked, "We are looking for work. Does anyone know where we can find work?"

The owner, a portly old man, came out from the kitchen. He introduced himself as Andros. He listened to their story and felt their pain. "Come with me" he told the young men. He in turn introduced them to the old Greeks that were playing cards and games. Andros asked if any of them could help. He appealed to them; "I know we have our own security to deal with; but I wanted make everyone aware of their situation. Also, go easy on the teasing." All the old men shook their head 'yes'.

The men at the kafenio knew these were serious times and they went easy on them. No unfunny jokes and teasing. They knew that these young travelers needed help. Everyone was afraid of the coming events that could morph into a major war and they were guarded about making commitments; but never-the-less they were willing to help young Greek men in need.

Andros told everyone, the old Greeks and a few old Russians, that he would make a temporary place for Peter and Steve in the kafenio. He would employ them and let them sleep on the chairs. He asked everyone to think about what they could do to help them escape from Russia before they were caught up in the revolt against the royal family.

He ended his appeal with something everyone already knew. Russia was destined to be engulfed in a major civil war for control of the country. It was a dangerous place to be.

THE MAGIC OF BOLDNESS

"The philosopher Goethe advocated: Whatever you can do, or dream you can, begin it. Boldness has genius, power and magic in it."

The ancient Greeks enjoyed many intellectual passions in their lives, including philosophy and poetry. They also expressed their truths in mythology and poetry. The ancient Greek poets of tragedy had a rational explanation of God's purpose in letting humanity make their own way. It was said that humanity created chaos in their lives because of the tragic flaw the Gods placed in humanity's character. It was believed that the gods placed it in us to help us achieve our purpose in life and to become wiser threw our suffering. Humanity was forced to be bold in facing the obstacles, hardships and suffering in life with courage and boldness and that boldness had magic in its enactment. The ancient Greek viewed 'timid' responses as self-defeating.

Andros led them to a stately old gentleman named Dr. Sotari, who was a retired professor of philosophy and history at the Taras Shevchenko National University in St. Petersburg. Dr. Satori was standing and shouting to get his ideas heard over the laughter and kidding by the other Greeks at his table and a couple of nearby tables.

He was defending the emerging communist movement. It was as if he was lecturing a class room. He stood up and addressed a bunch of old bored Greeks who just wanted to get back to their card game. His voice echoed through the Kafenio:

"Communism is rising from the conditions of economic deprivation and misery. It is another rebellious movement caused by human greed and economic disasters, ideological delusions. A major cause is the excessive concentrations of wealth, economic dislocations leading to extreme inflationary pressures and poverty. Communism corrects these problems and provides doe an equal distribution of wealth."

An elderly man named Stavros started shouting back at him; "It's a German trick to cause chaos in Russia. They want a civil war so that they can take over our country."

Dr. Satori answered; "The movement is about new ways at looking at old problems and it is a résistance to change by those who hold the power and don't want to give up control. New ideas posing as solutions of old grievances always have great appeal and power in changing the world to one class of people. And so, there is conflict between the new and the old ways. It is not a German plot to start a civil war in Russia."

With as much sarcasm as he could muster, Stavros said; "You intellectual are naive. It's a call to war. It is 'class warfare' and like tribal warfare it will be bloody with no mercy shown. It's a cry for vengeance for years of deprivation caused by the 'Royals' and the struggle is to the death."

Andros interrupted the shouting match and asked all of them if they knew of a way to get the two young men with him on a ship leaving Russian. Stavros turned his attention away from Dr. Satori to Andros. He asked if they had any experience on any type of ship or even a small boat. "If so, who did they train under as apprentices?"

Peter answered them; "We don't know anything about ships and how they work. "Stavros said; "I thought as much. Wrong answer, but it really doesn't make any difference. You two will just have to lie about your experience. Remember, you will not be in a confession booth. In life, you have to take chances to get what you want. Boldness has a magic about it. By the way do you know the names of any seamen from Greece?"

Peter answered; "Yes. We knew Costas and Yianni."

"I can make this work. I know the captain of a ship schedule to dock soon." Stavros seemed elated; "Perfect. You tell the Captain of the ship you trained under them Thar will clinch your chances of getting a place on his ship. If you guys want to leave Russia, here is your chance. He probably won't throw you overboard after the ship is on the 'high' seas. After all you are Greeks. He'll find something for you 'two drifters' to do."

He warned that the ship would leave immediately once they had a full contingent of experienced hands. Another old Greek who was listening told them to show up early in the morning before too many sailors found out about the openings. They were given the names of Costas and Yianni for references to the Greek captain. Tell him that you heard about the openings at the Kafenio the night before. It might help."

Stavros added; "He should be willing to hire some young hands, provided that they were somewhat qualified. He always said that he didn't want to endanger them and his ship with inexperienced hands. So play up your experience with Costas and Yianni."

All the while, Dr. Satori was listening to the conversation and then stood up to speak. He invited Peter and Steve to spend the nights with him until the Captain docked. He received immediate applause from the other men in the Kafenio for the gesture to help these two young men..

As they were leaving the kafenio, another old Greek who wanted to get in the action shouted, "Boys, you are about to hear the good Doctor's sermon that 'reality is an illusion'. After that 'brain twister', he may twists your brain around again with his stories about the 'shinning being of light'. If you have time come back here and we will help you regain your senses."

Dr. Sotari was a widower who lived in a small, but elegantly furnished apartment. Peter and Steve were impressed with his large bookcase and the statues that he had collected as well as a few oil paintings on the wall. He lived with a relatively attractive lady that seemed to be in his age-range and she prepared them all a light meal.

Steve and Peter were starved and couldn't wait to get

started. She recognized their thirst and hunger and went back into the kitchen to prepare more for them to eat. Life had brought them to their knees. A simple act of kindness gave them a small glimmer of hope about their circumstances and a feeling that they would survive the madness of war.

Peter asked Dr. Satori, "What are the protests and the fighting all about?"

He answered; "The main proponent of communism is an intellectual named Karl Marx, who is the leading light behind this new revolution. I sometimes fantasize and see him looking at the world as a bright green and beautiful garden. We are all at the garden gate and watch while he opened it wide to everyone – the poor, the workers who toil, the sick, the infirmed, the masses of people looking for a place and their share of the fruits in the garden."

He added; "He was a man who gained prominence with his concept of egalitarianism and his affirmation of equal political, economic, social and civil rights for all people. He was the philosopher who first planted the seeds of communism which eventually germinated and grew like weeds among the poor, the disenfranchised, the anguished, the deprived and the abused people of the working class.

He was the son of a prominent lawyer. He was brilliant, studied law and philosophy at the leading German Universities. His great passion was to mix constantly with intellectuals who spend their time discussing God and atheism, politics and reform, socialism and capitalism and complex philosophical and metaphysical issues. Many of his associates were socialists who believe all the people, not just the wealthy, should own the land, the natural resources, production and all the institutions of a nation. Marx believes that everything should be divided equally."

In a respectful way, Peter said; "I agree with you that communism is a fair way to run a country; but I think that Stavros had a point about communism was used as a rallying cry to class warfare. Steve and I witnessed the horrors of war. We wondered why God didn't show his hand and stop it. We had to load the mutilated bodies of young beautiful men onto carts pulled by mules to mass make-shift burial holes. It is hard for me to believe that there is a divine and worthwhile purpose for all that horror."

Dr. Satori didn't disagree; but he observed; "Let's not place the blame on God for mankind's cruelty to each other. It is mankind's fault for all the atrocities. It is sad that such madness and waste has gone on for thousands of years."

He saw that he was losing their attention to the smell and delivery of food. Peter and Steve rushed to the table and gobbled and devoured everything on their plates. Dr. Sotari smiled and seemed to feel good about helping them.

After dinner and while everyone was relaxing, Peter asked Dr. Satoru; "I'm curious about the comment made by one of the old Greeks when we were leaving the Kafenio. I think he said something about the 'Shinning Beings of Light'. Was he talking about angels or something like that?"

"Something like that. It's a long complicated story and somewhat controversial. The bible, classical mythology, the Koran, even folklore and religious texts all over the world tell the same story and that is humanity was genetically created by aliens from another planet. The 'Shinny Beings of Light' are the name given to these aliens by humanity. These reptilian aliens were mining the earth for gold and precious metals and they created humanity as a slave race to do the work for them."

Peter asked; "What happened to them?"

"It's a long history, but after many centuries of prohibited integration by some of the aliens with female human slaves the leaders of the aliens decided to 'wipe out' everything on earth with a great flood and start over. It didn't work; the same problem all over again. There was still conflicts between these aliens or 'gods' as the ancient Greek myths and religious writings refer to them. It was decided to put the hybrid aliens/humans in charge of the planet (the now royal families). They placed the planet under the eyes of the 'Watchers' and left."

Peter and Steve were 'spell bound' and speechless. Peter eventually asked; "Are you saying that the ancient Greek gods were really aliens?" Dr. Satori answered; "Yes." There was a pause to catch their breaths. Peter asked; "Does this mean that priests and churches were created by these aliens to control humanity?" Dr. Satori said they divided us with royal families, cartels, secret ruling cartels and countries and all the forms of control that we see in place. It's a 'divide and control' strategy.

Aghast, Steve said; "I'm scared. Reptilian aliens rule us and we don't even know it. All our history is hiding what you are telling us. We were created and are ruled by animals and reptiles?"

Dr. Satori realizes what he told them was too much for them to comprehend as theoretical and conjecture. Even though he believed it to be true, he tried to walk it all back and restore their perception of the world. He almost shouted; "Forget about the past. Forget about the disasters. Forget about who runs things. Nobody really knows what happened in the past. Everything vanishes in time. The past is gone in a second and is no more. The present is all we really have and it vanishes in no time at all. Life is short. Pursue your dreams, do what makes you happy. Follow your bliss.

Dr. Satori could see that they were fighting off fatigue and depression. He reached out and took them by their hands to the bedrooms. Peter felt grateful for his help and said; "Thank you. Thank you for helping us. We are not cheerful company. Right now, we are discouraged by the world and everything about it. The world may not be what we thought it was and the world powers are set on destroying each other again. To make matters worse, we are trapped in a strange country. Everything seems bleak. "

REALITY'S ILLUSIONS

"Aeschylus' historic quote about pain and suffering: *"Even in our sleep, pain which cannot forget falls drop by drop upon the heart, until in our despair. Against our will, comes wisdom through the awful grace of God."*

Many Greek seamen know a little bit about the Greek myths. Navigating the seas has always been an acquired skill. 'Even Homer's Odysseus had trouble sailing the Aegean Sea.' It was said that the struggle was with Poseidon – the Greek god of the Sea. Like the other Greek gods, he was a trickster. He attracted many people with the beauty of the seas, oceans and other bodies of water and set many traps in these beautiful attractions – currents, whirl pools, covered rocks with water- to entice and trap humanity and drag them to the depths of a watery grave.

They slept in as long as they could before guilt of

neglecting his host forced them to get up. After years of sleeping on the cold earth, the beds seemed to be heaven sent. And the scent of hot coffee was too much to resist and they woke up for early morning madness with Dr. Satori.

After gulping down too many cups to count, Steve had a question and couldn't wait to inject his thoughts in the conversation. He asked; "Dr. Satori, how did the ancient Greeks view the world and creation?"

Dr. Satori answered; "They believed that everything is spiritual even the planets as well as everything else in the universe. I won't go into that philosophy in great detail. It's getting late and we need to get going. But, let me give you my idea about creation. Reality, everything, is a spiritual stage play and an illusion conceived during your last 'life after death." Dr. Satori stopped at that.

Steve was perplexed with such a short and unbelievable answer. He persisted, "How is that possible?" Dr. Satori answered, "We are all spiritual beings and we are here in body to experience and learn from our experiences." Peter asked; "Everything seems so surreal. Please tell us how it all works. What makes you think reality is an illusion?"

Dr. Satori thought for a moment; then said; "Philosophers and scientists speculate that everything that exists existed before and will exist again. Past, present and future exist at the same time and in the same space. Within this construct, everything is connected by the thread of time; yet separated by this thread."

Steve excitedly said, "Wow! What about us humans?"

Dr. Satori smiled and said; "The Book of Life is replete with stories of rebirth of old souls; their constant deaths and rebirths and stories of reincarnation. He told them; "I have a copy of that book on the book self; do either of you want to read it so that we can discuss it more?" Peter answered; "Thank you for your offer. It is too much for me. I'm afraid to say I'd flunk your class. "

Dr. Satori smiled and continued his 'home' lecture. "The short stories of life changes; yet they constantly stays the same. Everything dies; yet lives again. Magically, within this mysterious and complex scheme of things. One last thing – nobody really knows anything about anything."

Peter squeezed in a question. Regarding our situation, what do you think we should do?" He responded immediately, "Leave Russia and Europe. More wars and bloodshed are about to happen. Let me give you both a word of advice. I heard it from my little angels who work in the shadows of government. You should leave Russia immediately. A world war is about to start. You must, take great chances to escape. Staying here is too dangerous. Become daring mariners and sail away."

Dr. Satori paused for a moment to organize his thoughts. He said, "To save yourselves, it will take daring action and strong and determined willpower. Think of yourselves adventurers, men who take calculated risks to achieve great things in life. Now is your time to be daring to complete your journeys and find your destined place in the world. Don't ever quit on yourselves. "

They showed up at the kafenio with Dr. Sotari. Their talk with made them ready to do what it takes to escape from Russia and find a secure place in the world. The old men had good connections and they found starting jobs for them on a ship leaving for countries in America, but the ship wouldn't dock for another two weeks.

He went on and said, "You came into the world with a story that was written for you long ago and far away. Your life is that story. You are an actor in a play. The world is the stage. You are not in control. Always remember, reality is an illusion. Mark my word, your chance will come. We always know the truth. You know where you belong and you will get there."

Steve said, "Wait. Wait! Are you saying that we were born with a life plan? And are you saying that life is all an illusion? How can that be?"

Dr. Satori was smiling when answered, "Many people believe in destiny. Your destiny' is your life plan. It is a Greek concept." Steve shook his head in agreement. He went on and said, "Consciousness is all there is. Everything else is an illusion." Steve asked, "Is consciousness God?" Dr. Satori answered, "It is for some people?

He told them that he dreamt that he was just standing still in the middle of a big square." He interpreted that to mean he was stable and could expect no major changes in his life. Steve said that he dreamed that he was back in Greece walking the beach with Cleis. Peter said he had a crazy dream of playing cards falling all over him. Nobody could think of what his dream meant.

Dr. Satori went to the kafenio for his morning dose of their thick, black Turkish coffee and then returned quickly for a piece of toast ro offset the acidic tasted. He told Peter and Steve that he was told that they caught a break. The men at the Kafenio arranged a meeting for Peter and Steve with the captain of a Greek tanker that was harbored at the port. Timing was good. The tanker was getting ready to leave and deliver goods and materials to South America. He needed a few more experienced mariners.

The Captain was concerned that the daily skirmishes that were taking place on the streets between the "Reds" (the

Bolshevik factions) and the "Whites" (the anti-socialistic factions) would break out into a full-fledged war and he was anxious to bring new hands aboard and leave the port before the fighting began.

The three of them rushed down to the kafenio. The old men at the kafenio asked Peter and Steve if they had any mariner experience. They said, "No". The old Greeks laughed. They told them to always say "Yes." They pointed out that it would be mostly hard labor; but eventually they would get the 'hang of it.' There was more chatter between the old Greeks and more laughs among the oldsters.

They were talking among themselves and to a man they all said that they would like to be there when the Greek captain found out that they were novices. He was a burly man known for his temper and he would be on fire when he found out that they were 'land lubbers'. They teased Peter and Steve by telling them that the captain was known for throwing people over board that he didn't like.

Following the advice, almost the continued insistence of the men at the Kafenio, they showed up at the docks early the next morning at daybreak. An old tough-looking man, the captain, was on the deck with a hot cup of coffee in his hands. He was a short burly man with a big mustache and what seemed to be a very much enlarged head. His face was a dark bronze with many deep wrinkles. He didn't have many teeth left and his gums seemed like gills. He was an old salt, a wanderer of vast oceans. The men at the Kafenio told them that he was as ugly as Socrates; but lacked the gifts that God had given to Socrates – brains, intellect and compassion.

One old man from the kafenio said, "He will ask you if you were trained by the Smuggler? If you say 'yes' just to get a job on the ship, he will ask what his real name is. It is a trick question. Nobody knows the Smuggler's real name or where he comes from." Tell him that you never heard of anyone by that name.

Peter wondered why anyone would choose to be a mariner and a sailor and live a lonely kind of life on the high seas and oceans. Looking at him he concluded that there wasn't anyone waiting at home for him. He probably had no real choices. The life of a sailor and a captain suited him. It gave him a chance to travel the world, stop in different ports and there would always be women available for hire. Not a bad life.

Being hired by the captain was a chance to leave Russia and get to the United States; but because of everything they heard about him they were a little apprehensive. But they had no other choices and they mustered the courage to approach him.

They introduced themselves and he responded cordially. He told them, 'call me Captain.' They had an advantage they were Greek and they were recommended by the men at the Kafenio. 'Do you know how to work the boiler room?' Without any hesitation they answered, "Yes of course."

He took them down to the boiler room and asked them, "Who did you train under and what training do you have? What ships have you worked on?" They gave him Costas name. He knew Costas as an experienced mariner and fisherman. Then they told him that they had been trained by the Smuggler from Lesbos. Surprisingly, he seemed impressed and reacted in a very positive way, "Very good, the Smuggler is one of the finest mariners in Europe. His men are trained to know every job on a boat."

The Captain told them that they would be leaving in the

morning and they must be ready to go. "Leave everything and everybody behind. We must grab the tide and be on the ocean early tomorrow without any delays."

As they raced from the port to say their goodbyes and collect their few meager belongings, Steve expressed his concerns to Peter, "We don't know anything about ships and boiler rooms." Peter told him that there are no other real choices and that they had to work their way out of one bad situations into another.

"What difference does it make? We all drown in the seas of our own makings. If he throws us off, the oceans will pull us down gently. If we stay here in Russia, life and even death will be much more painful."

Peter was becoming a 'story teller' and a 'poor man's' philosopher, a trait he retained all his life. He joyfully told Steve; "Can all this be true or is it just an illusion and a stage play called 'life'?"

PASSAGE XII

THE INSANITY OF LOVE

Chorus Foreword: The 'Needlepoint in Life

There is a 'needlepoint' in everyone's life.. David Spangler in his book: "The Call" describes the needlepoint of life as our lives are woven from a melody of calls that draw us out and help us to define ourselves. Can you see your tapestry emerging, hear your song? It is a song as old as the human race. Many immigrant souls have heard the call and made the sacred journey to a new land. This is a pilgrimage that stirs the soul, demands a leap of faith, and awakens joy at the start of the journey and reverence on arrival at the chosen new crossroad of life. If taken in this spirit, the journey is poetry begun, a winding road to meaning, and a promise of a better life."

Peter was trying to become part of the massive movement of brave illegal immigrants to America. This was the wave of immigrant who helped make this country the greatest one in the world. These immigrants (like the immortal immigrants of all time) all faced the perils and hazards encountered by migration to strange new shores to save themselves and their families. They were all brave souls who sailed and set off with only faith and hope as their compass and without any assurance that they would make it safely.

Like many of the other brave immigrants seeking a better life in America, Peter did not speak the English language;

he had no one to sponsor him, had no financial resources and had to face the animosity of many people who resented the huge influx of immigrants to their shores. But before he faced all these hurdles, he had to jump off the side of a large barge moored a great distance from the port area of New York City and swim through the cold dark waters of New York harbor to make it to safety. His survival would require enormous tenacity and guts.

After reflection of the moving events of his life, the underlying spiritual currents, his great passions and loves, his close calls with death and the mythical interplays of destiny, he gained a deep respect and a reverence for the supreme mystery that is called life. \ \

As he stared at the rough, cold waters, he dealt with the prospect of death made vitally real by the onslaught of his survival instincts. Confronting mortality paradoxically implies being alive. It also means willing to defy death and accepting whatever his fate was meant to be. It was important to him that he face the dangers of life and that if he was to die it would be a heroic death linked to the ancient Greek honor of dying properly.

He knew that it was a high-risk chance he was taking and that there would be no Greek gods to help him. He was on his own. But he heard Dr. Satori's words: "Be bold in life."

NOTHING TO LOSE

Boldness has its own power. It makes sense to take a chance when there are no good choices and nothing to lose."

Aspiring young Greek seamen had a 'needlepoint' decision to make when they boarded a fishing boat for the first time. When that grand moment came and they were hired, they were usually told to always be bold. They were selecting a life full of risks that required boldness and a fearless attitude. The old fishermen who had survived many risks and dangers would say; "Don't hold back, don't be overly cautious and don't allow yourselves to become victims of your own fear and inaction. There is safety in taking bold action. Freedom comes with having nothing to lose.

Dr. Satori and Stavros agreed to go with them to the Port and do what they could to help them get jobs on the ship. They would use what little influence they had on the Captain to help them. Peter and Steve arrived early at the Port in ample time and were enthusiastic and ready for their new journey, but they had to bridge the obstacle of 'no experience'.

Stavros led them to the Port and agreed to have a preliminary with the Captain and use whatever influence he had with the Captain. He said; "There are openings and all you have to do is convince him that you are experience."

Peter asked; "Where is the ship going?" Stavros answered; "They are going to the United States and then down to South America before returning to Greece." Both Peter and Steve yelled; "Perfect!" Stavros said; "The Captain will interview you both. Remember what we told you to say."

It was time to make a move regardless of their qualifications. It wasn't a job interview and Peter and Steve were not looking for careers. They didn't plan on coming back with the Captain or going any place else with him. It was destination America and a dream come true. Peter wasn't immersed in religion but the thought did occur to him that there was some divine foreshadowing and foreseeing of things beyond their reason and control. He had to take ownership of the opportunity even though acting on it seemed beyond all reason. But gauche he would be to the very end.

The Captain came down the gang plank and come over to them. He got right to the point and asked; "Do you guys have any experience?" Peter answered; "We trained with Costas and Yianni." The Captain asked his trick question; "Did you guys train with the smuggler?" Peter and Steve had been prepped by the gang at the Kafenio and answered; "We never heard of anyone who went by that name."

He asked them about their relationship with Costas and Yianni. Peter stepped forward and gave him a full briefing of the war and Costas' death. The Captain seemed to have no emotion about the news, but Peter felt his sadness over the news. The Captain asked another question; "Did you guys fight against the Turks?" Peter answered; "Yes." Then silence. The Captain told them; "You are both hired. Be here early tomorrow morning at Five A.M."

They left to say their goodbyes. Peter told Dr. Satoru, "South America is close enough for a first trip." Dr. Satori said, "Starting a dangerous journey requires some trust in your destiny and it also requires faith in themselves to be able to whether the storms that may arise. He went on to say that when a person commits to a dream involving his spiritual bliss, invisible hands will appear to guide the pilgrim dreamer. When a person harkens to a call for a journey and an adventure and when they follow their heartfelt bliss, the path will emerge where there was no path or way forward before.

There are times when there are few options and everything needs to be changed, to be done, to save and advance and to improve the fortunes of life. To make a move to change their fortunes, they needed to bluff their way aboard the ship and get passage away from Russia."

Everything seemed to be lining up for them and Peter was starting to believe that there are no coincidences in life. Every event had meaning. He felt Costas' presence and whispered to Steve; "I think Costas is here with us and helping us with the Captain." Steve said; "Don't talk about spirits and ghosts; it 'scares the shit' out of me."

They said their goodbyes to Dr. Satori and Stavros. They thanked for everything they did for them. They gave Dr. Satoru a special 'shout out' for all he did for them. Stavros said; "The Captain wouldn't tolerate any delays."

They took a short nap and got ready to go. They were at the dock in time and were met by the First Mate. He showed Peter and Steve the work area and told them to shovel coal into the boiler. He showed them the valves that must be turned off when the pressure got too high and other valves that were important to maintaining the safety of the ship. His parting words were, "Work hard, the ship needs power to leave the port."

Into the hot boiler room, they went. The men in that hellhole were overjoyed and eager and happy to be replaced. They were being assigned to the top deck; which was very pleasant work with the wind in their hair and vistas of ocean views.

Peter was smiling and somewhat relieved. He told Steve; "How hard can this be? We just shovel coal." And shovel they did. They were amazed when the ship started moving. The first mate yelled down, "Keep shoveling. More coal." And they did more shoveling. It was hard work but it seemed pretty easy. They were like two possessed demons keeping the fires in hell alive. The first mate left; but occasionally called down and told them to keep up the pace "for now."

"I told you Steve that there is nothing to worry about. It is hard work on a ship but not complicated" said Peter, now acting the part of the wise man. The ship was making good time. They went for hours. A call came down: 'This is the Captain slow the boat down!" Peter and Steve looked at each other and just shook their heads. They determined that he wasn't talking to them. "What did they have to do with boat speed?"

The heat in the boiler room was steadily rising. The boiler room was getting intense, almost flaming and potentially explosive hot. They were drenched in sweat. The air in the room had evaporated. It felt like the air had been sucked out of the room or had risen to the top and was hovering deathly still. There was no oxygen to inhale. They kept shoveling as ordered.

They were baking to death and there was no relief at hand. Not knowing what to do, they kept on shoveling. In their panic and ignorance, they didn't know whether to stop or not; but they only had one set of orders and that was to shovel hard and shovel they did. They thought that the ship would stop and sink if they didn't continue to shovel more coal into the furnace.

The first mate came running down the stairs yelling at them, "Can't you dopes see the temperature on the gauge is so high that the boiler is about to explode?" That was it; all they needed to know. Peter and Steve rushed to the stairs and were falling all over each other and pushing each other in their mad rush to get out of the boiler room. They climbed the stairs two at a time and were gone before the first mate knew what was going on.

He called for help. As Peter and Steve were rushing out of the room, other men were jumping into the boiler room to stem the pending disaster. Peter and Steve couldn't get far enough away from the boiler room and they hovered near the life boats. The Captain was on the deck screaming orders to find them. He would make them pay. It was not enough that the situation was under control they had to suffer.

Before long, the Captain found them. He was slapping them around with his hat and kicking them in the ass. They were running around in circles to avoid him. He was screaming, "I'll throw both of you overboard, make you walk the planks, you idiots." Then he paused for a moment, "No that's too good for you fools. I'll put you in the brig and starve you to death. We'll starve you and work you to death."

The sailors on deck were all laughing and clapping their hands in rhythm as they Peter and Steve ran around chased by the Captain. Eventually the Captain was tiring, breathing hard and he could barely walk. He was exhausted chasing them and trying to hit them with his arms, his feet, his hat and anything he could get his hands on to throw at them. Finally, he was completely spent. He sat down and just peered at them hiding behind the lifeboats and oil drums. His screaming and ranting seemed to give him some relief.

The other men aboard were laughing. The Captain started chasing Peter and Steve and yelling at them again. They looked like a bunch of clowns running around the boat; but Peter and Steve knew better than to laugh out loud. The Captain was screaming, "What the hell am I to do with these two idiots." After a short delay, one of the galley hands went to the Captain and told him, "I could use a hand in the galley."

He went on to say, "Salas was down. He's sick and is not able to work in the galley. It is a bad sign that he doesn't want food." The Captain was now calm and, after a moment, he too appreciated the grand comedy. He started to laugh thinking about them racing out of the boiler room in panic. "You morons – you could have killed us all." Steve whispered, "So much for being a gauche mariner."

They questioned Peter and Steve about their work experience. The young men gave garbled and somewhat contradictory answers. They were clearly confused and not sure what they should say, if anything. After this questioning which amounted to much about nothing it was concluded that they were just a couple kids who had a rough time of it and were just trying to find their way. They all soften. All these sailors had been there and they all wished that they had been given a better chance at life. They were trapped in lives that they didn't want to live.

After more discussion, it was determined that Peter would be assigned to the galley kitchen because of his prior experience with the butcher shop. He also seemed to have a knack for cooking food and he responded happily to his new assignment. Steve would be the cabin boy. His only experience was washing dishes and waiting on tables. He would wait on the Captain and do all the menial tasks. Perfect casting it seemed. Everybody was satisfied; except for the two mates that had to return to the boiler room.

Peter felt that guiding angels were involved in their lives, but seemed to be playing and teasing them with the craziness that took place with the Captain. Although not always pleasant and easy, unforeseen events and circumstances were unfolding and were becoming a positive force in their lives. Peter's experience in the kitchen would become important throughout his journey, as well as the passport of the deceased sailor named Salas that dropped to the floor as they dragged his body for a burial at sea.

REACHING FOR THE DREAM

"Turn away no more; the watery shore"– Blake

Nothing came easy for Peter. He always had to make hard decisions either to survive or to reach a goal. It seemed like he was always living and lodged in his dreams and that he was traveling over many cross roads seeking his place in the world. Like Odysseus, he had to make his way through a maze of life obstacles as he wandered by the currents and lone sea breakers. His journey was painful at times and torturous when considered in retrospect. What underlined his vision of the new world was derived from his dreams, his horrific experiences and his desire for the good life to be lived within a congenial order of existence that was love, family, home and hearth.

There was another such a moment before him. He was at the edge of time when he had to make a quick decision and he knew that in front of him was the dark abyss of a watery death if things turn out badly. He didn't know whether he would have to run, jump or stay still, whether to say yes or no, whether to take a chance or play it safe, whether to have faith or to listen to his inner doubts or whether to reach for a dream and risk it all.

Peter was preparing himself. They were arriving in New York City Harbor and he had to make a decision whether to jump off the ship or not. He didn't know anyone in New York City. He had no money. He didn't know where to go. He faced danger before and he was willing to take extreme chances. But he was bothered by the thought, "What if he made it and was caught. Would they put him in prison? Who would be there to help him?" He would soon come to one of those edges of time and have to make a fateful decision. If he jumped off would he fly or would he fall?

He remembered Doctor Satori's advice to be bold and that boldness will give him the power he needed. Steve seemed oblivious to it all. He never seemed to plan anything or look ahead; he had a reactive personality. Trouble always seemed to follow him. He had learned to run away from his problems and, so far like the trickster that he was, he was able to elude all the traps that he created for himself. The trip to him was somewhat pleasant and as was his habit he just enjoyed it without a care in the world.

So far the long voyage across the Atlantic Ocean had been uneventful; except for the tragic and unexpected death of their shipmate, Peter Salas who died of some undiagnosed disease. They were given the grisly tasks of cleaning his area and deathbed and wrapping his body in hard cloth for a burial at sea. As they were placing his personal items in his leather traveling bag for his next of kin, Peter noticed his French passport. Thinking ahead, he knew that there would be a time when it would be valuable. He pocketed the passport.

It was December 1918, when they pulled into the Port of New York City. Peter and Steve were overwhelmed and fascinated by the sight of the Statue of Liberty with her hand raised high holding the Torch of Liberty. Even the wonderful sight of Istanbul didn't compare to the glorious vision of this beautiful green lady framed by the great city behind her.

They arrived late at night and got into ship queue. The staging area was in the outer port area and they were waiting for their chance to dock, unload their cargo, reload, and then quickly leave. This procedure also gave the ship captain and his mates the means to control desertions. They quickly unloaded the cargo and then sailed back to the outer and distant reaches of the port harbor.

Even though it was night time, Peter could see that the Port area and the City were teeming with people and activity. It seemed colorful, exciting, and most of all it was the United States where according to rumors the men wore tailored suits and high hats, the women were all beautiful and sexy and the streets were paved with gold.

Everybody was on deck talking about the United States and asking the Captain if they could go ashore for one night. The answer was a firm "no". The ship had to leave as soon as it had its clearance and he didn't want any of the crew getting into trouble or disappearing. He had been there and done that and he wasn't going to make that mistake again.

Peter and Steve heard the rejection and were disappointed as they had high hopes of seeing Fifth Avenue and Broadway. Peter told Steve to wait there for him and he would be right back. He went below and came back with a small bag containing some of his personal items and the passport. He told Steve to do the same.

Peter whispered in Steve's ear that they were going to jump ship and swim ashore. He told him that, "We may not get another chance." Steve was unsure. They were outside the Port area and he was not of the mind that he could swim that far. The water was freezing and the cold would be another problem. He told Peter that he had to think about it. Having to swim so far in the middle of the night in freezing water was not what he was expecting or was confident that he could do.

There was something else holding him back. He never talked about it or told Peter; but he also missed Cleis. Whenever he thought about her he felt an ache in his heart. He was in love and he was ready to go back and fight for her hand in marriage. He had become a different person. Facing the many dangers and obstacles and surviving helped him to become more of a man. He never told Peter, but he even thought that his actions and antics in Istanbul were crazy; even somewhat disgusting. But on second thought it was an important life experience even though it was comical and he had played the part of the fool.

The thought of her waving a white linen handkerchief goodbye to him caused him a lot of 'heart-break' nights. She was a lovely vision and he couldn't get her out of his mind and his heart. Yet he loved Peter. He was his friend and the thought of going with him and continuing their adventures and their journey excited him. The fear of losing Peter, who he had come to depend upon, weighed heavily on him. Should he go with Peter or should he play it safe and stay on the ship?

They talked more. Steve confessed that he was scared to jump and didn't think he could swim that far. He told Peter: "Wait, let's come up with a different plan."

Peter was getting nervous and was uncomfortable with any more delays. He tied the laces of his shoes together and put it around his neck. He knew that the other deck hands would be looking for them and that he would lose the chance to jump ship if he waited any longer. He tried to persuade Steve; but to no avail. He couldn't get him to make up his mind and muster the courage to jump. Time was running out. He only had a few minutes left. His chance would be gone. There was only one thing to do. Peter hugged Steve who had become more than a friend - a brother and a comrade. Their life together was over. It was time to say goodbye.

Peter was at the edge of the rail and hesitated a moment before jumping. He was not willing to play it safe. It was all or nothing for him. His destiny was now going to be of his own choosing. They were both sad and crying. What they had gone through together taught them how to cry and express their sadness without being embarrassed or feeling any shame. Peter wished Steve good luck and then jumped into the cold waters. Steve yelled down to him, "Peter I'll be in Lesbos. Write me. Don't lose touch with me. I love you brother."

He vanished into the dark waters. Every now and then Steve could see Peter's head bobbing in the water; but after a few moments he couldn't see him anymore. Steve was left on the deck already missing his friend. It was pitch black and Peter was swimming somewhere alone in the dark, filthy waters of New York Harbor. Steve wondered if Peter would make it.

Peter had the 'last chance' will to survive. He felt that he had to grab this chance for a better life. No matter what happened; it would be worth the risk for he was convinced that otherwise he would have nothing – no real future if he went back to Europe. The past was gone. The present was intolerable. He only had the future and he had to reach for it no matter what.

He was in battling the tides and was getting tired. He was

suffering fatigue, had heart pains in his chest and yet there was only one thought in his mind and that was survival. He was swimming sideways – the Australian crawl – to conserve his energy and it seemed like an eternity. For one brief moment he was getting scared that he wasn't going to make it. He tried to get his mind off his fatigue and off the pains in his arms and body. He was trying to suck in large amounts of air to get fresh bursts of energy.

To take his mind off his fatigue and his fear that he might drown, he thought of what it would be like to die. And what is death? Is it no more than leaving a short lifetime and going into eternity?" Are we:

"Like wingless birds, we are swept into a city of cathedrals. These cathedrals are made entirely of a crystal substance that glows with a light that shines and radiates powerfully from within.   The first feeling is one of being awestruck into reverence for the divine. The place had a power that seemed to pulsate through the soul.

Peter was hearing the sweet sounds of the angels of death hovering over him, but he knew that he couldn't give up and go to them. There was no other choice but to keep swimming. He had to fight the danger was that he would get so tired that he would pass out from fatigue. He briefly thought that it might just be better to let go; but that scared him and he made a vow to himself that he would struggle to the end and never give up.

He kept looking up from the water and tried to see over the small waves which were blocking his vision. Finally he saw the Port lights and the docks up ahead. Surprise and amazement took over. He was going to make it. The truth was that he was a little proud of himself. He did it!

When he got to the dock area he climbed up gingerly. He

was exhausted and had a little trouble summoning up the strength to climb up. Once he was to the top, he looked around for police as he didn't know what they would do to him if they caught him sneaking into the country. The docks were vacant except for a few dock hands that were way down the block smoking and talking. "Were they guards?" he wondered. 'Would they see him walking in the dark soaking wet, cold and shivering?' He thought he must have been a scary sight. Where would he go? What would he do? His troubles had just begun.

Suddenly, he heard a muffled scream of surprise. When he turned he saw a well-dressed couple looking at him. They seemed terrified at when they saw him. He was dripping wet. Water was streaming down from his hair over his face. He looked like some monster from the sea. All his features were distorted and magnified by the darkness. To Peter's surprise they were talking in Greek. Peter said very calmly: "Please don't worry, I am not going to hurt you. I just jumped ship. I want to come to America. I am a good person."

They seemed relieved when they heard him talking Greek. From his accent they assumed he was from Lesbos. They asked where he was from and he told them Plomari. There was some small talk about that port town and Mytilene. They told him that there was fighting going on and everyone was hopeful that all Greece would be free soon. Peter said he knew; but didn't tell them that he was involved in the conflict and that the Greek army was succeeding. Their information was old; but there was nothing to gain by getting into that conversation.

Then they asked him how they could help. "Where are you going and what do you want?" they asked. "Where is the Greek kafenio?" he answered quickly and softly. The man laughed for he knew that was a place to get help. Many of them had gone through there; the Greek Ellis Island. He told Peter, "Don't worry. We won't call the police. Follow us and we will take you there."

It was not too long before they got there. They told him that he had to go into the door next to the grocery shop and climb some stairs to get there. They gave him a few dollars, wished him luck and watched him as he opened the door to go up the stairs to the kafenio. Peter found himself walking up the stairs again to the kafenio. He loved the smell of tobacco and old Greek men. It seemed like he was in an old dream. Had he gone back in time and was he in Lesbos again? He heard somewhere that life goes in cycles and maybe the gods were teasing him and spinning him around.

When he got to the top of the stairs he could smell the strong odors of Turkish coffee and cigarette smoke and the musky odor of accumulated filth. All these places have a similar odor and an unforgettable character. He felt safe. Once he got into the main room, he saw the usual assortment of old men playing cards. Some of them looked at him when he first walked in; but then went back to their card playing.

Peter stood there alone, dripping wet, wondering what should he do.

PASSAGE XIII

FINDING A LIFE STAR

Choral Foreword:
Taking Control Of Destiny

Many classical Greek myths have a background theme that there is a thin curtain or barrier between the spiritual world and the human world. Some of the myths tell of the crossover and interplay of the Greek gods with human beings to influence the lives and destiny of human beings. Special attention was given by the gods or spirits to individuals whose pre-birth life plan included an Odyssey or spiritual journey.

The highlight of the journey es the moment when the traveler must make the transition from the spiritual journey to a new dream-state. The traveler must overcome a great obstacle or struggle to prove his or her readiness and bravery to face and begin their life plan.

Homer pictured Odysseus as having to overcome the danger of the vicious waves of turbulent water. His boat toppled in the crest of a giant wave spinning him round with one tremendous blow. He went plunging overboard, the oar-haft wrenched from his grip. A gust that came on howling at the same instant broke his mast in two, hurling his yard and sail far out to leeward. Now the big wave a long time kept him under, helpless to surface, held by tons of water, tangled too, by the sea-cloak of Calypso. Long, long, until he came to the spouting brine, with streamlets gushing from his head and beard: but still be-thought him, half drowned as he was, to flounder for the boat and get a handhold into the bilge to crouch there, foiling death.

Once the obstacle is mastered, the Odyssey or spiritual journey is over and a new dream begins. This water passage is similar to a baptism symbolizing the holy act of taking control of one's destiny. It is a reflection not unlike Joseph Campbell's discussion in his book entitled the Labyrinth which describes these kinds of risk-takers as heroes:

"Furthermore, we have not even to risk the adventure alone, for the heroes of all time have gone before us. The labyrinth is thoroughly known. We have only to follow the thread of the hero path, and where we had thought to find an abomination, we shall find a god. And where we h a d thought to slay another, we shall slay ourselves. Where we had thought to travel outward, we will come to the center of our own existence. And where we had thought to be alone, we will be with all the world."

Peter's successfully faced and overcome the dangers of his water obstacle. The ship he was working on parked outside the New York harbor to discourage seamen from deserting and staying in the United States. He bravely jumped off the ship into the icy cold, dark water and began a difficult and long swim to the city. He didn't know anyone and couldn't speak English. He made it to the harbor wharf of New York City. Peter began his new dream by taking control of his destiny.

A NEW DREAM BEGINS

"Only chance can speak to us. We try to read the messages every day. Whoever the gods of fortune are, they will drop things in your path, but don't search for those things you will not find them."

Life produces men who are habitual 'risk-takers'. It is in their DNA. They don't always think things through, they usually end up in harm's way and then are forced to react quickly and turn many ways to survive. The word for these men is – poutropon – or polytropic literally meaning 'turning many ways'. The polytropic hero archetypes were mythical Jason for Steve and the wily Odysseus for Peter.

A million thoughts went through his mind as he stood there dripping wet. He was now an illegal immigrant without the glorious label of a pilgrim, a wanderer or a seeker in a bright new world. He had followed a warped path through life, a twisted track, but was always fortunate to find a door that was an opening to survival.

Peter could hardly believe that he found his way through and out of the Labyrinth of Eastern Europe and that he made it to the United States. He felt like a man who had completed the first step in his quest and a sacred pilgrimage and had survived the perils of a journey through hell. Now he was looking for a pathway in this new world. He had a fleeting sense of excitement when he made it to the kafenio; but this feeling of exhilaration was soon replaced by a concern about survival.

All aside, his was a journey of necessity and such journeys cannot be planned, they must be lived and there is no clear path forward, there is only a way. On this subject,

Buddha says: 'you cannot travel the path until you become the path.' Peter was all he had in his journey; he was his own guide, his lantern and became his path. He made his way forward by doing what he had to do. In his own exciting way, although not the stuff of great myths, he found ways to make the many turns in his journey and he was versatile enough to survive and to make it to 'the goal of his wanderings' determined to survive, to live the 'dream' and 'to follow the silk thread to happiness.'

Peter stood there for what seemed to be an eternity trying to collect his thoughts and determine his next steps. He was at a major crossroad when destiny played his card. To his surprise, a voice from the back of the Kafenio called out, "Peter is that you?" Someone was walking to the front of the Kafenio where Peter stood and he was asking in a voice filled with underlying tones of disbelief, "Are you really here in New York City? What are you doing here? Why are you soaking wet?"

It was Christos. Last Peter saw of him, he was running for the port area to board a boat and get to the mainland before he got arrested for killing Dmitri. Peter walked toward him, they met, hugged, kissed each other; they had both come through hell and the killing fields of war and they were ecstatic to see each other. Christos asked him again, "How did you get here?"

Peter looked around to see if anyone was listening and then whispered: "I jumped ship and swam to the port. A Greek couple found me and led me to this Kafenio." Christos smiled and said, "Ah, nothing to worry about. Most of the men here jumped ship and the rest of us got here one way or another. Good for you Peter. Be proud, you made it. Many tried, many didn't and who knows what happened to them."

Some of the old men were listening, smiling; some were even standing looking at Peter in approval. Christos and Peter were hugging each other and slapping each other on the shoulders. It was an unexpected and heart-felt reunion thousands of miles from their homeland. They all sympathized with Peter and they all experienced what Mohammed said long ago, "A journey is a fragment of hell."

The next few minutes were spent with Christos and Peter trying to talk over each other and tell each other their stories. This went on for a minute or so and then suddenly some awareness of Peter's fatigue. He needed some 'down' time to recover. Peter got real tired, went silent and let Christos tell his story.

Peter knew the first part of the story. It was as expected. Christos' lead-in was about the many young Greek men and boys that for a variety of reasons and motives joined the army in anticipation of the war with the Ottoman Turks. The Greek people were ready, the national anthem was sung in the schools, the horn was blown in the Churches. They wanted their freedom and it would require the death and sacrifice of many young men – the flower of the nation – before they were able to caress the sweetness of freedom. The Greek nation was mentally ready for the struggle to the death between these armies – battle-tested and the highly vaulted Turkish and Muslim armies against the hastily assembled Greek armies.

Like most Greeks he was upset with the European Powers who avoided direct support and participation of their armies. It was not expected that the Greeks by themselves would prevail. Then came a 'tipping point' and Greece was joined by their Balkan cousins who rushed to assemble their armies. This created a multi-front war for this classic struggle giving the combines forces of Greece and the Balkan Nations some degree of hope. Behind the scenes were the Great Powers – England and France – and the Russians supporting the Greeks and the Balkan nations and arrayed against them was powerful Germany supporting the Ottoman Empire.

Christos told Peter that he was in the infantry and was part of a unit that operated behind enemy lines getting information and when necessary making 'hit and run' attacks on Turkish supply lines and the deployed artillery units and, most important, disrupting logistic operations. He said that it was dangerous work, but he found it exciting.

Then it all changed for me. We were no longer engaged in guerilla tactics. My unit was watching the Greek army make a very bloody and suicidal attack on the Ottoman lines and it was wonderful to see their lines break and the Turks chaotically running and trying to reassemble their forces at a fault line they had hastily established. We were ordered into action and given the job of 'mopping up' the rear units the Turks left behind to slow the fast advancing Greek army. Our group managed to get behind a Turkish staging area and moved quickly to attack these small fire units before they could deploy and get entranced. As I was running across the field to attack a machine gun position, I took a hail of fire. They took out my right leg and grazed my head. That's all I remembered.'

Peter couldn't get many words in the conversation not even when Christos took a breath. He resigned himself to being the audience; but he didn't mind as he was tired and even in his fatigue he listened to and found Christos' account interesting. He asked Christos, "What happened after that and how did you get to the United States?"

"The next thing I remembered was waking up in a cart with some other wounded soldiers. There were moans and groans and blood all over us and the pain magnified as these carts were being drawn by mules across dirt and bumpy roads. I was sick, dehydrated, bleeding, sweating and didn't have any room to move around. Then I passed out again.

When I woke up again, we were going into a small town where some make-shift hospital units were set up and that's where they took me. It was a big tent and a number of operations were being done and a few doctors and volunteer nurses were scrambling around trying to tend to everyone. They gave us some alcohol they found in town as painkillers and then it was my turn to go under the knife. I lost the bottom half of my right leg, but not the pain that remained."

Christos got up and went and got them a couple of more drinks. Peter could tell that he was deep in thought and it had to be about the war and the pain of reliving the horrors of his operation. It seemed to Peter that the Greek men who fought in the war were united in a common bond that was beyond explanation and none of them, nobody 'risks the adventure alone' and there were many heroes that showed up for the war including 'the heroes of all time that have gone before us.'

He returned, sat down again, and pushed another drink in front of Peter. He smiled and said, "Then God sent an angel to help me. He must have felt sorry for me. She was a volunteer nurse and I later found out that she was a princess from the Phanariotes family.

You know Peter, at that point in my life, I would have fallen for anyone who gave me some tender loving care; but to be sent a beautiful and regal princess to care for me was beyond my wildest dreams." Christos continued, "It turns out that her family, the Phanariotes, was considered royalty. Through marriages and investments during a century and a half they took over political and administrative leadership in the Danubian provinces of Wallachia and Moldavia in present Rumania. These Greek rulers inherited the title of Hospodars (meaning princes) and started the movement to free Greece and revive the Byzantine State.

She told me that when the war started many members of her family and other Greek notables in Istanbul and other towns were murdered and massacred by the Turks. The younger male members of the Phanariotes joined the Balkan armies and the girls went to the front lines to help the brave Greek wounded recover.

We spent a great deal of time together and she gave me a history lesson about the Greek tribes from the Balkans. The four Greek tribes from the Balkans spread out and settled all the Greek islands and southern Italy. That is part of the reason there was a natural affinity between the Greeks and the Balkans.

If I marry her, I may claim to be part of the royal Greek family from the Balkans." Peter smiled and said; "I'll do the same."

The kafenio was closing and they had to leave. Christos told Peter he could stay with him until he was on his feet. Peter was relived and thanked Christos for his offer and help. As they were walking to Christos' apartment, they continued the conversation. By that time Peter was really gone-tired, but he listened out of kindness to his host. Christos saw his fatigue and told him, "Peter we'll talk more tomorrow."

Christos realized that Peter had changed and was a man

now. He was 'much traveled' and, by the grace of God, he lived through many harrowing situations. He was a man. He was no longer helpless and hapless; he grew to be versatile and shrewd. Like Odysseus, he became cunning and resourceful. There were many twists and turns that he made along the way; but in classic Greek style Peter always chose what turned to be the most precarious and difficult way to go; but he ultimately made his way forward on his Odyssey. Christos felt that Peter was divinely inspired.

LOVE LONGS FOR ITSELF

"The longing you express is the return message "– Rumi

They were excited to see and be with each other again. That morning they got up early, had some coffee and toast and engaged in a little pleasant chatter and conversation about this and that. The apartment was small but large enough that they could be comfortable sharing it. Peter had no clothes other than what he was wearing when he jumped ship. Christos offered to share his clothes with him; more kindness from his country man.

It was time to organize their living arrangements, finish their personal hygiene, dress and then head to Fifth Avenue and Greek town. Peter was really excited to see New York for the first time and in the common light of day it was imposing, immense, spectacular and a vision splendid with people rushing about with faces of determination and with orange auras of preoccupation and anxiety.

They found a small Greek restaurant that was opened for breakfast. Peter asked Christos if the story he told him last night ended up being a love story. Christos answered, "Yes of sorts." He told Peter that when he was ready to be released from the make-shift recovery house, he asked her out for coffee. The town where his recovery house was located was showing some activity again and a few shops were open for business. She agreed and after that they became a couple.

He was released from the Greek army and they went off happily to see her family in Romania and get permission to get married. Christos said, "That didn't go so well. Everything about that family was power, money and control. She was a princess and a bargaining chip that could be used for the basis of a merger with another powerful family and extend their base." Christos seemed a little agitated when he said, "They were going to make her the consideration in a business deal."

She agreed that she would not get married until the war was over and she in return got them to use their influence and help me get into the United States. The family received what they wanted. They quickly made the arrangements, gave me a ticket, gave me money and to their great relief they plied me away from her.

Peter didn't know if he should ask the question or just leave it alone, but wanted to know the current status. He asked, "Is it over?" Christos was pensive for a moment but he eventually answered, "No, we are writing each other. God bless her. She knows that I don't have much money so she sends me what she calls "tokens of love" to help with the rent. I love her and she holds the strings to my heart. I'm like a monkey on a string – up and down and can't go anywhere. I am not sure if I go after her or just stay here until she makes up her mind and comes to me." Christos added the thought, "Or maybe I will just give up and try to find another woman to love."

They finished breakfast and went over to the kafenio. Both of them felt a little depressed talking about the past and how they missed Lesbos. Peter told Christos about his love for Antigone and what happened to her. Christos understood as he too had lost his love. They both agreed that they had to accept their losses and move on with their lives. There was a sense of longing that they felt and a calling to return to Greece. There were too many loose ends in their lives and they didn't feel quite right about what was happening to them.

The discussion shifted. Peter talked a little about his experiences in the Greek army and the battles he participated in and the personal losses that he still can't get over. The rest of his story was simple. He told Christos that after their release from the army, they went to Russia, that they didn't like the country, the politics, the war; but they loved the women who were varied in looks, most were exotic, all of them attractive and many were beautiful beyond belief. He told Christos, "But there was one problem in this land of beautiful women — no money, no girl."

Peter continued with his story and said, "Eventually an opportunity came to leave Russia and find a way to get to the United States." He also told Christos the funny stories about the Captain, how they finagled their way into a job, the boiler room disaster and the trip from Russia to South America and then up to New York where he jumped ship, swam to the port area and then over to the kafenio.

In retrospect, it was a hilarious situation and Peter was at a point where he could laugh heartily about it. Although it didn't seem like much in the telling, but it was a great deal more poignant in the living. But Christos got caught up with Peter's infectious laugh and they both roared. When they got to the kafenio and went upstairs Peter could hear Greek music playing. All the old men were standing, having a good time and it looked like party time. Christos told Peter, "It is a party for you." Peter suddenly felt like he was home. Back in Greece. He felt alive again.

They went to a table up front and there was Greek chicken soup, warm grape leaves with meat not just rice and covered in a tasty avgolemono sauce. There was a bottle of ouzo, wine and Turkish coffee. For the drinks it was one-part alcohol to two parts water as done in Greece. They turned up the music; everyone was singing, laughing, eating and enjoying themselves. Peter laughed and shouted, "Where are the belly dancers?" Two old Greek men got up and started dancing crazy and acting like little kids again. Christos said, "That's not much but two old men dancing is the best we can do." They were now all up laughing and dancing.

It was a wonderful moment. Peter who now had a habit of letting a few tears go when he was extremely happy or depression sad was clearly touched and felt the warmth and love for the men of the kafenio. They were friends, comrades, brothers, amigos and they too had left their homeland and missed the warm hearts, the sun and the fields, the sheer rock cliffs and the dark blue waters of Greece.

When the party was over, Peter and Christos went to the back of the kafenio to their table. Christos huddled over the table and asked, "Well Peter, my good friend, what is it you want to be and do with your life?" It was the central question. "What is going to be your way forward?"

Peter thought a while and told Christos, "Don't know

about my life yet and there are not many jobs I can do. I don't speak good English and that is a problem. I guess I could become a cook at one of the Greek restaurants. They would have to teach me some dishes. I did learn quite a bit about cooking on the ship, but thinking back it was all a rehash of garbage."

He went on, "I worked as a butcher in Russia and know how to do that job." Christos interrupted Peter, "What is it you love and want to do?" Peter paused, "What was it he wanted to do with his life?" Christos said again, "Tell me what you want to do; not what you think you could do." Peter didn't hesitate for a minute, "I love playing cards. It is about chance. There is intensity about the play. There is always suspense. All we Greeks love 'risk-taking'. A job and an ordinary life are not for me."

He was engaged mentally and emotionally with the thought of playing cards for a living and went on to say, "For now, I'd rather play cards than do anything else. The cards bring with them the mysteries. The order and play are fascinating, the strategies are complex and reading the body signs adds to the mystery of the play. Body language tells what is going on in the minds of the other players. You cannot be a fool and play the game.

That is what I would like to do. I already play a good hand and can almost memorize the cards. But it is mostly for fun." Peter went on to say, "No matter how good I get I don't think I can make a living playing cards. I only have one stake, my gold cross. I'll take it to the pawn shop. Chance plays too big a role. One bad night and I could lose everything."

Christos spoke up again: "If we could make the god 'Chance' work for you and if the old Greeks at the kafenio show you how to sort, stack and read the cards would that get you started?" Tomorrow night a very special person will come to the kafenio and I will introduce you to him. He teaches people how to mark and read the cards. If he thinks you are a good card player, he could also arrange some card games with the 'high rollers' for you. It could be all you need to get started."

The night was over and they were walking slowly over to Christos' place. On their way, Peter asked; "Do you love her enough to risk everything and go to her?" Christos was quiet for a moment then answered, "Yes, I still love her. We write. She promises to come here so that we can be together. I have become her captive and she holds my heart in her hands. My thoughts are only of her. My heart won't let me separate from her. These are the chains that destiny has placed on me."

Peter was a little surprise at his response. He always thought of Christos as a 'macho' type of guy - free, handsome, independent, someone with many loves – that kind of a Greek character. But maybe he wasn't. It was clear that Christos got emotional when he talked about her. Peter found him to be sincere in his affections, but he wasn't sure that he would be loyal and faithful to any woman not even the one he loved.

Christos asked Peter if he was ever madly in love with any woman. Peter's first thought was of Antigone, but she was gone and had become just a legend. He answered, "No, not really". Christos asked, "Would you be interested in meeting a very beautiful girl named Agape? She is a student at a local school and is one of the girls who works for me selling carnations and flowers at the hotels and restaurants around the City. I think that you two would pair up nicely.

She has a good heart."

Peter responded immediately, "Yes, of course. What are the New York women like?" Christos answered with a smile, "The ones who work at the financial district are 'Pandora' types. They'll rip out your heart, eat it and spit it out. But the other ones, the waitresses, the students, the nurses are where the sweet Muses are to be found. They live together because it is too expensive to live alone. These sweet Muses will inspire you and make you feel like a god. I've been told that the word 'inspire' means 'in spirit' and these ladies will inhale your essence, inhabit your body and become one with you in spirit. They are intense."

THE TRICKSTER

"The trickster myth derives creative intelligence from appetite." – *Lewis Hyde*

The Trickster myths appear in many cultures. In Greek mythology he sets traps to capture his prey. He is driven by greed and a great appetite. Although his motives are malevolent, they usually end up with the prey escaping and benefiting from the experience. There are many different tales of the Trickster with complicated plots many of whom are humorous with powerful life lessons.

Christos and Peter had breakfast in the morning at a Greek deli on 5th street. The next stop was a 'high-end' clothing store where Christos treated Peter to new suit, shirt and a pair of 'black patented leather' shoes. Christos sadly told him, "This is for your help with that tragic moment with Dmitri. I wish that it never happened. I got caught up with the hellish tradition of preserving the family honor." Peter said, "Leave it alone. It's over."

They took a little time to walk around New York City and enjoy the sights. Peter was overwhelmed by the size, mass and heights of the buildings. Istanbul was impressive, but it lacked the strength of the steel mammoths were like something out of the Greek myths. As they were walking around, Christos said, "I've made arrangements for you to meet the trickster. He the man I told you about. He knows how to change the play in a card game and how to read the mystery of how the cards are stacked and dealt."

Peter asked, "Is that a nice way of saying he will teach us the mysteries of playing cards?" Christos said, "Peter, use nice words to make it sound legitimate. Otherwise the dark forces will be attracted to you."

Christos continued, "He is an old man who spends his time wandering around New York City and going into and out of the kafenio, the bars, restaurants and card games talking to anyone who stops to talk to him. Peter asked, "What does he talk about that is so important?" Christos answered, "He considers himself to be an authority on everything. He talks about mythology, religions, philosophy, poetry, prophecy and the other wild hallucinations handed down by the ancient Greeks and Jews."

After they arrived, Christos went to the tables where the old Greeks were playing cards and table games. He told the old Greeks that he had invited Margolis to meet him at the Kafenio to discuss business. There were a lot of 'Oh's and 'Ah's' and 'awe shit'. It was obvious that the old Greeks didn't want their games interrupted by Margolis' taking and showing off.

To quiet them Christos told them what the meeting was

about. He told them that he wanted Peter to meet Margolis the trickster and become a pro-gambler. The old Greeks all said, "We can teach Peter how to play." A couple of them added, "We all know how to cheat too."

As they were talking, a white-haired man with a full goatee came into the Kafenio and walked right up to the front grand table. Surprisingly, the bored old Greeks and Margolis were pretty cordial to each other at first. It wasn't long before everyone at all the tables and Margolis were arguing and calling each other names.

This was not what Peter expected to see, but he suspended judgment as this was new territory for him. Christos and Peter sat down and listened and waited. Peter looked a little perplexed by everything that was happening and was having trouble making sense of it all but he relaxed when Christos put his hand on his shoulder and told him to enjoy the show. The more he looked and listened the more he was amused by what seemed to be a live comedy involving Margolis the trickster and story teller and a 'make-shift' captive audience of old Greeks.

As he listened to all the noise and chaos of the old Greeks interrupting and arguing with Margolis and each other made Peter feel like he was back in Lesbos. He enjoyed their shouting, their playful nature and their disruptive mannerisms. He couldn't tell if the old Greeks were at all serious about their noise and questions, but it was good theater and everyone seemed to be enjoying the interactive show.

Christos went over and got three cups of coffee and some muffins and brought them over to their table. Then he went over and pulled Margolis over to their table. Peter was excited to meet him. Introductions were made and Margolis sat down at their table. Peter was fascinated by this well-dressed, diminutive man with a large shock of wavy white hair, matching goatee framing a face that seemed to have a permanent smile. He seemed to have a very pleasing demeanor which was embolden by an aura of self-confidence. All and all he seemed to be an interesting person. After his round with the old Greeks and everyone's laughter he held the promise of being a joyous person to be around.

Christos introduced him as Margolis and told Peter that he came to the United States many years ago from Athens. He spoke excellent 'Greek' and during their conversations he was able to capture Christos and Peter's dialect. Margolis came across as a very intelligent man who played to his audience and who maintained a constant stage presence, spewing out a dialogue of literary imperatives, which were given more weight by his loud, clear and pronounced enunciation of his words. He was purposely being over-dramatic and without any embarrassment at all he deliberately maintained a pompous air demanding attention and a required acknowledgement of his acquired wisdom, and his many apparent intellectual gifts. All of this he made apparent by his haughty bearing and practiced delivery.

Peter asked Margolis the obvious question, "Why do they call you the trickster?" One the old Greeks who overheard the question shouted, "Because he is a thief."

Margolis shouted back, "Listen and learn. The road that we tricksters travel is in a spirit world as well as a road in this world. But I am not an adept who can move between heaven and earth. It sometimes happens that the road to where I must go is not open and then I must travel as a thief if I am to survive in this world."

The old Greek shouted back, "That's skata, pure bull shit."

Passage XIII

Margolis turned to Peter and Christos and said, "We tricksters are thought of as the complement to fate. We represent the elements of life not accounted for by destiny. We change the cosmic rules, we trick the gods of Wall Street and we give to mankind what they need, what they deserve, an equitable break even if it is not part of fate's preordained plan."

Christos ad Peter patiently listened to Margolis pontificate and once he was done Christos got right to the point. He asked Margolis to tutor Peter and teach him how to play cards the way the professionals do it. He told Margolis that Peter was a good friend. He also told him of Peter's journey, his difficulties, his language barrier, his acute financial situation and his need to find a way to make a living. Peter added, "I love playing cards. I'm curious and fascination by the mysteries of chance and I want to learn how the cards should be played and how a game should be managed."

Christos then said something that Peter didn't expect. Christos in a heart-felt manner told Margolis, "Peter helped me with an instance of 'honor' and a 'life and death' situation and I owe him for being there to help me when I needed it."

Margolis realized what Christos was trying to accomplish and quickly took control of the situation. He told Peter that he could teach him a trade, give him a technique that would give him control over the cards – what he described as taking the destinies of the cards away from the gods and putting the final outcomes into Peter's hands.

Not being sure of what was being said; Peter looked quizzically at Christos who smiled and did an interpretation, "Margolis has agreed to show you how to 'mark and play' the cards for a living. However, this is to be a business arrangement. In return for the training Margolis wants fifty percent of your winnings for a period of two years. For that he will get you some games to hone your skills and make a few dollars." Peter readily agreed.

Peter believed that playing cards was a good outcome for Peter. Given his circumstances it was the only possible workable one. He only needed to know a few English words, it gave him a livelihood, some economic security, freedom to travel the cross roads of the United States and a trade that he could always fall back on and make what he needed to survive.

Peter asked, "Is this legal?" Margolis answered: "It is not illegal" He added the caveat, "It is not illegal as long as you are not caught. Your tracks must be hidden and you cannot let them know who and where you live. A disguise is always necessary and you should appear as a butcher or restaurant worker when you come into the game room and sit down to play. If you think that playing cards is a game, you're wrong. It is serious business if you are caught cheating at cards. Many times, the losers will kill you."

Margolis wanted to allay his Peter's concerns and also justify what he was going to do. He went on to say that he loves the United States; but it is a country of tricksters and con men. He added the thought, "Many of American leaders are crooked tricksters. These guys are everywhere. They are disguised as politicians, bankers, priests, businessmen. Wall Street is plagued by many con men. All these tricksters have mastered their art, their con, their trade and justify their activities under the rubric called "capitalism." Margolis stopped talking. He was smiling and seemed pretty impressed with himself.

Peter was confused, "What is he talking about? He believed that America was rich and powerful and it was built by settlers and brave immigrants. Peter was getting lost in all the rhetoric. When Margolis realized that; he suddenly 'mellowed out' and let things get a little more sanguine. He had gone too far in his attacks on the rich people that he disliked.

He calmly changed the subject and said, "Okay we have a deal. But there is one condition. You must play cards at least four nights a week with the old Greeks. They will trach you how to read the cards, count them, mark them, play them and all other manner of tricks. If you learn to hold your own with them you will be successful in this business. I'll do the finishing work and get you into some good games. Peter agreed to the terms.

It was getting late and the Kafenio was getting ready to close. Margolis wanted one last shouting match with the old Greeks. He quickly pulled a chair near the lead table and got up on it. He started shouting, pontificating and preaching to a group of tired, bored old Greeks. He was causing a great deal of commotion by waving his hands for broad effect, jumping off and on his chair to get their attention and shouting above the small group of men who were laughing with or at him and enjoying the closing act.

Peter and Christos left him and the old Greeks shouting obscenities at each other. Peter asked, "Is he crazy?" Christos answered, "He's a genius at play."

THE PLAY OF THE GAME

"I was led into captivity by the bitch business – the game is to tangle, lure and snare." C.H. Sisson

Peter needed a job during his training period playing cards with the old Greeks Spending money was a must. Funds were necessary just to live. He couldn't keep on relying on Christos. He had to get on his 'feet' and enjoy the excitement of this great city. Money would help him feel free and enjoy the nights and bright lights of New York City.

After a little searching, he found a job at a high-end Greek restaurant in New York City. He worked in the kitchen, cleaned tables off, functioned as maître' de and did whatever else was needed. There was no pride or hubris only thankfulness that he was able to have a job where language was not a barrier and food was always available, Greek music was there for inspiration and sentimentality, and the job served as a wonderful cover for his true vocation – playing cards with an unfair advantage.

Peter played cards with the old Greeks and learned some of the 'tricks of the trade.' Margolis was right he learned how to play a winning hand and manage the game.

But Peter knew he couldn't take a chance on promises. He needed a job at this stage in his life. He needed spending money and needed to get on his 'feet' and enjoy the excitement of this great city. He needed money to feel and enjoy the brightness of this land and country.

It was an interesting learning experience about an old trade – gambling. Peter had already learned much about game techniques by watching the tricks played by the old men at the kafenio in Greece and elsewhere; but now he would be playing at a very sophisticated level and for high stakes. He had to know more about the trade if he was to play with the 'night-time' high rollers.

Peter turned out to be a 'quick study' and a natural at the game. He learned how to mark the cards by bending the corners of cards, how to use sandpaper hidden under a ring to scratch the cards, how to poke them and how to memorize cards played and held. Most important he was taught how to play a hand, how to never change expression or talk with his body movements and how to know the fine art of bluffing.

He had met Margolis' terms. It was time to meet with the master trickster. Peter was excited. He was about to become one of Margolis' trickster. Christos contacted Margolis about meeting Peter at the Kafenio and he showed up as promised.

Margolis first lesson was about He was going to be taught the 'play and the con' of the game. He then went on to teach him that even in a 'professionally managed' game of chance, the player must still get a good hand to play; but if he didn't, he had to know when to bluff or when to throw in the cards. Managing the game meant controlling the risks, minimize losses and maximize gains. It required good judgment and mastering the art of deception.

One of Margolis' rules was to 'hide' the winnings. During the game there would be losing hands and, if not, the 'card playing' con required that some losses be taken to demonstrate the for authenticity of the player. Large wining should not be left on the table and the players should hide their winnings on their person. Most times large bills go into a player's shoe or pocket as the game progressed.

Then there was the play of partners and they discussed the concept and positioning of a partner at the table. The partner always sits to the right of the player and takes the 'bad' cards until a 'good' card shows and can go to the lead player. The partner knows when to take a bad card by looking at the right hand of the player to see if the thumb and forefinger are connected or separated. If they are separated, the partner takes cards as long as possible without drawing suspicion.

They went over game etiquette and, very simply, it was last in first out. Margolis said, "If you get into a game and you see marks on the cards you must leave if you are the last one into play." They worked together for over six months before Margolis told Peter that he was ready for his first game. As part of the service, he promised to arrange Peter's first game, and, of course, for a large percentage of the earnings.

Margolis felt like he had to address Peter's innate honesty. He started with a qualifier. He told Peter that he loved the United States, but he needed to warn him about the con men. They exist and they have the money which they probably got it by taking advantage of small investors and people. He told him, "Don't have any qualms about taking their money. They take from others. Remember, the game is not about getting rich; it is to help you make some money, help you to survive, maybe make some money to start a business or another, engage in a little commerce. And along the way, try to help others if you can."

It was time to go. Margolis was tired of talking and they were tired of hearing him talk.

During his short tenure with Margolis, Peter confirmed what he already knew. Margolis was a master trickster. He followed a grand design - that of creative play between chance and necessity. He knew and recited the mythical lies that reveal the eternal truths about all the other con men. Margolis had attitude and maybe he was a closet-idealist. No doubt. he always caused mischief and did tricks to reveal other people's hidden purposes. But he did show Peter the way to make a living – and made it possible for him to buy some 'fruits and the meat of the gods' to satisfy his needs. Peter had learned how to control and capitalize on the play of the cards.

Margolis promised to arrange the first card games. Peter would soon be in action perfecting his skill as a professional gambler. Everything was in motion

There was even time for play. While they waited for the first game, Christos and Peter enjoyed the night life together and became even better friends in the process. Both of them were tinged with the excitement of the City and Peter's debut as a professional gambler. There was the promise of meeting new people, new places to go and things to do. Peter was confident and ready to take control of his life. For the first time, Peter believed that he had found the way to have a life plan, which would be of his own choosing and making.

TRAVELING THE CROSS ROADS

"I've known rivers ancient as the world and older than the flow."
— Langston Hughes

Gambling is one of mankind's oldest activities and evidence of it has been found across the globe throughout the ages. It is as old as known history itself and was first mentioned in Greek literature. Everyone, from the upper elite to the peasants and the slaves enjoyed gambling. Playing cards was not just considered to be a game of luck and chance, but it was believed that the play was controlled by the gods. The casting of dice was a way of choosing rulers, making predictions and betting on circumstances. Games later developed which became pleasurable forms of gambling and grew in popularity through to the middle ages and right through to the present day.

Peter was now embroiled in an 'edge of life' game. He chose a profession that was based on calculated risk, chance and necessity. He was now a trickster in his own right.

However, he needed a huge stake; but there was only one asset that he had and that was the gold cross that Antigone left him. He had to make a decision whether to let go of the only physical remembrance he had of her and of their moments together. But there was really no choice for him, he had to pawn the beautiful gold cross to get his stake and give himself a fighting chance to make a living in hectic New York.

He always believed that he would retrieve the cross from the pawn shop, but when he went back to retrieve it he found out that it was sold. After he found out he was left feeling guilt, sadness and remorse. He buried his feelings about the gold cross knowing that life doesn't offer many or even any choices. It was ironic that he had to let go of the gold cross.

Peter was saddened by what he had to do. He remembered when he took the gold cross from the Orthodox Church and told Father Paris that the Church should give the gold to the people and only have wooden crosses. He now believed that he was the object of the lesson and he too was only entitled to a wooden cross. His golden spiritual keepsake and reminder of Antigone was gone forever.

The moment had come to pass. It was Antigone's gift from the past. Peter had his stake and was playing cards in cities along the East Coast. He was going from one place to the other in search of the elusive 'card game' and the opportunity to sharpen his skills and put together enough money to move up to the professional games in New York City and Boston. He spent lonely years on the road between Florida and Boston, Massachusetts and he met all manner of men playing game after game and experiencing a number of adventures which were more like close calls.

He was developing his 'standard model' going from city to city and game to game, and one close encounter after another and then the great escape.

The games he had in the South were dangerous. They hated immigrants and especially immigrants who could barely speak English. Peter flashed his passport – the one with the name Peter Salas that he obtained on the ship that brought him from Russia to the United States – but that didn't make much difference to these racist Southern country boys. He was a foreigner and even though their ancestors were once immigrants this country was theirs and no damn foreigners were going to take it from them and no damn foreigners were going to take their money from them.

Peter found that these 'good old boys' were pretty confident in their skills and their ability to mark. He was surprised at how proficient they were at markings the cards. But they were no match for Peter. Over the years in game after game around the country, he learned and developed defensive skills and counter-markings to sabotage and modify a marking system. His opponents never realized that they were getting false signals, changing everything to Peter's advantage.

The good old boys were usually joyful and happy. They had a new source; a 'pigeon' with fresh money. This was 'edge of the seat' moments as they were willing and anxious to teach this foreigner a thing or two about 'down country' play. They "would wipe and whip this guy until he had nothing left."

At the beginning of play, Peter would loss a few hands as he was concentrating on learning their system. This worked to his advantage as the ante was being raised with every hand. Then everything changed. He started winning and winning, but to keep them interested he loss a few hands to keep them in the game. By early morning most of the 'old boys' had gone home a lot lighter in their pockets. Peter won a lot of money and now had to find a way to 'unwind' and get out of the game and town alive. He lost a few more hands to the remaining players and that seemed to quiet them.

Then he asked for a break, He told them that he was going out for a smoke, some breakfast and to wash up. As soon as he was out of the game and gone from the premises, he was running for his life. He barely got out of their clutches with his winnings. The good old boys didn't know what happened and started blaming each other. They all went home thinking that they would see Peter again, they would be better prepared and the results would be different. They would fix that damn foreigner for good!

A MAN POSSESSED BY HIS SPIRIT

"Democritus, who was known as the laughing philosopher, described the life as everything existing in the universe is the fruit of chance and necessity."

Passage XIII

After a long tour of smaller cities, he returned to New York City and went directly to the Kafenio. An excited Margolis greeted him on his arrival and told him about a major game about to happen in Pittsburg. He had already arranged for him to be invited. He also told Peter that he should take a partner as the guys he would be matched against were real pros and very skilled in their play. And, oh yes, they were very rough boys if they are on the losing end of a game so he needed to be careful.

Margolis introduced Peter to a player named Johnny as his potential partner for the big game in Pittsburg and suggested they get to know each other. There was a lot of 'meet and greet' talk and then Peter and Johnny agreed to sit down and determine whether they could work together or not.

Margolis explained, "There are games, circumstances and times where a partner is required and plays a major role in controlling the flow and play of the cards. The partner provides flexibility and allows the play to go in one direction or another. You already have the knowledge of cards before they are played and your partner will function as the 'hinge' moving the flow of specific cards to him or away."

Peter didn't like partners and he usually played alone. He didn't feel comfortable managing the unknowns of a partner — his emotional makeup, his mind set, capabilities strategies, directions, reactions – all uncontrollable and dangerous factors; but as he moved up to larger and larger games he realized that he needed a hand that could take bad cards away from him and change flows and outcomes.

Johnny and Peter took a private table in the Kafenio and ordered drinks. Peter ordered Turkish coffee and Johnny order a coca cola and some sweets. Peter started with some small talk and asked: 'how old are you Johnny?' Johnny smiled and told him: 'thirty years old.' And then he kept talking and talking about himself, his life, his skill, his divorce, his girlfriend and Peter couldn't turn him off.

Once he released or 'dumped' all his personal 'stuff' on Peter he relaxed a little and let Peter get in, say something or ask more questions. Peter asked him: 'how do make your marks on the cards?' Johnny showed Peter a big gold ring with a large green opal in the middle and told him that he puts a small piece of sandpaper between the ring and the bottom side of his finger so that he could quickly scrapped the card without being too obvious. Johnny said, "Margolis told me that he sent the cards to the dealer and that the cards were solid without a white border. This will make it easy to mark the right cards."

Peter asked him, "Can you remember the cards?" Johnny said, "I've tried but I'm not good at that. We can't rely on my memory; but I can mentally influence the cards. It's a "trick of the mind, a trick of the light." I learned how to do this in the Philippines. All the old holy man can do things, change things, become part of the spirit world. We can all cause events and influence matter by using intense concentration. You'll see. We will get all the good cards when we play together.'

Peter didn't believe anything he said and was a little worried that he was going into a serious game with some rough men with a nut by his side. He excused himself and went to the back of the kafenio and interrupted the dialogue between Margolis and Christos, who he assumed were devising new schemes and 'hatching' new plans and adventures. Peter asked them, "Is this guy serious? That's crazy talk about the spirit world and how he can will and mentally move the cards around. We could lose a lot of money or worse get killed."

Margolis told Peter, "Relax. He is good with the cards and he is one of the best on the streets today. Play with him and you will see."

Peter left them and walked back to the table where Johnny was and said, "Let's play cards and get to know each other." They played and practiced together at the kafenio for most of the night and over the course of the evening they worked out their strategies and body signals to govern the play of the cards. It was good.

They closed the cards down. Peter told Johnny, "Don't mix and deal the cards so quickly. You will make everyone suspicious. Show a little ignorance and be respectful; it will go a long way in helping us to get out of there."

After the play they got some refreshments and went back to the table to talk some more. Peter asked him, "Aren't you scared to play in Pittsburg. You will walk into Hell and you better be prepared to face all your demons and control your fears." Johnny smiled, "I will have my God with me. We exist in His mind and we live again and again. So there is nothing to fear."

Peter was acquainted with all of the madness of the Greeks; now here was a priest without a collar, an unfrocked one, and a madman from the Philippines. He thought, "The whole world must be filled with crazy people."

Johnny was rubbing his gold opal ring and was thinking of other things. Peter interrupted his actions as a sign of nervousness or maybe he had moved into his own thoughts and into other realms. Johnny got up and told Peter, "I will see you in the morning. We can have breakfast together and take the train to Pittsburg."

Christos was smiling when they got outside. Peter asked, "Why are you smiling?" He told Peter, "I heard that this guy Johnny is into the mysteries. Certainly, you as a Greek know about the Mystery Schools. All the 'movers' of the world – Plato, Aeschylus, Alexander the Great, Caesar Augustus, Cicero and the others were practitioners of the occult and initiates in the secret philosophies. They used different techniques, sensory deprivation, breathing exercises, sacred dance, drama, drugs – you name it – to induce altered states of consciousness and influence the story of their world and change their destinies. You are in for a ride through a lot of craziness."

"That and this is all madness. I have to walk into this game with a holy man who is posing as a professional gambler."

Christos asked Peter, "Can he play cards?" Peter thought for a moment, "Yeah, I had a little trouble staying in the game with him. He got all the cards." They both laugh together. Christos said, "It's hard to know who the real madmen in this world are. He'll be a real asset to you in a tough and complicated game. And who knows he may bring some spiritual help with him."

HUBRIS WAS HIS TRAP

"The long days store up many things nearer to grief then joy ... death at last the deliverer." Sophocles

The next day, Peter and his new sidekick jumped on a train and soon after arrived in downtown Pittsburg. It was bleak. Peter didn't like the feel of the city and had a sense of foreboding. Johnny was happy, smiling and excited to get started.

They didn't waste any time and went straight to the game. They didn't even bother to check into a motel as they knew that they would leave town as quickly as they could.

Peter was a little nervous when they arrived at the bar. He sensed that something was not quite right.

They were directed to the second floor where the game was taking place. Peter was surprised by the size of these men. There were steel workers mostly, some merchants and businessmen playing a very serious card game. The stakes were high and the betting was fierce. Players were coming and going. Many of them did not last long. They liked the action and just became observers.

Johnny was excited. He saw the large sums of money that three of the players had amassed on the table. It pushed his 'greed button'. It was a dream come true.

Peter was thinking that they should leave. He was already looking for an escape route out of the building in case everything went wrong and he was feeling some degree of panic when he didn't see a way out. If they started to play rough; Peter's thought was to let the money go. It was not wise to 'test the fates for just paper money.'

They stepped into the game room and everything was set in motion. They no longer had choices, they had to take a place at the table and let destiny play the hand out. The night went as expected. Peter and Johnny won most of the hands played and pocketed a number of large cash pots. It was coming too fast. The cards were falling in the right way and they could almost win just with skill, knowledge and experience.

When they had a break, Peter whispered in Johnny's ears

that it was time to lose some money and get the hell out of there. Johnny wouldn't hear of it. He wanted it all. Peter told him to give him his large Opal ring and he would clean it in the bathroom and get rid of the sandpaper. Johnny said, "Okay but I am going back and play some more and milk those steel men."

Peter went to the bathroom to clean the ring and think about their escape plan. He found a small window, opened it and looked down. He was on the second floor and he peered down at a cement patio below. It would be a leap and a long fall and he wasn't sure that it was worth the risk. Then he heard a lot of yelling, what sounded like fighting and then silence after some shots were fired.

They were pounding at the bathroom door and trying to break it down. Peter's heart was racing, he had a massive internal release of adrenalin and his body started trembling as it surged through him. He was a little dizzy and out of sorts as he dealt with the reality that everything was closing in and crashing on him.

Cement landing and all, he was out the small window and landed clumsily on the cement below. He hurt his ankle, but that didn't stop him from mustering everything he had and managing to skip-limp into the night and over to the train station. He asked the old man at the ticket counter, "When will the next train get here?" The ticket man asked him, "Where do you want to go?" Peter hastily replied, "I don't care. Get me on the next train. I'll go wherever the next train goes."

Peter was lucky. He was able to purchase a ticket to Buffalo just as the train arrived. In no time he was aboard, seated, fidgety and feeling crazy tensions. In what seemed to be an eternity, the train moved slowly out of the station and he poked his head up to see the station quickly disappearing behind him. It was pure relief, he didn't care where he was going, he had a pocketful of money and he was safe.

He slouched down in his seat when he saw a bunch of men running into the station looking for him. The gods were with him and he hoped that Johnny was with his God. Poor Johnny was left in that 'hell hole.' He never heard from Johnny again; nor did anyone else.

When Peter finally got back to New York, he went straight to emergency to have his foot treated and a soft cast put on his foot. Then he went to the kafenio to find Christos and Margolis. Christos happened to be there and he immediately went to meet him. He was surprised to see Peter walk into the kafenio with a soft cast on his ankle and a walking cane to keep the pressure off his foot and leg. "What happened?" he asked. Peter said, "The doctor told me that he couldn't cast an ankle, too many small bones. It's called an incurable ankle."

"What happened at the card game?" Peter answered, "It was Johnny's greed and his excessive ego that got us into trouble. We had complete control of the cards and we could easily read and play them to our advantage. Our winnings mounted up. The power to dominate these tough steel workers at cards went to his head and made him feel like he had supernatural powers. He was slamming the table every time we won a hand. It was like spitting in their face. I warned him and told him to lose some hands. I wanted to get out of there as quickly as possible. It didn't feel right."

Peter paused for a moment and then said, "Margolis is also to blame for putting us in a 'no-win' situation. I am going to call him 'on it' and tell him that I can't work for someone who doesn't care about my safety. It is all about the 'buck' with him."

Christos gave Peter a word of caution; "Be careful. You need his contacts to find and get into games. Be diplomatic. Think about what you say to him. Words have power. You could be standing in the night with nothing to do if he abandons you."

"Christos, love you like a brother and value your advice; but my first goal is to get out of his trap and be on my own."

PASSAGE XIV

THE SWEETNESS OF LOVE
– AND ITS MADNESS

Choral Foreword:

Much of the discussion about the madness of love was offered by 'old' Greek philosophers who spent much of their time discussing the various attributes of love, beauty, truth, destiny and fate. They wanted everyone to believe that love's passions are a kind of divine madness sent to us by the gods, a madness that is brought by the gift of bliss. It may be that their age and experiences made them cynical about pure and true love which they believed is twinge with traces of madness. In the dialogue entitled Phaedrus, Socrates expressed his belief in the value of madness in life and beyond:

"There is a third form of possession or madness, of which the Muses are the source. This seizes a tender, virgin soul and stimulates it to rapt passionate expression, especially in lyric poetry, glorifying the countless mighty deeds of ancient times for the instruction of posterity.

But if any man comes to the gates of poetry without the madness of the Muses, persuaded that skill alone will make him a good poet, then shall he and his works of sanity with him be brought to naught by the poetry of madness, and behold, their place is nowhere to be found."

Plato echoed the call that the poetical hypnotism instilled

on men by the Muses is a form of possession and madness by noting that, "He who without the divine madness comes to the doors of the Muses meets with no success, and the poetry of the sane man vanishes into nothingness before that of the inspired madmen."

He preached that the gifts and conditions of lust and love were given by the gods to the Muses and that these gifts were to be used to torture Greek men. In fact, some brooding Greek men believe that many women enjoy torturing them with their fragrance, their beauty, their succulent bodies and the controlling promises of pleasure. They went so far as to say that a woman may have a romantic soul and the spirit of a muse aching for true love; but their reality and motivations are not ruled by a compassion for men. here were other Greeks who recognized the spirituality of true love as witnessed by the poems of ancient Greece which are replete with tributes to the divine mistresses of love and pleasure. Clearly the myths of Greece conclude that love's passions are flashes of fire in the heart leaving an eternal flame that cannot be quenched, for love is more powerful than death.

Like many Greek men and women, Peter believed that, in its extreme state, love can drive the lover and the beloved to commit acts of folly, foolishness and stupidity which can lead to the destruction of the precious relationship they were trying to preserve. The Greek view is that love in its extreme leads to madness and Peter during his life subscribed to that view, but he did so with an acceptance of the humorous insanity of it all.

THE TRICKER'S TRAP

"All knowledge and ideas are hidden in the soul. Plato"

Peter's new life as a professional gambler was a lonely, brutal grind, night in and night out. He was in the Trickster's trap and looking for a way out, but he had no immediate way to 'trip' the trap and escape.

Even though Christos was telling him to be cautious with Margolis because he controlled (bribe) the inside men who controlled access to the card games. But Peter was of a different mind. He wasn't going to keep risking his life playing against the good old boys. Margolis sold Peter by telling him that he would be playing against the Wall Street crowd who could afford to lose money and who didn't come after you with a gun if they lost money in a card game. Peter didn't like taking money from the workers; he wanted the Wall Street crowd.

It was time for a confrontation with Margolis. Peter was willing to risk his business relationship with Margolis. He made Margolis a lot of money over the years he worked with him. If he wasn't a valuable asset to the Trickster by now; then it was time to move on and find something new.

Deep inside Peter was feeling pretty good about himself. He had emerged from a young boy on the run – his Odyssey – to a man controlling his destiny.

He set up a meeting with Margolis at the Kafenio and was on his way to meet him. Christos was also going, not to help Peter with Margolis; but as an observer. This was 'high' Greek theater. Whatever the outcome, they were going to the Greek nightclub that night to celebrate Peter's victory or his escape from the trap. Peter was in a good state of mind for his negotiations – he didn't care how it turned out.

Peter and Christos arrived at the Kafenio before Margolis and were drinking Turkish coffee – a dark, hot bitter coffee. Christos asked Peter, "What wrong? You seem down?" Peter asked, "Can someone be sad and happy at the same time?" Christos answered, "There is a very thin line of reality between the two feelings. I guess the answer is yes. Why the question?"

Peter answered, "I received a picture from my mother of my father, my brother and mother together. They were very happy and it was great to see that my father made it home. I am sad because I missed them all and wish I could be with them?"

Christos smiled and said, "We'll celebrate your father's return tonight and do what all Greeks do in these kinds of moments. We'll go listen to Greek music and drink." Peter smiled at the thought he just got and said, "That reminds me of something my Yaya told me. She told me that when a Greek is happy, they listen to Greek music, drink and cry. When a Greek is sad, they listen to Greek music, drink and dance." Christos said, "We'll do both."

At that moment, Margolis came in the door with his usual flair and a joyous look on his face. He was heading toward Peter when the old Greeks called him to their tables. Peter waved his hand in such a way as to tell him it was okay to go first to the old Greeks.

They heard the old Greeks in unison ask Margolis to tell them a story, or recite a Greek poem or sing a song. Margolis was smiling as he stood on a chair. One of the old Greeks yelled out, "Margolis you should have been a performer not a thief." Margolis seemed to take some offense to that remark and said, "I'm not a thief; I'm a trickster and if you knew anything about mythology you would know that tricksters' tricks always backfired on him to the advantage of his victim. The cards are always stacked up against him. He starts action, but the gods always make him lose."

Some of the other Greeks told the old Greek who made the remark to 'shut up' and let Margolis say his piece.

Margolis said, "I've been doing some thinking about our lives and I reached the conclusion that we were 'night crawlers'. We sleep during the day and come out at night. In fact, there are many of us who work and play at night. Just the opposite of most people. The old Greeks were shaking their heads 'yes' but it was clear that they were not thinking it was a good thing, but that it was an accurate observation.

Margolis went on with his talk. By then, everyone was serious and thinking of their own situation. They were also disappointed that he had not brought them his usual comedy routine. He was preaching to these old Greeks; perhaps, a waste of time but Margolis was determined to make his point and give them some awareness of hos they were living their lives.

He said, "I have a poem which tells the story of the of night life. It is a poem entitled: "Acquainted with the Night" by Robert Frost that describes the lonely road traveled by many people:

> "I have been acquainted with the night. Night life.
> I have walked out in rain – and back in rain.
> I have out-walked the furthest city light.
> I have looked down the saddest city lane.
> I have passed by the watchman on his beat

And dropped my eyes, unwilling to explain.

Once he got off the chair, an old Greek asked him if he talks to everyone he sees. Margolis answered, "I talk to anyone who will listen. I'm like Socrates, except he was a Greek and admitted that he didn't know 'nothing'. I'm a Jew and, of course, I know everything."

Another old Greek asked, "What's worse. Someone who doesn't know anything or someone who thinks he knows everything." Another old Greek answered, "Someone who thinks that he knows everything, but really knows nothing." Another old Greek laughed and said, "Like all of us. We think we know it all, but we know nothing. Socrates was right."

Margolis had a laugh with the old Greeks and left them and came over to Peter and Christos. He held his hand up and said to Peter, "I know what you are going to say. And you are right. I let you and Johnny down. I'm to blame for what happened to him. It is on my karma."

He added, "And Peter, I'm sorry. I took advantage of you and put you in harm's way. Not only that I promised you one thing and gave you another. From now on, I'll arrange games in the big cities like Boston and New York."

Margolis said his piece and went silent. Peter thought for a moment and said, "We're good." There were smiles all around.

"To tell the truth, the poem was not for the old Greeks. Their time is almost up and there is no time or value in remorse. It was for you two. You are two bright, handsome guys and your life is ahead of you. The night life is not for you guys. You'll want to be in love, have a family and live a life that you can live with them. You can't do that having to crawl the streets at night."

Peter and Christos didn't expect that. There was no hidden agenda or devious motive. It was straight from the heart. It was a sweet moment of love and honesty, which doesn't come too often in life. It was a moment when men let their guard down and within their silence, they conveyed to each other that they cared and valued one another.

Peter and family in Lesbos

THE SWEETNESS OF LOVE

"Love is a flame and ashes; love is a moan and a grudge" From a Greek song

"The ancient Greeks described Love as a strange feeling. It is captivating madness. When unfulfilled, there is a burning in the heart. It is a soul thing; an expression of true love can be a simple act like having a hand reach out and press it to a loving heart."

Peter and Christos were relieved that the confrontation with Margolis went so well. They left the Kafenio and were on their way to the Greek nightclubs on Fifth Avenue. Christos said, "I have a few surprises to share with you. I've been doing a lot of thinking about my life and what I want to do with it. When I ask myself serious questions, I am always surprised by what the answers I get. This time was no exception."

They found a table in a corner with a good view of the band and dance floor. It was always fun to watch a group of people hold hands and dance in rhythm to Greek music. They were excited, ordered drinks, some food and were set for an 'Opa" night.

Peter told Christos that he was fascinated by the many beautiful young ladies in New York City. Lesbos was never like that. The girls were pretty, but the girls in New York were like pained dolls. They were 'high heels' tall, beautifully dressed, hair perfect, and sexy. They knew it and it gave them attitude and attitude made them even more alluring.

They had a few too many drinks and the Greek music

Passage XIV 433

took hold of them. Greek music is magical and creates wonderful moods. Once in this mood, the mind goes to wonderful places.

Christos and Peter were listening to a new song whose words dug deep into their hearts and opened old wounds:

"Night after night, truckload after truckload I barged into life too late to be able to deny it now, a great love and terror. In the night I get drunk, I am dazzled by headlights, who's after my life?

My heart wants to fly, to fly and be like a God,

End and beginning, my grey soul, love is a flame and ashes"

Peter asked Christos, "What do you think this crazy thing called love is — a 'flame', a 'flame' and the 'ashes' of a broken heart?"

Christos said, "It may be that I am a fool in love, but I think true love is about finding and being with your soul mate.

Love yearns for an intimate relationship with a soul mate. It is not that I don't enjoy 'one-night stands'; but I've had my fill of them. Falling in love with the wrong woman can start the 'flame' in a person's heart. The 'ashes' are what's left of a burned heart.

Playing cards taught Peter how to read someone's mental state and Christos' response indicated that he was under emotional stress of some sort. It was either time to discuss his problem or change the subject. Peter decided to keep it light and he change the subject.

He interrupted Christos and told him that he had a comical story to tell about the old Greeks, "A funny thing happened to me when I first arrived in the States. I asked the old Greeks what are the women like and how do I approach them. They could only talk about the women of the streets. They were possessed by the thought of the naughty girls and warned me not to fall in love with one of them. They told me that there were many women available for a price. These women know how to handle immediate needs; but do not fall in love with them. They are tender traps."

I told them, "I want to know how to find and approach a girl in the States. Not warnings about prostitutes and the naughty girls of the night."

One of the old Greeks answered me by saying you can't know what true love is until you know what it isn't. We are giving you warnings. What you do is your own business. . The girls we are talking about are as beautiful, and even more so than other girls; but just because they give you all they got, doesn't mean that their 'giving' is the same as love. They may be down on their luck or they may have chosen or were forced into the streets, but it is best to start with innocent girls instead of risking a lifetime of remorse that will surely come with the experienced ones."

Christos was back into it and said, ". The old Greeks had some advice for me. s. But I soon realized that they were just 'too full' of themselves. They tried to make me think that they were 'great lovers' - the usual 'bullshit' of old men way past their prime. I knew they had brains. They had survived the trip to the States and made a living; but their thoughts about women were better suited to Greece and the tradition of arranged marriages. Frankly, I can't imagine somebody else picking my wife and my being married to a stranger."

Peter said, "I made the same mistake; except I talked to Margolis. I quickly found out that he didn't know anything about love. I wanted to know how to attract women in the

States. How different was it from Greece? The old cynic gave me 'crazy talk' about attracting, dating and making love. He told me that dating in the States was subject to the laws of averages. It was a little like baseball. First, you had to get up to the batting plate as many times as you can and then it was all about your batting average. You'll make passes at women and expect to strike out many times; but you only need a hit or two along the way to stay in and enjoy the game. It is about percentages. Forget about the strike-outs, concentrate on the hits and scores."

Peter added, "I also had a good talk with the men at the restaurant. They told me not to hurry the process. When you are ready and when destiny calls your number, the right girl for the moment or longer will show up. They said that I needed to become successful. Women adore power and money and are looking for a good provider who can afford to build a nest with them. The good girls were mostly about love and having children.

Christos said, "Let's stop talking about the 'bull shit' of fools. They are too old to remember what love was. I have something that has been bothering me and I need to talk with you about it. In fact, you are the only one I can talk to about it. The tragedy is what I did to Dimitri and my sister. I ruined their lives and I can't get over it."

What brought this all back to me was Steve, your friend and traveling companion. You told me that Steve had a chance to make it to the States and instead went back to Greece to be with the young girl he had a relationship with. You also told me that he couldn't even take care of himself and, yet, he was willing faced up to her powerful father because he loved her."

Peter concurred, "I did say that."

"My heart broke when I heard that. Dimitri probably would have gone back to my sister. I destroyed their relationship. It was wrong of me to interfere with love for tradition. I cause so much damage. I want so badly to be wrong and be told that I did the right thing, but down deep inside I know it was wrong of me. My pain is my truth."

Christos stopped talking and looked at Peter for an answer. Peter said, "There are questions we can't answer. Your destiny and journey are far bigger than us." Christos persisted and said, "Yes, I know all that but what do you think?"

Peter weighed in on the discussion. "There is a major difference between Steve and Dimitri. It was about love. Steve never stopped loving her and did everything he could to be with her. Dimitri was different. He seemed to be running away from your sister. Maybe Dimitri would have had a change of heart, but more likely he was either too scared or just running from the responsibilities or, sadly, not in love."

"Thanks Peter. That helped, but my pain is still there and probably always will be."

Peter reached out and laid his hand on Christos' arm as a sign of support and understanding. Christos said, "There is more to talk about. In her last letter, Cleis said that she wanted me to return and come to her. She still loves me and wants to start a life together. She is ready to leave and come back to America with me."

Peter asked, "Isn't that what you have been waiting for? Go to her!" Christos replied, "It is a little more complicated than just leaving and going to her."

Christos ordered another round of drinks. He stopped talking and listened to the Greek music. That damn Greek music made him sad when he thought of Helene.

Not being with her was like the flame that was slowly turning him into ashes and he had no choice. He needed to fly back to Europe and be with her. He realized that she was his soul mate and he had to fight for their love and life together. He had one sickening thought and that was his karma. Would he be denied and even killed for what he did to Dimitri?

Peter knew it would just be a matter of time before Christos went back and seek some resolution with her. Unfortunately, she was a captive of her family and a valuable asset to be used through the right marriage to consolidate the power of the royal family. He was captive. Peter believed that it was madness to return to her and find a solution to the battle he would be facing. But he knew that Christos had to find a way to be with her.

Peter didn't feel the same pain that Christos was feeling, but he knew that he would have his own pain and a song to sing when his time for a new love beyond all reason came.

On his way home Peter passed a homeless man and he gave him enough money for a week of meals. Peter always felt sorry for anyone who was down on their luck. This was his way of acknowledging the needs of others and giving back. Whenever he could, he would give a share of his winnings to the unfortunate people on the streets. He thought of himself as taking from those who have and giving a share to those in need.

The Greek are mysteries people. They are superstitious and always aware of a spiritual presence. No doubt, Peter was aware that, but for the grace of God, he could be among those in need. But it was more than that for him. He always had an open heart and an open pocket book for those in need.

PETER'S CALYPSO FANTASY

"Every heart sings a song and waits to hear a heart sing back."
Author

Peter didn't hear from Christos for almost a month. He didn't think too much of it, but was pleasantly surprised to hear from him and accept his invitation to join him that night at the Greek nightclub. He told Peter that he had a couple of surprises for him.

That night Peter went to the club and was greeted at the door by a smiling Christos. There were smiles and hugs hello. Both men had become genuinely fond of each other and couldn't wait to have a few drinks together, talk and listen to some lively Greek music.

After the evening got started, Christos told Peter that he had made up his mind and was leaving the States in the next few days. He decided that he was going to Helena and try to make his life with her. Peter was surprised, but as he thought about it he wasn't. It always felt right for Christos to go to her.

Peter tried hard not to come across as lecturing him, but felt compelled to warn him about the danger. Her family was very powerful and could have him killed. Christos said, "I thought about that, but I can't really help myself. Love is a compulsion and a form of madness. The ancients were right about love being a form of bliss and bliss is a form of possession and possession as driving a person to madness.

After all that was acknowledged and said, Christos seemed relieved and even joyous with the thought that he had made a major decision and was free. Peter knew that a good part of his joy was seeing and being with his soul mate, as he described her.

Christos sang a Greek song that the band was playing:

*"Spread your wings and fly away;
fly softly to the heart and mind."*

At that moment, a pretty waitress cama up to him and started to sing with him.

*"Spread your wings
And escape from where the darkness lies
where the prison is
Oh Lord, give me the wings to save myself
Hold me tight not to lose myself."*

Christos and the waitress smiled at each and hugged each other tight for a short moment. She left and he sat down with Peter, who had a big grin on his face. Christos said, "Try singing to a woman someday. See where it takes you." The word back from Peter was *bravo*.

Peter said, "I was told by a beautiful woman that I knew in Turkey that 'Every heart has a song to sing.' She also told me that the word 'song' meant many things. It could be an expression of love or it could mean a journey or it could just mean a wonderful moment together with someone."

"Yes, I guess so. I never thought of all that." Christos said, "I have a surprise for you. Not sure I'm doing you a favor, but I decided to turn my nighttime carnation and flower business over to you. It will be a good source of additional income for you, but there are a few things I should tell you. The girls are all going to college and there is pretty rapid turnover. A lovely lady named Agape is the leader of these ladies and she is very strong and runs my business with a tight hand. She is a Sicilian Greek and their families should be avoided. As is their habit of these Sicilians they do a lot of things with kisses."

Peter asked, "What do you mean?" Christos smiled and said; "If she likes you and accept you as my replacement, she'll kiss you on the cheek. If she doesn't kiss you before the night is over, then she won't do the deal. Oh, and coming in the door is that surprise."

It was more than just a surprise for Peter. A beautiful young lady followed by a number of other beautiful women were coming in the door and heading to their table.

Much to Peter's delight, they all seemed friendly with broad and captivating smiles on their faces. He could hear their chatter and their laughter which was going on 'non-stop'. There were four ladies who were young, heavenly and divine in appearance. But he knew that he had to be careful as they could turn in a' New York' minute. He knew that they were probably reserved in attitude and, behind their appearances, each of them was complicated, apparently intelligent, no doubt interesting, passionate and inviting, and of course very needy.

Agape gave Christos a kiss on the cheek and each of the ladies did the same. Agape went to Peter and greeted him with a smile and a short tight hand shake. No kiss on the cheek yet. All the ladies did the same thing.

Agape said, "Peter these beautiful girls are my friends and roommates. This is Callie, our poetess and intellectual. Next to her is Melody who sings and writes songs. She is everyone's good friend and is very funny. She makes us all laugh. It is hard to believe that someone so pretty makes us laugh at her and at ourselves. And this serious lady is Poly, who tells us that there is more to the world than we can imagine."

Christos said, "Peter they are all roommates and the personification of Hesiod's Muses. For your safety, you should know that there are no secrets between them."

Peter smiled, said hello to each of them, sat down next to Agape and instantly forgot everyone's names. He could see that these ladies were special. Even though they were in 'lock step' with Agape; they had their own aspirations and possessed unique qualities, which were enhanced by inherent feminine intuition and inherent psychological understanding of people's nature.

Drinks were served. Dinner was served to those who were not watching their weight. The chatter was intense. Christos and Peter didn't know which way to turn his head and who he should listen to. Most of the time he didn't even what was going on with everyone. But he acted like he knew what was being said and he did what any wise man would do – he smiled at everyone and had 'make believe' conversations with them.

Finally, Agape made a move and asked everyone to get up and dance. She asked Peter to lead the line.

Peter was an average dancer; not a fluid and natural one. He tried hard, but he was slow and deliberate in his steps. He was pleasantly surprised when Agape took over and it was clear that she knew the graceful rhythms of Greek dancing. Peter stayed as the second in line and keep the beat going as she improvised her steps.

They danced the steps of the song together and at the

same time she continued to lead the line of dancers. Peter was pleased that she added a degree of sophistication to the dance. With Peter in the lead everyone would have stumbled over 'moving' feet and bumped into each other. A disaster was averted.

On the way back to the table, Peter tanked her for taking control of the line dance. This simple act of humility sealed the deal. She kissed him on the cheek and gave him a hug. All the girls followed suit at the same time and Peter was in his glory surrounded and mauled by all these beautiful ladies.

When the magic moment was over and they were seated at the table, Peter asked Agape, "Are you the ringleader of these lovely ladies. Are they your loving Muses?" She replied, "Yes. They are my roommates and we are all good friends. We go to school together. We are inseparable. But sadly, when someone graduates, they leave and we don't see each other again."

Christos took Agape aside and she confirmed their acceptance of Peter as his replacement. She told Christos that she cared for him and reluctantly kissed him good bye.

Peter and Christos conveniently met at the men's bathroom. Christos asked, "Do you want all this madness?" He made the only decision a man in his right mind could and said, 'yes'.

Agape made the announcement. To all the girls. They gleefully crowded around Peter, made a fuss over him and showered him with kisses. They hugged him and their soft energies overpowered him and made him a little dizzy. Agape stood back and couldn't be more pleased. Peter had some difficult times in the past, but this was a major accomplishment. Calypso and these lovely Muses were not ordinary women. They were classic Muses who had strange inspirational powers over Greek men. Peter felt that power. His childhood fantasy had come true. Like Odysseus, Peter found his Calypso and her muses. He would spend many wonderful years with them before destiny claimed them back again.

Christos was smiling; almost laughing. He said, "Good luck Peter! You will need it. Your life will never be the same. Remember, you wished for this fantasy and the gods decided to punish you by making your wish come true." All Peter could do was shrug his shoulders.

Peter wondered what the future would bring. He suddenly knew why Odysseus turned down Calypso's offer of immortality and her loving company and that of her maidens. He would lose his ego, his identity, and he would be no more. The ancient Greeks believed that once a Greek loses his identity. He is gone. He is dead and no one remembers him. It is as if he had never existed. Pretty scary.

In spite of the madness, Peter decided, "There was no better way to go. He would lose himself in a perfumed paradise." It was time for Peter to experience 'young love' with its unbridled desires, its soaring passions, its 'breath-taking' excitement and its uncontrolled madness.

Yet, his Odyssey was still a search for his 'soul mate', for true love and for its spiritual meaning.

AS IN A DREAM

"The entire visible Cosmos is a sympathetic reflection of the divine in matter, time and space". K. Stein

Young life was over. Peter started to realize that something was missing. He was living a full life in New York City, but he was approaching 'thirty years of age' and felt empty inside. His mother recently wrote and told him that his father had returned to Greece. He was sure that this was the reason for his loneliness. He missed Greece, his home and his family. There was a 'hole' in his heart.

That night Peter had trouble falling asleep. Against his will, from deep inside his being, Peter was hearing the call of new voices. He dreamed that he had lost his real identity in New York City. That it was time for him to become who he really was and to find his rightful place in the world. His dream images were strange and unfamiliar sights of new places.

He felt like he was being drawn to something new in his life, but what? He continued to toss and turn and was overwhelmed with the feeling that he was connecting to higher planes of reality, and that he was being prepared and drawn to new life directions.

He woke up early and made his morning cup of coffee, took a few moments to relax and read the paper from Greece. In the back of his mind, he was trying to figure out what was happening to him. He recalled that his mother told him that intense feelings meant something 'unusual' was going to happen to him and that he should expect major changes in his life.

Peter was a creature of habit. He did what he always did during these moments in his life; he went to the port and the harbor to be near and with the water. He found a spot where he could see the Statute of Liberty, that grand lady and listen to the roar of the ocean. He was taken back to Greece when he felt the cooling mist from the waves hitting his face. The sounds of the crashing waves helped him to relax. Even the fishy smells from the harbor were delightful. It was a moment.

That night he got ready for a long night of cards. He put his uniform on — the three piece black suit, the freshly clean and pressed white shirt, an under stated dark tie, polish shoes. Underneath his elegant attire, he wore his beige silk underwear. He was ready for a long night and a morning game with the 'high rollers.'

He was anxious to play and he arrived at the hotel a little early. It gave him time to have a mid-day dinner and sometime after dinner to relax before his opening act at the card table started.

While he was in the restaurant drinking coffee and reading the newspaper from Greece; Agape came into the restaurant and walked up to him. She came to him and made believe that she was trying to sell him a carnation, but all she really wanted was to connect with him and give him a small kiss for good luck. She whispered to him that he looked very handsome and didn't want to say goodbye. Peter was puzzled. She never came to him before a game. He reached out and held her hand. They smiled at each other and then she left.

Then it came to him. Was this the goodbye kiss that Christos warned him about? They were together for four happy years and he couldn't imagine that she was leaving him. She was always happy, even loving, when she was with him. He remembered what Christos told him, "She was a Sicilian Greek and her family controlled her life. Perhaps, she was called to an arranged marriage.

After he finished eating, Peter was feeling a little odd again. Maybe it was too much coffee, too much anticipation, too much energy around him; he wasn't sure what was going on and what he was feeling. Maybe he was upset about Agape. Whatever it was he had to turn all of it off. Game time was approaching and he had to make his way to the main ball room.

Like all game players, he was superstitious and followed a routine that he thought gave him a little energy and protected him from bad luck. He brushed down his 'three-piece' suit with his open hand, took his black fedora off and folded the crease, pulled the gold watch out of his vest pocket and checked the time, He adjusted the white shirt under his vest and lastly neatly tightened his tie. Now he was ready to engage and take on some great card players.

As he was approaching the 'hat check' counter. he felt a strong burst of energy overcoming and attracting him. That force got stronger and more intense the closer he got to the counter. For some unknown reason, he was surprised to see a beautiful lady at the counter and he felt like he was being drawn to her. His focus and energy had shifted away from getting ready for a long night of cards and his attention now was concentrated on her. He couldn't know that sympathetic energy was in full expression around him and that his life was being changed at a spiritual level.

When he got to the counter, she was singing a Greek song that he knew. The words were typical Greek melancholy and sad events. He smiled and started singing with her. She was pleasantly surprised to see a handsome man in front of her singing along with her.

The lyrics were not exactly right for someone new; but it was a song for the moment:

"If you only were in this fire you started

You'd be burning in my arms
And when the flames covered you
It'd be the sweetest torture
I'm standing in your fire
But you don't want to join me"

Vera put her hand over her mouth to hide her singing. Actually, she was covering her smile. Peter jokingly did the same thing. She said, "I don't want my boss to hear me singing with a customer." Peter said, "I understand. Thank you for the moment."

Peter usually had control of his emotions, but a wave of intense attracting energy was overcoming him. He sensed a burning in his heart. Peter was sweating from the heat. That lady seemed to be the consuming flame.

He asked her, "What is your name?" She smiled and when she did Peter felt a positive force go through him. He thought it was just the energy of confidence. She answered, "My name is Bessie. No, now it is Vera." Peter paused for a moment and said, "Okay…. Vera it is nice to meet you."

She didn't ask him for his name, so he volunteered it. "My name is Peter." No real response. He stayed in the conversation and asked her, "Where are you from?" She answered, "I'm from Boston and my family is from Lesbos." Peter got a little excited at the thought that she came from the same island that he did. He asked her in Greek, "What town?" She answered him straight away in Greek, "We are from Aghiasso." He laughed and excitedly said, "I am from Plomari. What a coincidence! We had to come thousands of miles to meet."

Vera couldn't hold back talking about a deeply held belief. "My mother used to say that there is no such thing as a coincidence - only destiny. She used to say that a coincidence is always meaningful and that something mysterious happens when events that are 'spiritually related' take place."

Peter asked, "What does all that mean?" Vera answered, "It could mean a lot of things. It could mean that we are connected because we are both from Lesbos." Peter interrupted and said, "And the surprising thing is that we met in the big city of New York at the Waldorf Astoria. Who could have predicted that?" Vera said, "It could also mean that like attracts like. That we are from the same tribe, that we have the same blood and that we have similar feeling and energies. Like attract like."

Peter said, "How can that be? We don't know each other and it doesn't make sense to me that people who don't really know each other can attract and find each other in this great big world."

Vera said, "I remember asking my mother that question? She said that everything in the universe is connected. God connected us to each other spiritually and that we are guided our feelings." Peter asked, "How does your mother know all these things?" Vera said, "She is an old Greek lady who talks to the Other One on the other side who tells her all these things.

Peter wondered, "What a crazy conversation?" He asked, "Who is the Other One?" She said, "Not sure. She mentioned the name Apollos, the Greek mythical god of prophecy."

He didn't want to hurt her feelings by telling her that no one can read the future because it hasn't happened yet. So instead, he said, "She sounds like an interesting lady. I'd like to meet her someday." Vera answered, "If it is meant to be, you will."

Passage XIV

For some unknown reason, he felt a little embarrassed. He tried to change the subject with a little humor and asked, "Isn't Aghiasso way up in the hills? Are you a Hill Billy?" Vera didn't answer him. She dropped her arms by her side and gave him a "dead pan" look. Peter said to himself, "Oh! Oh! That was not funny." He smiled at her and said, "I'm sorry. I am not very good at making jokes." She smiled back when she heard his sweet apology and then reached out and shook his hand. "OK we're friends, no offense taken."

They were silent staring at each other. Suddenly she said, "Hey, I've seen you before. You were that well-dressed man who danced alone to a sad song at the Greek nightclub. Everyone was looking at you because you were dancing with your overshoes on. I had the strongest feeling to join you and almost got up and danced with you."

Peter smiled and said, "When a Greek man dances alone, it is because he is dancing with his soul. When I dance, I struggle to become one with my inner self."

Vera asked, "Do you dance to forge?."

Peter answered quickly, "Sometimes, but most times I dance to remember. Over the years, Greek people learned that the men who had to leave Greece never returned. These kinds of goodbyes are "an agony" for everyone to bear. Saying goodbye forever is a kind of death. Many times, leaving home means parting with loved ones; perhaps, forever. We believed that life will slowly dissolve them and that they will disappear. The road back home is usually never traveled and the past becomes nothing more than just "a sad goodbye in a tragic dream."

Peter added, "Once the music starts, the solitary dancer makes his way to the dance floor. Having enjoyed a few too many drinks, he is feeling a "release of life's pain." By this time, he is ready to dance. He is already in touch with the sadness of leaving the loves of his life and everything that was his life. As soon as he makes it to the center of the dance floor, he stretches his arms out as if they are wings and then he begins his dance, head down spinning slowly in circles."

Peter suddenly realized that it was time for him to leave. "He quickly said, "Perhaps, we will meet again and sing another song together."

Vera was surprised by her emotional surges and she too was struggling to get control of her senses. She reached for his hat with her right hand to show her ring finger. It was a "stop sign" and a signal that there was no going forward. He got the message, took a deep breath and told her, "I enjoyed meeting you."

The encounter left him with the strange feeling that he may have relived moments from his past or that he was getting a glimpse of the future. But these were strange thoughts for him. He was more of a realist and he quickly let go of them. He told himself that it was just another instance of meaningful Greek madness.

As they shook hands goodbye, a burst of energy surged through them. It was a connecting link of 'sympathetic feelings. They both knew that it was far more than mere emotional attraction. There was a "like-to-like" recollection of past lives. There was a "heart-to-heart" bonding that found existence in a spiritual plane of reality.

He now understood the reason for his dizziness and confusion. At some level of consciousness, a strong connecting bond had been forged between them. He found what he didn't know he was looking for and he would never be the same again.

Myths are the spiritual stories of life connected throughout the history of humankind by: 'the threads in time'.

EPILOGUE: CELERBRATING THE ODYSSEY

Peter's tale is a story of his struggle to survive and become who he was meant to be. His story starts with his youthful experiences and journey. It is connected to the past by the trials and tribulations that are similar to the life and death experiences of Odysseus, the main character in the tale of the Odyssey.

The overarching theme of Peter's story is his struggle to be free and find his rightful place in the world. He had to overcome many obstacles and dangers. His story started with a long journey, which is an historic undertaking of many Greek men and boys of his time and his journey turned out to be similar to the myth of Odysseus, the hero of the poet Homer's tale- the Odyssey

Looking back, his story was a quest and struggle to be free. He was an immigrant and his story is filled with many harrowing events and changes of fortune which occurred over his long wandering journey.

Peter's tale is the horrors of warfare. He was forced to experience these horrors at an early age. His tale took a look at the troubles of his world. He learned that we are cursed by our 'tragic flaw' and our greed and thirst for power/

There is a Greek word for the 'tragic flaw'. It is the Greek word – 'hamartia' — which means the tragic flaw in humanity. It is the same word that early Christians used for original sin, which is the sin that we are born with and that is beyond any human being's control. Humanity's hamartia is the tragic flaw that is the cause of humanity's eternal struggles.

The myths of life are the spiritual histories of our world, which are destined to repeat themselves because of humanity's tragic flaw. Their message is that our karma is driven by our belief that we must 'destroy to survive' and that life's purpose is to overcome our tragic flaw and to evolve in of the myths to spiritual beings of love and goodness.

THE MYTHMAKER

EPILOGUE: THE POETRY OF PETER'S TALE

The Odyssey
We are the myth-makers
We are the heroes of dreams
Hearts that spread their sails
To shadowy islands anywhere

We are born as innocents
Children of fate, we set sail
Into life's crashing waves
We ride the tides of our tale

We crave love's sweetness
Cursed to feel its heartaches
Overwhelming us with madness
We are cursed to feel life's pain

Our dreams pile on dreams
Dreams that are only illusions
Yet, inspire Odysseys of hope
Sailing into struggles of life

Prayers and cries go unheeded
The struggles become our myth s
And in our myths we find truth
And the purpose of the Odyssey

We are the myth makers of life
We are the heroes of dreams
Hearts that spread their sails
To shadowy islands anywhere

-Charles Peter Zaloumis
Myth Maker

ABOOKS

ALIVE Book Publishing and ALIVE Publishing Group
are imprints of Advanced Publishing LLC,
3200 A Danville Blvd., Suite 204, Alamo, California 94507

Telephone: 925.837.7303
alivebookpublishing.com

www.ingramcontent.com/pod-product-compliance
Lightning Source LLC
Chambersburg PA
CBHW020939230426
43666CB00005B/84